# Discovering

CONNECTIONS 3

# Discovering

EDITED BY

Richard Davies and Glen Kirkland

 PUBLISHING LIMITED
TORONTO ONTARIO CANADA

ISBN 0-7715-1162-0

DESIGN
Frank Newfeld

ILLUSTRATIONS
Dianne Richardson
Frank Newfeld

COVER
Frank Newfeld

2 3 4 5 6 7 8 9 BP 85 84 83 82

Printed and bound in Canada

# Contents

## Individuals and Society

## Here Comes the Future!

# Relationships

## The Road Ahead

# Individuals
# and
# Society

Robert I. Brownstein

# The Nonconformist

For the second time in one day and
the second time in his life, Don ran in
sheer terror with fear gripping at his heart.

I t was sweltering in the schoolyard, but the ranks of students remained rigidly at attention though their shirts were drenched with the sweat that poured off their lean bodies. For they all were lean, dressed the same, standing in the same position. It was a blissful picture of conformity except for one error, one movement that

twisted uncomfortably in the precise lines. This single error of psychological instruction was Don 12.

However, in this case the heat was not the irritant; Don always writhed in mental agony during public executions. His muscles would contort and strain against his conscious will as the victim mounted the gallows, and then as the trap door opened and the sound of a neck snapping reached his ears he would relax instantaneously and march with the others back to Quarters. At the present time the victim had twice committed the most abhorred crime known to man. The penalty was death for the evil, cruel, insane, and fiendishly vile nonconformist. It said so in the textbooks at school so it must be true. The fiend was now swinging at the end of a rope with a broken neck. It was lucky, mused Don, that they had caught this one before he developed. He might even have caused dissension in the ranks. Detection of nonconforming students was improving. It had been a long time since they had hanged an eight-year-old.

Don returned to his section, stood beside his bunk, and waited for the buzzer. When it did go off, as it always did, at precisely six seconds to seven each morning, he walked, as he always did, to class. As was customary the instructor began by giving a strong lecture on the evils of nonconformity, and then told the students to be glad that the vigilant detectors had spotted this menace to society so he could be disposed of. Then he went on to his real subject, mathematics. Don was only fourteen, but intelligent for his age; he had already mastered the multiplication tables up to eight times twelve and was beginning to grasp long division. Of course, it never entered his mind to do extra-curricular studies and go beyond his classmates. They must all maintain the same intelligence quotient.

The mathematics course began as the teacher snapped a question at the class.

"What is the product of seven times nine?"

Naturally no one volunteered the answer. To do so would be an attempt to place oneself above the other members of the class, thereby practising nonconformity in one of its most hideous forms. The instructor selected a student who stood up, bowed, said by your most gracious and illustrious leave, and gave the correct answer.

Science class was next on the agenda. Don

had no knowledge of science in the real sense of the word. As he entered the classroom and seated himself at the desk he saw a reading assignment on the board. Ever since Don could remember there had been a reading assignment in science class. He picked up and opened his textbook in unison with the rest of the class and read. The first sentence seemed to move back and forth, back and forth, as a colorful vortex appeared in the centre of the page and seemed to draw him into it while a voice droned on.

"Your eyes are getting heavy, you are sleepy, sleepy."

In minutes Don was hypnotized and the voice changed to the familiar tone of his instructor.

"All that I tell you now you will wholeheartedly believe for it is the truth, the only truth. The nonconformist is vile, is the low of the low. The glory of life belongs to those who conform. Conform to society! Conform to life! Conform! Conform! Conform!"

When the buzzer sounded Don returned to his bunk. He rested there until food was served which he, though famished, devoured slowly in perfect rhythm with his roommates. Then another buzzer sounded, the trays were removed, while Don and the others reclined and waited. Fifteen minutes later a bell, not a buzzer, sounded and Don got up, walked through the dim corridors, and left the building.

Don's feet moved mechanically as he walked toward the production station. For two hours he must tend the hydroponic plants and then return for the evening class. He walked on the same streets, as usual making sure that he skirted the "slums." The slums were hotbeds of nonconformity but were slowly being destroyed by the ever-increasing government raids.

He plodded on until he reached the station, entered his room, changed to work

4 | clothes, and reported for his assignment. It wasn't difficult work, to be sure, tending the plants that meant survival for an empire. Without them famine would strike, as other sources of food were few and far between. So on Don toiled, slowly and solemnly, till two hours had gone by and a buzzer sounded. Don returned to his room, changed back into uniform, and left the station. He then began walking toward the school. Suddenly the air erupted into a torrent of blisteringly hot air as heat beams flashed over his head. Don continued to walk in the same conforming steps, slow and patient, but the beams blasted closer and closer. He began to shake uncontrollably while sweat poured from his body. His tortured mind screamed run, his subconscious told him to walk slowly in simple, patient, conforming steps. Don stopped, stumbled in a moment of indecision, then he ran blindly from the blasts right into the path of a raid from the slums. He tried to dodge but a thick arm grabbed him around the throat. Pressure increased on his windpipe as he gasped for breath. Then he felt a powerful blow on his head....

Don 12 awoke. Immediately he was overcome by nausea so he lay down and rested, trying to co-ordinate his thoughts. He had not reported for evening class, he was missing without explanation. He had run in blind fear, committed nonconformity; the detectors were already after him. At the next execution his body would dangle as others' had at the end of a rope. Suddenly his mind settled down, returned to, and dwelt on, a single thought. He had committed nonconformity, he was evil, vile, the low of the low. Don tottered on the brink of madness and just managed to manoeuvre himself back into sanity. He got up slowly and realized he had a problem, was in an awful predicament. He did not have the slightest idea where in the world he was. The only buildings he had ever remembered being in were the school and the production station. The only places he knew of were those on the route between these two buildings. He was near none of these places, hopelessly lost.

Don walked; all he could do was walk, and hope that he would stumble on a familiar street. Then he saw two people walking. Something nagged at his mind as he hurried toward them to ask directions. They didn't walk in the slow, precise steps of students and adult conformists. They were talking, motioning with their hands, not acting in a conforming manner at all. Suddenly he looked at the buildings around him. They were shabby and each was different. This wasn't a normal street. He was in the slums.

For the second time in one day and the second time in his life, Don ran in sheer terror with fear gripping at his heart. Finally, however, he realized that his frantic manoeuvres were only drawing attention to him and perhaps taking him deeper into the slums. Reason, for the first time since his awakening, pierced his thoughts. He must endeavor to make himself as inconspicuous as possible. He must return to the school, and the people in the slums might prevent him from doing this. But how could they stop him? Unnecessary physical contact was nonconformity in one of its many hideous forms. Yet did this apply to the slum people? They were nonconformists and then again he was a nonconformist. He was evil, vile, the low of the low! Reasonlessly he wandered for over four hours.

There was no hope in his tortured mind, not that he understood the implication of the word in the first place. But then he was doing the only thing he could in attempting to return to school. His mind had only one beaten track, and to fit himself once more safely and sanely into that groove was Don's only chance for survival.

"Don 12 report! Don 12 report!"

He froze in his tracks, now alert and thinking. That was the detectors' mobile squad calling him to report. They must have discovered his absence and were looking for him. A wave of relief overcame him as he hurriedly made for the speaker. He would be taken back to school and everything would be all right. Tomorrow they would call an assembly in the yard, and take him to the gallows, and put a rope around his neck, and pull a lever and...! Don stopped. He didn't want to be hanged. Yet he couldn't stay the way he was, and the detectors would catch him anyway. Perhaps if he turned himself in, they might be lenient. But no. There was no mercy for his crime. Death would be inevitable.

The loudspeaker sounded nearer. They were tracing him, were picking up his signal. He pounded his skull, futilely realizing they had picked up his brain waves and that he couldn't hide now. In the slums he might be safe but he didn't know which way was the slums. He turned, fearfully surveyed the foreign surroundings, and began to walk. Diligently the loudspeaker followed him, so he walked faster and faster, finally breaking into a run.

"Don 12 report!"

The voice came from in front of him. Other loudspeakers sounded all around him. Don listened again and found there was no sound coming from his left. He ran in that direction, hearing the detectors set off in pursuit. Don was going as fast as he could, but how could he evade a mobile unit? Suddenly a large building loomed up before him. He ran toward it, then stopped. It was the school. He screamed and ran toward the gate, but found it was closed. He attempted to climb it, but fell. Relentlessly Don banged at the bars, yelled at them, implored them to open and let him through. He tore at the steel till his hands, scraped and bruised, began to bleed. He stared at them unbelievingly. Never before had he been even slightly hurt. Pain fogged his brain. He stood there, staring dumbly before him until hands took his arms and led him away. One of them took something out of a small leather box and pricked his arm with it. Don felt dizzy and tired. Then he blacked out.

When Don awoke, he found himself sitting in a small room, unfurnished except for the single chair he occupied. The dizziness he had encountered before he blacked out did not occur again during his awakening. Don wondered if his execution would be held in public or in some secluded area without the usual formalities. But then a section of the wall slid away and two men entered. They took Don through a dim corridor into a well-lighted room. There a young man questioned him about the raid that was responsible for his present predicament. As Don remembered nothing, the interview terminated shortly and he was taken back to his room.

Several hours later four men took Don from his room out into the courtyard. All the students were assembled and the solid steel gallows glistened in the sun. Oddly enough Don no longer felt any of the fear or confusion he had experienced before his capture. He was at peace with the world as he mounted the steps and stood above the trap door....

It was sweltering in the schoolyard, but the ranks of students remained rigidly at attention though their shirts were drenched with the sweat that poured off their lean bodies. For they all were lean, dressed the same, standing in the same position. It was a blissful picture of conformity except for one error, one movement that twisted uncomfortably in the precise lines. This error of psychological instruction was Don 13.

F. R. Scott

# Examiner

The routine trickery of the examination
Baffles these hot and discouraged youths.
Driven by they know not what external pressure,
They pour their hated self-analysis
Through the nib of confession, onto the accusatory page.

I, who have plotted their immediate downfall,
I am entrusted with the divine categories,
ABCD and the hell of E,
The parade of prize and the backdoor of pass.

In the tight silence
Standing by a green grass window
Watching the fertile earth graduate its sons
With more compassion – not commanding the shape
Of stem and stamen, bringing the trees to pass
By shift of sunlight and increase of rain,
For each seed the whole soil, for the inner life
The environment receptive and contributory –
I shudder at the narrow frames of our textbook schools
In which we plant our so various seedlings.
Each brick-walled barracks
Cut into numbered rooms, black-boarded,
Ties the venturing shoot to the master's stick;
The screw-desk rows of lads and girls
Subdued in the shade of an adult –
Their acid subsoil –
Shape the new to the old in the ashen garden.

Shall we open the whole skylight of thought
To these tiptoe minds, bring them our frontier worlds
And the boundless uplands of art for their field of growth?
Or shall we pass them the chosen poems with the footnotes,
Ring the bell on their thoughts, period their play,
Make laws for averages and plans for means,
Print one history book for a whole province, and
Let ninety thousand reach page 10 by Tuesday?

As I gather the inadequate paper evidence, I hear
Across the neat campus lawn
The professional mowers drone, clipping the inch-high green.

Paul Simon

# I Am a Rock

A winter's day
In a deep and dark December,
I am alone,
Gazing from my window to the streets below
On a freshly-fallen, silent shroud of snow.
I am a rock.
I am an island.

I've built walls,
A fortress steep and mighty,
That none may penetrate.
I have no need of friendship; friendship causes pain.
It's laughter and it's loving I disdain.
I am a rock.
I am an island.

Don't talk of love;
Well I've heard the word before.
It's sleeping in my memory.
I won't disturb the slumber of feelings that have died.
If I never loved, I never would have cried.
I am a rock.
I am an island.

I have my books
And my poetry to protect me.
I am shielded in my armor,
Hiding in my room, safe within my womb.
I touch no one and no one touches me.
I am a rock.
I am an island.

And a rock feels no pain;
And an island never cries.

# Constance L. Melaro

# R U There?

## Dear ANYONE human:
### WILL YOU PLEASE TAKE YOUR HEAD
### OUT OF THE COMPUTER LONG ENOUGH TO READ THIS?
### I DON'T OWE YOU THIS MONEY!!!

August 17

Dear Madam:
Our records show an outstanding balance of $2.98 on your account. If you have already remitted this amount, kindly disregard this notice.

THIS IS A BUSINESS MACHINE CARD.
PLEASE DO NOT SPINDLE OR MUTILATE.

August 19

Gentlemen:
I do *not* have an outstanding balance. I attached a note with my payment advising you that I had been billed *twice* for the same amount: once under my first name, middle initial, and last name; and then under my two first initials and my last name. (The former is correct.) Please check your records.

September 17

Dear Madam:
Our records show a delinquent balance of $2.98 on your account. Please remit $3.40. This includes a handling charge.

THIS IS A BUSINESS MACHINE CARD.
PLEASE DO NOT SPINDLE OR MUTILATE.

September 19

Dear Machine:
You're not paying attention! I am NOT delinquent in any amount. I do *not* owe this money. I was billed TWICE for the same purchase. PLEASE look into this.

October 17

Dear Madam:
Our records show you to be delinquent for three months. Please remit the new charges plus $4.10. (This includes a handling charge.) May we have your immediate attention in this matter.

THIS IS A BUSINESS MACHINE CARD.
PLEASE DO NOT SPINDLE OR MUTILATE.

October 19

Dear Machine:

MY attention! You want MY attention! Listen here, YOU ARE WRONG!!! I DON'T owe you $4.10. *CAN YOU UNDERSTAND THAT*? I also DON'T owe you the new charges of $13.46. You billed ME for my MOTHER'S purchase. Please correct this statement AT ONCE!

November 17

Dear Madam:

Our records now show you to be delinquent for four months in the total amount of $17.56 plus $1.87 handling charges. Please remit in full in ten days or your account will be turned over to our Auditing Department for collection.

THIS IS A BUSINESS MACHINE CARD.
PLEASE DO NOT SPINDLE OR MUTILATE.

November 19

Dear Human Machine Programmer –
Dear ANYONE human:

WILL YOU PLEASE TAKE YOUR HEAD OUT OF THE COMPUTER LONG ENOUGH TO READ THIS? I DON'T OWE YOU THIS MONEY!!! I DON'T OWE YOU *ANY* MONEY. *NONE*.

December 17

Dear Madam:

Is there some question about your statement? Our records show no payment on your account since August. Please call DI 7-9601 and ask for Miss Gilbert at your earliest convenience.

THIS IS A BUSINESS MACHINE CARD.
PLEASE DO NOT SPINDLE OR MUTILATE.

December 18

*...Deck the halls with boughs of holly...*
"Good afternoon. Carver's hopes you enjoyed its recorded program of carols. May I help you?"

"Hello. Yes...My bill is...should I wait for a 'beep' before I talk?"

"About your bill?"

"Yes. Yes, it's my bill. There's..."

"One moment, please. I'll connect you with Adjustments!"

*Good afternoon and Merry Christmas. This is a recorded message. All our lines are in service now. If you will please be patient, one of our adjusters will be with you just as soon as a line is free. Meanwhile, Carver's hopes you will enjoy its program of Christmas carols....Deck the halls with...*

December 26

Dear Machine:

I tried to call you on December 18. Also the 19th, 20th, 21st, 22nd, the 23rd, and the 24th. But all I got was a recorded message and those Christmas Carols. Please, oh, please! Won't you turn me over to a human? *Any* human?

January 17

Dear Madam:

Our Credit Department has turned your delinquent account over to us for collection. Won't you please remit this amount now? We wish to co-operate with you in every way possible, but this is considerably past due. May we have your check at this time.

Very truly yours,
Henry J. Hooper, Auditor

January 19

Dear Mr. Hooper:

You DOLL! You gorgeous HUMAN doll! I refer you to letters I sent to your department, dated the 19th of September, October, November, December, which should clarify the fact that I owe you nothing.

February 17

Dear Madam:

According to our microfilm records, our billing was in error. Your account is clear; you have no balance. We hope there will be no further inconvenience to you. Though this was our fault, you can help us if, in the future, you will always include your account number when ordering by mail or phone.

Very truly yours,
Henry J. Hooper, Auditor

February 19

Dear Mr. Hooper:

Thank you! Oh, thank you, thank you, thank you!

March 17

Dear Madam:

Our records show you to be delinquent in the amount of $2.98, erroneously posted last August to a non-existent account. May we have your remittance at this time?

THIS IS A BUSINESS MACHINE CARD.
PLEASE DO NOT SPINDLE OR MUTILATE.

March 19

Dear Machine:

I give up. You win. Here's a check for $2.98. Enjoy yourself.

April 17

Dear Madam:

Our records show an overpayment on your part of $2.98. We are crediting this amount to your account.

THIS IS A BUSINESS MACHINE CARD.
PLEASE DO NOT SPINDLE OR MUTILATE.

Richard Davies

# It Looks So Good, You'd Hardly Know It's a Disaster

WHY TAKE LESS?
MAKE THE BIG STRIKE
DISCOVER GOLD
GET RICH QUICK
EASY PROFITS
       BE SLIM AGAIN WITHIN MINUTES
       50% OFF
       LAST TWO DAYS
       HURRY HURRY HURRY
ARE YOU LONELY? UNATTACHED?
BALDNESS WORRY YOU?
THEN SELL IT LIKE IT IS
THE NAME OF THE GAME IS MORE CASH FOR MORE PEOPLE
       WHY EVEN LOVE HAS A NEW RING TO IT
       (only $999 sales tax not included)
       YES FOLKS IT'S DOLLAR DAZE
       AND HE'S DREAMING OF A BEAUTIFUL GIRL
       WHILE SHE'S DREAMING OF A BEAUTIFUL DIAMOND
EVERYTHING MUST BE SOLD
DON'T DELAY SHOP TODAY
CALL FOR A FREE ESTIMATE
NO INTEREST FOR ONE FULL YEAR
       TO BE OR NOT TO BE
       THAT IS THE QUESTION
       TRANQUIL TERRACE
       THAT IS THE ANSWER
SCENIC VIEW
EXECUTIVE STYLE
PRESTIGIOUS LIVING
HARD TO BEAT
CAN'T REFUSE
WHILE THEY LAST
IMMEDIATE DELIVERY
ON THE SPOT INSTALLATIONS
IT'S YOUR LAST CHANCE
HURRY WHILE STOCK LASTS
       (Offer expires yesterday)

## Katherine McGillivray

# Women in Advertising

**Show us as intelligent human beings, not as if we had had prefrontal lobotomies.**

I'm fed up to my head and shoulders with advertising that insults women. And I'm also puzzled, to the tips of my Revlon-painted toenails, by an advertising approach that holds fifty-one percent of its customers in utter contempt. We are shown as kitchen lackeys – and while the woman does the menial work, there's a man doing the voice-over. Man sells, woman slaves.

The time has come for advertising men to liberate themselves from their false idea of women. Don't they realize how many working-age women are out working today? Half the women in the country are simply not at home when the Man from Glad drops in. They're at their desks, their factory benches, or their seats in the boardroom.

Now, I really don't think that all advertisers are male chauvinist pigs, but I do think that they're missing out on their market. Contempt for their female fifty-one percent of the buying public leads them into some very curious advertising. Do they really think we believe in fairies? Like that awful Man from Glad? Do they think we sit at home, hoping Mr. Clean and those other weirdos will drop by?

When they go home to their wives and girlfriends, do they ask them, "Seen the White Knight today, honey?" Do they look out of their picture windows and shout, "Hey! It's a white tornado!" If not, why not? If they don't talk to their own women that way, why do they do so to the rest of us?

Why have they created this extraordinary image of us? How long will it be before they liberate us women from this hopelessly distorted picture they present of us? It had better be soon. For I believe that this liberation is a great deal more important than they seem to imagine.

Published with the kind permission of Black Rose Books, Montreal, from the book *Mother Was Not a Person*, Margaret Anderson, ed.

What kind of homes are advertisers forcing upon us? With floors that mustn't be stepped on, kitchens where nobody cooks, with an atmosphere like a hospital ward.

Correction. Somebody is allowed to cook – but only grandma. And only cake mix. You see the old bag leering over her steel-rimmed glasses. Mother doesn't cook. She serves. She serves Instant Breakfast to a bunch of lay-abouts who can't crawl out of bed ten minutes earlier to get to the office or school on time. She beams with motherly pride as her children stuff their faces with food. She's forever shoving food down people. Usually cheap food, closely followed by expensive aspirins and remedies for acid indigestion. Which is probably why one seldom sees her eating.

Even when there's a party, she's there with her tray. Fetching and carrying like crazy. Then her husband turns round and shouts at her because she's bought bitter coffee. Or the Ajax has turned blue. Or she's starched his socks. And her daughter whines: "Wouldn't you know – my big chance! A date with George, and I'm all out of mouth-wash!" What a crew! My grandmother the cake-mix cook. My husband Attila the Hun. My son the gobbler. My daughter the gargler. Family life of a wife and mother, courtesy of the advertising industry.

Thanks a whole lot. We haven't come as far as you might think, baby.

Have they ever stopped to think of the overall picture this approach presents of Canadian womanhood? A sort of white female Stepin Fetchit, a lackey chained to her kitchen, with underarms like the Sahara, her scalp as flake-less as a billiard ball, breathing hexachlorophene over the Man from Glad, comparing the whiteness of washes from dawn till dusk with some seedy idiot with the microphone, doling out cardboard cornflakes and great dollops of monosodium glutamate, and carrying plates, carrying trays, carrying, carrying. Not much of a picture, is it? No wonder so many daughters, alarmed at the prospect of living like this, are taking off to communes.

So far, I've done nothing but complain about the image advertising men have created of women. But now I'm going to unburden myself of some advice which, if followed – and I have no reason to doubt that it will – will liberate us women from where we sit. At the bottom of our broken pedestals. Here's what advertisers can do for us. Show us as intelligent human beings, not as if we had had prefrontal lobotomies.

Stop portraying us as ill-mannered witches who sneer at the whiteness (or non-whiteness) of each other's laundry and sniff for cabbage smells. Show us with a reasonable standard of human behavior and decent feelings.

Stop talking down to women. Talk *to* us.

Keith Laumer

# The Walls

When Harry came, she would show him how it was.
He would see that the Full-walls weren't enough.
They all had them, and they were all unhappy.

Harry Trimble looked pleased when he stepped into the apartment. The lift door had hardly clacked shut behind him on the peering commuter faces in the car before he had slipped his arm behind Flora's back, bumped his face against her cheek, and chuckled, "Well, what would you say to a little surprise? Something you've waited a long time for?"

Flora looked up from the dial-a-ration panel. "A surprise, Harry?"

"I know how you feel about the apartment, Flora. Well, from now on, you won't be seeing so much of it...."

"Harry!"

He winced at her clutch on his arm. Her face was pale under the day-glare strip. "We're not...moving to the country...?"

Harry pried his arm free. "The country? What the devil are you talking about?" He was frowning now, the pleased look gone. "You should use the lamps more," he said. "You look sick." He glanced around the apartment, the four perfectly flat rectangular walls, the glassy surface of the vari-glow ceiling, the floor with its pattern of sink-away panels. His eye fell on the four-foot-square of the TV screen.

"I'm having that thing taken out tomorrow," he said. The pleased look was coming back. He cocked an eye at Flora. "And I'm having a Full-wall installed!"

Flora glanced at the blank screen. "A Full-wall, Harry?"

"Yep!" Harry smacked a fist into a palm, taking a turn up and down the room. "We'll be the first in our cell block to have a Full-wall!"

"Why...that will be nice, Harry...."

"Nice?" Harry punched the screen control, then deployed the two chairs with tray

Reprinted by permission of Robert Mills, New York.

racks ready to receive the evening meal.

Behind him, figures jiggled on the screen. "It's a darn sight more than nice," he said, raising his voice over the shrill and thump of the music. "It's expensive, for one thing. Who else do you know that can afford..."

"But..."

"But nothing! Imagine it, Flora! It'll be like having a...a balcony seat, looking out on other people's lives."

"But we have so little space now; won't it take up..."

"Of course not! How do you manage to stay so ignorant of technical progress? It's only an eighth of an inch thick. Think of it: that thick..." – Harry indicated an eighth of an inch with his fingers – "and better color and detail than you've ever seen. It's all done with what they call an edge-excitation effect."

"Harry, the old screen is good enough. Couldn't we use the money for a trip...."

"How do you know if it's good enough? You never have it on. I have to turn it on myself when I get home."

Flora brought the trays and they ate silently, watching the screen. After dinner, Flora disposed of the trays, retracted the table and chairs, and extended the beds. They lay in the dark, not talking.

"It's a whole new system," Harry said suddenly. "The Full-wall people have their own programming scheme; they plan your whole day, wake you up at the right time with some lively music, give you breakfast menus to dial, then follow up with a good sitcom to get you into the day; then there's nap music, with subliminal hypnotics if you have trouble sleeping; then..."

"Harry...can I turn it off if I want to?"

"Turn it off?" Harry sounded puzzled. "The idea is to leave it on. That's why I'm having it installed for you, you know...so you can use it!"

"But sometimes I like to just think...."

"Think! Brood, you mean." He heaved a sigh. "Look, Flora, I know the place isn't fancy. Sure, you get a little tired of being here all the time; but there are plenty of people worse off – and now, with Full-wall, you'll get a feeling of more space...."

"Harry..." – Flora spoke rapidly – "I wish we could go away, I mean leave the city, and get a little place where we can be alone, even if it means working hard, and where I can have a garden and maybe keep chickens and you could chop firewood...."

"Good God!" Harry roared, cutting her off. Then: "These fantasies of yours," he said quietly. "You have to learn to live in the real world, Flora. Live in the woods? Wet leaves, wet bark, bugs, mould: talk about depressing..."

There was a long silence.

"I know; you're right, Harry," Flora said. "I'll enjoy the Full-wall. It was very sweet of you to think of getting it for me."

"Sure," Harry said. "It'll be better. You'll see...."

The Full-wall was different, Flora agreed as soon as the service men had made the last adjustments and flipped it on. There was vivid color, fine detail, and a remarkable sense of depth. The shows were about the same – fast-paced, bursting with variety and energy. It was exciting at first, having full-sized people talking, eating, fighting, taking baths, making love, right in the room with you. If you sat across the room and half-closed your eyes, you could almost imagine you were watching real people. Of course, real people wouldn't carry on like that. But then, it was hard to say what real people might do. Flora had always thought Doll Starr wore padded brassieres, but when she stripped on Full-wall there wasn't any fakery about it.

Harry was pleased, too, when he arrived home to find the wall on. He and Flora would dial dinner with one eye on the screen, then slip into bed and view until the Bull-Doze pills they'd started taking took effect. Perhaps things *were* better, Flora thought hopefully. More like they used to be.

But after a month or two, the Full-wall began to pall. The same faces, the same pratfalls, the same happy quiz masters, the puzzled prize-winners, the delinquent youths and fumbling dads, the bosoms – all the same.

On the sixty-third day, Flora switched the Full-wall off. The light and sound died, leaving a faint, dwindling glow. She eyed the glassy wall uneasily, as one might view the coffin of an acquaintance.

It was quiet in the apartment. Flora fussed with the dial-a-ration, averting her eyes from the dead screen. She turned to deploy the solitaire table and started violently. The screen, the residual glow having faded now, was a perfect mirror. She went close to it, touched the hard surface with a finger. It was almost invisible. She studied her reflected face; the large, dark eyes with shadows under them, the cheekline, a trifle too hollow now to be really chic, the hair drawn back in an uninspired bun. Behind her, the doubled room, unadorned now that all the furnishings were retracted into the floor except for the pictures on the wall: photographs of the children away at school, a sunny scene of green pastureland, a painting of rolling waves at sea.

She stepped back, considering the effect. The floor and walls seemed to continue without interruption, except for a hardly noticeable line. It was as though the apartment were twice as large. If only it weren't so empty....

Flora deployed the table and chairs, dialled a lunch, and sat, eating, watching her double. No wonder Harry seemed indifferent lately, she thought, noting the rounded shoulders, the insignificant bust, the slack posture. She would have to do something in the way of self-improvement.

Half an hour of the silent companionship of her image was enough. Flora snapped the screen back on, watched almost with relief as a grinning cowboy in velvet chaps made strumming motions while an intricately-fingered guitar melody blared from the sound track.

Thereafter, she turned the screen off every day, at first only for an hour, later for longer and longer periods. Once, she found herself chatting gaily to her reflection, and hastily fell silent. It wasn't as though she were becoming neurotic, she assured herself; it was just the feeling of roominess that made her like the mirror screen. And she was always careful to have it on when Harry arrived home.

It was about six months after the Full-wall had been installed that Harry emerged one day from the lift smiling in a way that reminded Flora of that earlier evening. He dropped his briefcase into his floor locker, looked around the apartment, humming to himself.

"What is it, Harry?" Flora asked.

Harry glanced at her. "It's not a log cabin in the woods," he said. "But maybe you'll like it anyway...."

"What...is it, dear...."

"Don't sound so dubious." He broke into a broad smile. "I'm getting you another Full-wall."

Flora looked puzzled. "But this one is working perfectly, Harry."

"Of course it is," he snapped. "I mean you're getting another wall; you'll have two. What about that? Two Full-walls – and nobody else in the cell-block has one yet. The only question is..." – he rubbed his hands

together, striding up and down the room, eyeing the walls – "which wall is it to be? You can have it adjacent, or opposite. I went over the whole thing with the Full-wall people today. By God, they're doing a magnificent job of programming. You see, the two walls will be synchronized. You're getting the same show on both – you're seeing it from two angles, just as though you were right there in the middle of it. Their whole program has been built on that principle."

"Harry, I'm not sure I want another wall...."

"Oh, nonsense. What is this, some kind of self-denial urge? Why not have the best – if you can afford it. And by God, I can afford it. I'm hitting my stride...."

"Harry, could I go with you some day – tomorrow? I'd like to see where you work, meet your friends..."

"Flora, are you out of your mind? You've seen the commuter car; you know how crowded it is. And what would you do when you got there? Just stand around all day, blocking the aisle? Why don't you appreciate the luxury of having your own place, a little privacy, and now two Full-walls...."

"Then could I go somewhere else? I could take a later car. I want to get out in the open air, Harry. I...haven't seen the sky for... years, it seems."

"But..." Harry groped for words, staring at Flora. "Why would you want to go up on the roof?"

"Not the roof; I want to get out of the city – just for a little while. I'll be back home in time to dial your dinner...."

"Do you mean to tell me you want to spend all that money to wedge yourself in a verticar and then transfer to a cross-town and travel maybe seventy miles, packed in like a sardine, standing up all the way, just so you can get out and stand in a wasteland and look back at the walls? And then get back in another car – if you're lucky – and come back again?"

"No – I don't know – I just want to get out, Harry. The roof. Could I go to the roof?"

Harry came over to pat Flora awkwardly on the arm. "Now, take it easy, Flora. You're a little tired and stale. I know. I get the same way sometimes. But don't get the idea that you're missing anything by not having to get into that rat race. Heaven knows *I* wish I could stay home. And this new wall is going to make things different. You'll see...."

The new Full-wall was installed adjacent to the first, with a joint so beautifully fitted that only the finest line marked the junction. As soon as she was alone with it, Flora switched it off. Now two reflections stared back at her from behind what appeared to be two intersecting planes of clear glass. She waved an arm. The two slave figures aped her. She walked toward the mirrored corner. They advanced. She stepped back; they retreated.

She went to the far corner of the room and studied the effect. It wasn't as nice as before. Instead of a simple room, neatly bounded on all four sides by solid walls, she seemed now to occupy a stage set off by windows through which other, similar, stages were visible, endlessly repeated. The old feeling of intimate companionship with her reflected self was gone; the two mirror-women were strangers, silently watching her. Defiantly, she stuck out her tongue. The two reflections grimaced menacingly. With a small cry, Flora ran to the switch, turned the screens on.

They were seldom off after that. Sometimes, when the hammering of hooves became too wearing, or the shouting of comics too strident, she would blank them out, and sit, back to the mirror walls, sipping a cup of hot coflet, and waiting – but they were always on when Harry arrived, some-

times glum, sometimes brisk and satisfied. He would settle himself in his chair, waiting patiently enough for dinner, watching the screens.

"They're all right," he would declare, nodding. "Look at that, Flora. Look at the way that fellow whipped right across there. By golly, you've got to hand it to the Full-wall people."

"Harry – where do they make the shows? The ones that show the beautiful scenery, and trees and rolling hills, and mountains?"

Harry was chewing. "Don't know," he said. "On location, I suppose."

"Then there really are places like that? I mean, they aren't just making it up?"

Harry stared at her, mouth full and half open. He grunted and resumed chewing. He swallowed. "I suppose that's another of your cracks."

"I don't understand, Harry," Flora said. He took another bite, glanced sideways at her puzzled expression.

"Of course they aren't making it up. How the devil could they make up a mountain?"

"I'd like to see those places."

"Here we go again," Harry said. "I was hoping I could enjoy a nice meal and then view awhile, but I guess you're not going to allow that."

"Of course, Harry. I just said..."

"I know what you said. Well, look at them then." He waved his hand at the screen. "There it is; the whole world. You can sit right here and view it all...."

"But I want to do more than just view it. I want to live it. I want to be in those places, and feel leaves under my feet, and have rain fall on my face...."

Harry frowned incredulously. "You mean you want to be an actress?"

"No, of course not...."

"I don't know what you want. You have a

home, two Full-walls, and this isn't all. I'm working toward something, Flora...."

Flora sighed. "Yes, Harry. I'm very lucky."

"Darn right." Harry nodded emphatically, eyes on the screens. "Dial me another coflet, will you?"

The third Full-wall came as a surprise. Flora had taken the 1100 car to the roboclinic on the 478th level for her annual checkup. When she returned home – there it was. She hardly noticed the chorus of gasps cut off abruptly as the door shut in the faces of the other wives in the car. Flora stood, impressed in spite of herself by the fantastic panorama filling her apartment. Directly before her, the studio audience gaped up from the massed seats. A fat man in the front row reached inside a red plaid shirt to scratch. Flora could see the perspiration on his forehead. Farther back, a couple nuzzled, eyes on the stage. *Who were they*, Flora wondered; *How did they manage to get out of their apartments and offices and sit in a real theatre....*

To the left, an owlish youth blinked from a brightly lit cage. And on the right, the M.C. caressed the mike, chattering.

Flora deployed her chair, sank down, looking first this way, then that. There was so much going on – and she in the middle of it. She watched for half an hour, then retracted the chair, deployed the bed. She was tired from the trip. A little nap...

She stopped with the first zipper. The M.C. was staring directly at her, leering. The owlish youth blinked at her. The fat man scratched himself, staring up at her from the front row. She couldn't undress in front of all of them....

She glanced around, located the switch near the door. With the click, the scene died around her. The glowing walls seemed to press close, fading slowly. Flora turned to the one remaining opaque wall, undressed slowly, her eyes on the familiar pictures. The children – she hadn't seen them since the last semi-annual vacation week. The cost of travel was so high, and the crowding...

She turned to the bed – and the three mirror-bright walls confronted her. She stared at the pale figure before her, stark against the wall patched with its faded mementos. She took a step; on either side, an endless rank of gaunt nude figures stepped in unison. She whirled, fixed her eyes gratefully on the familiar wall, the thin crevice outlining the door, the picture of the sea...

She closed her eyes, groped her way to the bed. Once covered by the sheet, she opened her eyes. The beds stood in a row, all identical, each with its huddled figure, like an infinite charity ward, she thought – or like a morgue where all the world lay dead....

Harry munched his yeast chop, his head moving from side to side as he followed the action across the three walls.

"It's marvellous, Flora. Marvellous. But it can be better yet," he added mysteriously.

"Harry – couldn't we move to a bigger place – and maybe do away with two of the walls? I..."

"Flora, you know better than that. I'm lucky to have gotten this apartment when I did; there's nothing – absolutely nothing available." He chuckled. "In a way, the situation is good job insurance. You know, I couldn't be fired, even if the company wanted to. They couldn't get a replacement. A man can't very well take a job if he hasn't a place to live in the city – and I can sit on this place as long as I like; we might get tired of issue rations, but by God we could hold on; so – not that anybody's in danger of getting fired."

22

"We could move out of the city, Harry. When I was a girl..."

"Oh, not that again!" Harry groaned. "I thought that was all threshed out, long ago." He fixed a pained look on Flora. "Try to understand, Flora. The population of the world has doubled since you were a girl. Do you realize what that means? There are more people alive now than had been born in all previous human history up to fifty years ago. That farm you remember visiting as a kid – it's all paved now, and there are tall buildings there. The highways you remember, full of private autos, all driving across open country; they're all gone. There aren't any highways, or any open country except the TV settings and a few estates like the President's acre and a half – not that any sun hits it, with all those buildings around it – and maybe some essential dry-land farms for stuff they can't synthesize or get from the sea."

"There has to be some place we could go. It wasn't meant that people should spend their lives like this – away from the sun, the sea..."

A shadow crossed Harry's face. "I can remember things, too, Flora," he said softly. "We spent a week at the beach once, when I was a small boy. I remember getting up at dawn with the sky all pink and purple, and going down to the water's edge. There were little creatures in the sand – little wild things. I could see tiny fish darting along in a wave crest, just before it broke. I could feel the sand with my toes. The gulls sailed around overhead, and there was even a tree...."

"But it's gone now. There isn't any beach, anywhere. That's all over...."

He broke off. "Never mind. That was then. This is now. They've paved the beach, and built processing plants on it, and they've paved the farms and the parks and the gar-

dens – but they've given us Full-wall to make up for it. And..."

There was a buzz from the door. Harry got to his feet.

"They're here, Flora. Wait'll you see..."

Something seemed to tighten around Flora's throat as the man emerged from the lift, gingerly handling the great roll of wall screen.

"Harry..."

"Four walls," Harry said triumphantly. "I told you I was working toward something, remember? Well, this is it! By God, the Harry Trimbles have shown 'em!"

"Harry – I can't – not four walls..."

"I know you're a little overwhelmed – but you deserve it, Flora...."

"Harry, I don't *want* four walls! I can't stand it! It will be all around me...."

Harry stepped to her side, gripped her wrist fiercely. "Shut up!" he hissed. "Do you want the workmen to think you're out of your mind?" He grinned at the men. "How about a coflet, boys?"

"You kiddin'?" one inquired. The other went silently about the work of rolling out the panel, attaching contact strips. Another reached for the sea-scene....

"No!" Flora threw herself against the wall, as though to cover the pictures with her body. "You can't take my pictures! Harry, don't let them."

"Look, sister, I don't want your crummy pictures."

"Flora, get hold of yourself! Here, I'll help you put the pictures in your floor locker."

"Bunch of nuts," one of the men muttered.

"Here, keep a civil tongue in your head," Harry started.

The man who had spoken stepped up to him. He was taller than Harry and solidly built. "And more crap outa you and I'll break you in half. You and the old bag shut up and keep outa my way. I gotta job to do."

Harry sat beside Flora, his face white with fury. "You and your vaporings," he hissed. "So I have to endure this. I have a good mind to..." he trailed off.

The men finished and left with all four walls blaring.

"Harry," Flora's voice shook. "How will you get out? They've put it right across the door; they've sealed us in...."

"Don't be a bigger idiot than you have to." Harry's voice was ugly over the thunder from the screens. He went to the newly covered wall, groped, found the tiny pin-switch. At a touch, the panel slid aside as always, revealing the blank face of the lift-shaft safety door. A moment later it too slid aside and Harry forced his way into the car. Flora caught a glimpse of his flushed, angry face as the door closed.

Around her, the walls roared. A saloon fight was in full swing. She ducked as a chair sailed toward her, whirled to see it smash down a man behind her. Shots rang out. Men ran this way and that. The noise was deafening. That man, Flora thought; the vicious one; he had set it too loud purposely.

The scene shifted. Horses galloped across the room; dust clouds rose, nearly choking her in the verisimilitude of the illusion. It was as though she crouched under a small square canopy of ceiling in the middle of the immense plain.

Now there were cattle, wild-eyed, with tossing horns, bellowing, thundering in an unbroken sea across the screens, charging at Flora out of the wall, pouring past her on left and right. She screamed, shut her eyes, and ran blindly to the wall, groping for the switch.

The uproar subsided. Flora gasped in relief, her head humming. She felt faint, dizzy; she had to lie down – everything was going black around her; the glowing walls swirled, fading. Flora sank to the floor.

Later – perhaps a few minutes, maybe hours – she had no way of knowing – Flora sat up. She looked out across an infinite vista of tile floor, which swept away to the distant horizon in all directions as far as the eye could see; and over all that vast plain, hollow-eyed women crouched at intervals of fifteen feet, in endless numbers, waiting.

Flora stared into the eyes of the nearest reflection. It stared back, a stranger. She moved her head quickly, to try to catch a glimpse of the next woman – but no matter how fast she moved, the nearer woman anticipated her, interposing her face between Flora and all the others. Flora turned; a cold-eyed woman guarded this rank, too.

"Please," Flora heard herself pleading. "Please, please..."

She bit her lip, eyes shut. She had to get hold of herself. These were only mirrors – she knew that. Only mirrors. The other women – they were mere reflections. Even the hostile ones who hid the others – they were herself, mirrored in the walls.

She opened her eyes. She knew there were joints in the glassy wall; all she had to do was find them, and the illusion of the endless plain would collapse. There – that thin black line, like a wire stretched from floor to ceiling – that was a corner of the room. She was not lost in an infinitude of weeping women on a vast plain; she was right there, in her own apartment – alone. She turned, finding the other corners. They were all there, all visible; she knew what they were....

But why did they continue to look like wires, setting apart the squares of floor, each with its silent, grieving occupant...?

She closed her eyes again, fighting down the panic. She would tell Harry. As soon as he came home – it was only a few hours – she would explain it to him.

24

*"I'm sick, Harry. You have to send me away to some place where I'll lie in a real bed, with sheets and blankets, beside an open window, looking out across the fields and forests. Someone – someone kind – will bring me a tray, with a bowl of soup – real soup, made from real chickens and with real bread and even a glass of milk, and a napkin, made of real cloth . . . ."*

She should find her bed, and deploy it, and rest there until Harry came, but she was so tired. It was better to wait here, just relaxing and not thinking about the immense floor and the other women who waited with her. . . .

She slept.

When she awoke, she sat up, confused. There had been a dream. . . .

But how strange. The walls of the cell block were transparent now; she could see all the other apartments, stretching away to every side. She nodded; it was as she thought. They were all as barren and featureless as her own – and Harry was wrong. They all had four Full-walls. And the other women – the other wives, shut up like her in these small, mean cells – they were all aging, and sick, and faded, starved for fresh air and sunshine. She nodded again, and the woman in the next apartment nodded in sympathy. All the women were nodding; they all agreed – poor things.

When Harry came, she would show him how it was. He would see that the Full-walls weren't enough. They all had them, and they were all unhappy. When Harry came . . .

It was time now. She knew it. After so many years, you didn't need a watch to tell when Harry was due. She had better get up, make herself presentable. She rose unsteadily to her feet. The other husbands were coming, too, Flora noted; all the wives were getting ready. They moved about, opening their floor lockers, patting at their hair, slipping into another dress. Flora went to the dial-a-ration and all around, in all the apart-

ments, the wives deployed the tables and dialled the dinners. She tried to see what the woman next door was dialling, but it was too far. She laughed at the way her neighbor craned to see what *she* was preparing. The other woman laughed, too. She was a good sport.

"Kelpies," Flora called cheerily. "And mockspam, and coflet . . ."

Dinner was ready now. Flora turned to the door-wall and waited. Harry would be so pleased at not having to wait. Then, after dinner she'd explain about her illness. . . .

Was it the right wall she was waiting before? The line around the door was so fine you couldn't really see it. She laughed at how funny it would be if Harry came in and found her standing, staring at the wrong wall.

She turned, and saw a movement on her left – in the next apartment. Flora watched as the door opened. A man stepped in. The next-door woman went forward to meet him. . . .

To meet Harry! It was Harry! Flora whirled. Her four walls stood blank and glassy, while all around her, the other wives greeted Harry, seated him at their tables, and offered him coflet. . . .

"Harry!" she screamed, throwing herself at the wall. It threw her back. She ran to the next wall, hammering, screaming, "Harry! Harry!"

In all the other apartments, Harry chewed, nodded, smiled. The other wives poured, fussed over Harry, nibbled daintily. And none of them – not one of them – paid the slightest attention to her. . . .

She stood in the centre of the room, not screaming now, only sobbing silently. In the four glass walls that enclosed her, she stood alone. There was no point in calling any longer.

No matter how she screamed, how she beat against the walls, or how she called for Harry – she knew that no one would ever hear.

# James Stevenson

**"Night-night. See you in the morning."**

## Elizabeth Brewster

# Home for the Aged

The old men sit, five of them on a bench,
Half sleeping, half awake, dazed by the sun,
In the muted afternoon, between one broadcast ball game and the next.
Their thoughts are leaves that drift across a sky perpetually autumn.
Their hands are folded: they have done with the Sunday papers.

Decorously shabby, decently combed and clean,
They watch with half-closed eyes the passers-by,
The loitering lovers, the boys on bikes, the cars
Rushing eagerly to some scene of active life.

Their lives are folded up like the papers, and who can know
Whether their years passed sober and discreet,
With the measured, dutiful, regular click of a clock,
Or whether some old violence lingers still
In faded headlines on their dusty brains?
What boyhood do they wander in, what middle age forget?
And do they watch their dwindling stock of time
With hope, or resignation, or despair?

Reprinted by permission of the author.

# Harold Pinter

# Last
# to
# Go

"Yes, it was
the *Evening News*
was the last
to go tonight."

*Characters*     BARMAN     MAN

*A coffee stall. A* BARMAN *and an old* NEWSPAPER SELLER. *The* BARMAN *leans on his counter, the* OLD MAN *stands with tea*.

*Silence.*

MAN: You was a bit busier earlier.
BARMAN: Ah.
MAN: Round about ten.
BARMAN: Ten, was it?
MAN: About then. *(pause)* I passed by here about then.
BARMAN: Oh yes?
MAN: I noticed you were doing a bit of trade.

*Pause.*

BARMAN: Yes, trade was very brisk here about ten.
MAN: Yes, I noticed.

*Pause.*

MAN: I sold my last one about then. Yes. About nine forty-five.
BARMAN: Sold your last then, did you?
MAN: Yes, my last *Evening News* it was. Went about twenty to ten.

*Pause.*

BARMAN: *Evening News*, was it?
MAN: Yes. *(pause)* Sometimes it's the *Star* is the last to go.
BARMAN: Ah.
MAN: Or the...whatsisname.
BARMAN: *Standard.*
MAN: Yes. *(pause)* All I had left tonight was the *Evening News*.

*Pause.*

BARMAN: Then that went, did it?
MAN: Yes.

From *Last to Go* by Harold Pinter. Reprinted by permission of Eyre Methuen Publishers.

*Pause.*

MAN: Like a shot.

*Pause.*

BARMAN: You didn't have any left, eh?
MAN: No. Not after I sold that one.

*Pause.*

BARMAN: It was after that you must have come by here then, was it?
MAN: Yes, I come by here after that, see, after I packed up.
BARMAN: You didn't stop here though, did you?
MAN: When?
BARMAN: I mean, you didn't stop here and have a cup of tea then, did you?
MAN: What, about ten?
BARMAN: Yes.
MAN: No, I went up to Victoria.
BARMAN: No, I thought I didn't see you.
MAN: I had to go up to Victoria.

*Pause.*

BARMAN: Yes, trade was very brisk here about then.

*Pause.*

MAN: I went to see if I could get hold of George.
BARMAN: Who?
MAN: George.

*Pause.*

BARMAN: George who?
MAN: George...whatsisname.
BARMAN: Oh. *(pause)* Did you get hold of him?

MAN: No. No, I couldn't get hold of him. I couldn't locate him.
BARMAN: He's not about much now, is he?

*Pause.*

MAN: When did you last see him then?
BARMAN: Oh, I haven't seen him for years.
MAN: No, nor me.

*Pause.*

BARMAN: Used to suffer very bad from arthritis.
MAN: Arthritis?
BARMAN: Yes.
MAN: He never suffered from arthritis.
BARMAN: Suffered very bad.

*Pause.*

MAN: Not when I knew him.

*Pause.*

BARMAN: I think he must have left the area.

*Pause.*

MAN: Yes, it was the *Evening News* was the last to go tonight.
BARMAN: Not always the last though, is it, though?
MAN: No. Oh no. I mean sometimes it's the *News*. Other times it's one of the others. No way of telling beforehand. Until you've got your last one left, of course. Then you can tell which one it's going to be.
BARMAN: Yes.

*Pause.*

MAN: Oh yes. *(pause)* I think he must have left the area.

# William Witherup

# Freeway

An infected vein
carrying filth to and from the city;

a funnel
draining a huge operating table.

Even the light here
is the color of pus.

All the late models
have tinted windows to shield the murderers

and the chrome is honed
to slash and carve.

The city has complied
by drawing a rubber curtain of shrubbery

to enclose the view
and muffle the screams.

Reprinted by permission of the author.

Bruce Cockburn

# Going to the Country

Look out the window, what do I see?
cows hangin' out under spreading trees
ZOOM! they're gone behind the sign
white letters pointing to the long white line
and I'm going to the country
o, la la la la la
I'm going to the country
sunshine smile on me

I can smell the grass growing in the field
wind in my hair tells me how it feels
farmhouse, silver roof flashing by
tractor-trailer truck says goodbye with a sigh
and I'm going to the country
o, la la la la la
I'm going to the country
sunshine smile on me

Birds singing, I'm singing in my bones,
doesn't much matter now where I'm going
get it when I get there is what I'll do
if I get enough I'll give some to you
and I'm going to the country
o, happy as can be
I'm going to the country
sunshine smile on me

Reprinted by permission of Bytown Music Ltd.

# Berton Roueché

# The Lug Wrench

*I saw him coming at me again
and I swung the wrench.*

"Oh, *no*," Gail said.

"It sure feels like it," I said, and shut off the engine.

I got out on the edge of the road and walked around to the back. It was the right rear, and it looked as if somebody had been at it with a knife. It was halfway off the rim. Gail had followed me back. She stood there in the weeds, looking down at the tire.

"Oh, no," she said.

"It isn't as bad as all that," I said. "I can change a tire."

"I know," she said. "But – I just wish it hadn't happened. We were making such good time."

"So do I," I said. "But I told the Petersons around seven, and it isn't even six yet. We're O.K." I tried the handle on the trunk. "Be a good girl and go get me the keys."

A pickup truck went by going fast. There was an outboard motor clamped to the tailgate. I watched the truck disappearing up the road. The road ran for about a mile between potato fields and a pasture overgrown with cedars, and then cut down to a creek. Beyond the creek, about five miles

Reprinted by permission. © 1969 The New Yorker Magazine, Inc.

back, was Loomis. Loomis was where we had turned off the highway. Up ahead was another mile of fields climbing up to a wooded ridge and the junction with Route 17. Gail came back with the keys, and I opened the trunk.

"Is *that* the spare?" she said. "That old thing?"

"It's good enough to get us there," I said.

I gave her my jacket and rolled up my sleeves, and tried the lug that held the tire in its frame. The lug was loose enough to turn. I worked it off the bolt and picked up the tire and bounced it down and leaned it against the bumper. It had a good, hard bounce. I got out the jack and got down on my knees and got it under the bumper. It was a good thing I was just wearing chinos. My suit was in my bag. I hiked the jack a couple of notches with my finger, and got up and went back to the trunk for the lug wrench. It wasn't there.

"That's funny," I said.

"What's the matter?" Gail said.

"I can't find the lug wrench. You know – to hoist the jack and unscrew the lugs. It isn't here. It's gone."

"Are you sure?"

"Give me a cigarette," I said. "Of course I'm sure. It's gone."

"How could it be?" she said.

32

"I don't know," I said. I lighted the cigarette. "Maybe somebody at the garage..."

"Jack," she said. "What are we going to do?"

"I can't change a tire without a lug wrench," I said.

"But what are we going to do?"

"I'll just have to borrow one," I said. "I'll get one of these cars to stop and let me use their wrench."

"Oh," Gail said. Then her face changed. "But suppose nobody stops? Jack – this is terrible."

"Hush," I said. I put on my jacket and brushed off the knees of my pants. "I'll get somebody to stop. We'll be O.K."

The road was empty in both directions. We stood there and waited. I finished my cigarette and ground it out in the blacktop rubble at the edge of the road. I tried not to worry. This wasn't a deserted road. It always carried a certain amount of traffic.

"I think I see a car," Gail said.

I saw it, too. It was coming down the ridge, and I could see the windshield shining through the trees. We watched it come out of the woods, and it seemed to be moving very slowly, and then all of a sudden it was almost on us. It was a blue station wagon with two women in front and a little boy in back. I stepped out in the road and waved my arms. It didn't stop. The little boy turned his head and stared, but the women looked straight ahead.

"Well," I said.

Gail didn't say anything.

"Those were women," I said. "I wouldn't really expect a woman to stop."

Another car came down through the woods, and two cars moving close together came over the rise from the creek. The second of the two cars was a telephone-company truck. All three cars were going fast and all of the drivers were careful not to look at me, and none of them stopped. Gail went up to the front of the car and came back with her sweater. The sun was still well up in the sky beyond the creek, but the feel of the air had changed. It had the feel of evening. I looked at my watch. It was almost six-thirty. We had been here almost half an hour. A big trailer truck went by, and then another car. The car was an old sedan with big tail fins and racing stripes, and the driver was a boy with a girl in the crook of his arm.

"That makes six," Gail said.

"I don't know what else we can do."

"I know," she said. "But what happens when it gets dark?"

"It isn't dark yet."

"We could be here all night."

"Somebody will stop," I said.

A car came down from the ridge. We stood and waited and waved and watched it go by.

"Well," I said, "that makes it seven."

"And the one after that will be eight," Gail said. She looked at me. "Jack, I've got an idea. What if I tried it alone? Maybe a man would stop for me. I mean, for a girl."

"I know what you mean," I said.

Gail smiled. "All right," she said. "But seriously. What do you think?"

"I think you're probably right," I said. "I think it's a good idea."

"You do?" she said, and took a deep breath. She pulled down her sweater and straightened her skirt. "You really think it might work?"

"I think it's a good idea," I said.

"At least, I could try and see," she said.

"That's right," I said.

"Then get out of sight," she said. "Go get in the car."

"O.K.," I said.

I went up and got under the wheel and slid down low in the seat. I slid down as low as I could. I'm six feet one, but I managed to get my head pretty well out of sight. I could just see over the top of the dashboard. The road up ahead was empty. I reached out and adjusted the side mirror to give me a view of the road behind. The rearview mirror on the windshield was blocked by the lifted lid of the trunk. Gail was standing just off the blacktop with one hand cupped on her hip. In the sharp evening light, her hair looked almost red. She was really quite a sight. I saw her tense and turn. A car was coming from up ahead. I slid down low, and listened. I heard the car come up – and go by. But that didn't prove anything. Maybe the driver was a woman.

The next car came from the other direction. In the mirror I watched it coming and Gail stepping out, with her red hair blowing, and waving her hand. The car came up and slowed, and moved on, and then slowed again, and swung off the road. It was a green Mustang convertible with a broken back bumper and a rip in the top patched with tape. It backed up along the shoulder and stopped about a car length ahead. A man got out. He had short blond hair and he had on a longshoreman's jersey and an old green Air Force windbreaker. He looked about twenty-five. Gail came running and walking past my window. She didn't look at me. I slipped down in the seat as low as I could get.

I lay there and listened. I could hear them talking, but I couldn't hear what they said. I heard the man laugh. Then nothing. Then I heard a car door slam. Then they were talking again. It was uncomfortable lying there hunched under the wheel, and I wondered what they were talking about so long – what the man was talking about. I could hear Gail's voice every now and then, but the man was doing the talking. He laughed again. But it wasn't exactly a laugh this time. It was more like a grunt or a snort. Then Gail

said something, and I heard them coming my way. They came down along the shoulder of the road. I turned a little and raised my head. They were walking single file, with Gail in the lead and the man a step or two behind her, swinging a hammer-headed lug wrench. I started to sit up – and my heart gave a jump. Behind the man was another man. He was about the age of the other, and he had a round, pink, smiling face, and he wore glasses. He had a can of beer in his hand. I watched him go by. I felt a little funny. But he looked all right. They both looked all right. And it had worked. Gail had got us a lug wrench.

I opened the door and got out and walked on back and around. The three of them were standing there with Gail backed up against the side of the car. She had a kind of frozen smile on her face. They heard me coming, and the two men turned. I smiled and nodded and said hello. They stared at me.

"Oh," Gail said. She sounded out of breath. "This is my husband."

The man with the lug wrench looked at her.

"Yeah?" he said, and looked at me again. He put a cigarette in his mouth and lighted it and blew out a stream of smoke. There was beer on his breath and his eyes were bright and shiny. "And where you been all this time?" he said.

The other man gave a snorting laugh. "I know where he's been," he said. "He was hiding in the car, Les. I thought I saw something setting in there when we come by." He took a drink of his beer. "Ain't that right, fella?"

"Yes," I said. "That's right. I . . ."

"How about that, Les?" he said. "He was hiding in their car."

"Yeah," Les said.

"I'm sorry, boys," Gail said. "I'm afraid

it's all my fault. I'm afraid I played a trick on you."

"Yeah?" Les said. "What kind of trick was that?"

"I guess I sort of gave you the impression that I was all alone," Gail said.

"Yeah," Les said. "And now you're sorry."

"She don't sound sorry," the other man said. "Not real sorry. Does she, Les?"

"You know what I mean," Gail said. "I only meant..."

"Never mind, Gail," I said. "They know what you mean." I turned to Les. "Look — it's getting late. Let's be serious. You know what happened. We had this flat tire and somebody seems to have swiped my lug wrench. I'm sure my wife told you all that. So I tried to flag somebody down and borrow his wrench, but nobody stopped and – well, my wife thought maybe she might have better luck."

"She did, huh?" Les said.

"Yes," I said. "So she – and then you were nice enough to stop."

Les smiled. "You got a cute-looking wife," he said.

"Real cute," the other man said.

"My wife told you she was sorry," I said. "And I'm sorry, too. But you can understand how we felt. We were stuck here and it was getting late. We had to do something."

"We could have been here all night," Gail said.

Les dropped his cigarette between his feet and ground it out with his heel. He was wearing Wellington boots. He looked at the other man. "You know something, Billy?" he said. "I wonder if she really is his wife. I think she's too cute-looking."

"She said she was," Billy said.

"She said a lot of things," Les said. "Didn't you, Red?"

"I don't know what you're talking about," Gail said. "And don't call me 'Red.'"

Billy laughed. "Listen to that redhead temper, Les."

"Yeah," Les said. "That's another thing I like about her."

"All right," I said. "That's enough. Cut it out."

Les turned his head and looked at me.

"Look," I said. "This isn't getting us anywhere. Why don't you just give me that lug wrench and let me change this tire. Then we can all be on our way."

"Give?" Les said. "You want me to *give* you my wrench?"

"O.K.," I said. "I want to borrow your wrench."

He smiled. "Say 'please,'" he said.

"Oh, for God's sake," I said.

He laughed. "I was just kidding," he said. "Here – you want to use my wrench, take it."

He held out the wrench. I reached to take it, and he snatched it back. He smiled and shook his head. "You forgot to thank me," he said.

I stood there for a moment. Then I shrugged. "O.K.," I said – and I lunged. He tried to move, but he wasn't ready. I got a grip on the wrench and gave it a fast backhand twist and he couldn't hold it. He let it go and stepped forward and kicked me in the shin. I stumbled and fell and went down on one knee. I saw him coming at me again and I swung the wrench. I felt it hit and heard the crack of bone. He took a long, sliding step and sat down hard on the grass. Something moved behind me. I remembered Billy, and turned. But it wasn't Billy. It was Gail, with her mouth hanging open. Billy was up the road, running for their car. I turned back to Gail. Her mouth was still hanging open and she was staring down at Les. He lay on his back looking up with an empty look on his face, and there was blood running out of his ear.

# Jacques Prévert

# Family History

TRANSLATED BY E.A. LACEY

The mother knits
and the son goes to war
and the mother thinks "That's what sons are for."
And the father? What does the father do?
He runs a store.
His wife does knitting
his son goes to war
he goes to the store –
and the father thinks "That's what men are for."
And the son? The son and heir?
What does he think, the son and heir?
Why, nothing at all. He doesn't care.
His mother does knitting,
his father keeps store,
he makes war.
When he is through making war
he and his father will run the store.
On knits the mother,
on goes the war,
on goes the father running the store.
But the son is killed: he goes on no more.
So the mother and father go in their car
to the churchyard and think "That's the way things are."
And life goes on, with knitting and wars
and stores
wars and stores and knitting and wars
and stores and stores and stores
and wars.

From *Paroles* by Jacques Prévert. © Editions Gallimard 1949.

George Giles

# Letters from a Soldier

I don't think a man
appreciates his home and
family until he is away
from them a while and
then he begins to think
what he has missed.

**M**y dear girl – Still travelling east though slow. We won't be in Halifax till tomorrow, Monday. We are travelling through Nova Scotia now. The scenery all through Quebec is the most desolate ever I saw but it is improving now. We haven't been off the train since we left London except at Montreal where they marched us through Montreal for thirty minutes for exercise. I'm kicking well. Hoping you are and the kids. Goodbye. Fond love, George.

We are getting much better grub now [in England] than we did at first though I don't like the way we get it served out. (We have to line up at the cookhouse and take our turns, then beat it to your tent, sit down on a kit-

bag and go to it.) No plates no cups or tables just a canteen or mess tin and after eating, Oh Lord, I've got to go out and wash my tins. Just imagine me trying to dig the grease off a canteen with nothing but cold water and mud. You know how I would wash dishes at home where there was lots of hot water and soda, etc. Gee, don't I curse sometimes and wish I was back in little old Sarnia and able to hand that nice greasy tin over to you.... But we are quite used to it by now and there's absolutely no use kicking so we have just to grin and bear it and comfort ourselves with the fact that the worst is yet to come when we go over to France which will be in about two months. Well, dearie, I'll have to quit now; (this is my last piece of paper and supper is ready and if I hang around at all I'll be too late to get any). How is every little thing going on over there? Do the kiddies look for me coming home weekends yet or are they forgetting? I suppose they are, it

Reprinted by permission of Robert Nielsen.

doesn't take long for little ones to forget but I'll soon make 'em remember when I get back. I don't think a man appreciates his home and family until he is away from them a while and then he begins to think what he has missed.

I don't feel much like writing this evening as I am dog-tired. We have been out shooting all day. (Got up this morning at half past three and arrived down at the range at six o'clock and stayed there till one o'clock when we had to march back to camp over the damnedest hilly road imaginable.) The rest of the fellows are all asleep now but I thought I had better write now (than put it off till I feel better for fear I might not get a chance to write again before the Canadian mail goes....)

I'm waiting patiently for those photos of the kiddies in khaki; I'll bet they look well, especially our Lily. How is that little duck getting on? Is she still as saucy and looking for Daddy yet? I can picture that little coon jumping at me every time I went into the house when on a weekend from London. I hope you have no trouble with her this summer as there was heaps of it last year, but you will want to watch the fruit and see she doesn't get any green stuff down her as that's liable to cause the trouble with her any time. I think I'll have to cut that group picture down so that it will fit in my pocket for it's only getting spoiled in my kit-bag and it's got to go with me wherever I go. I hate to do it but I'm afraid it's got to be done....

We are liable to go to France at any time but if we go to school well we are likely to be here a couple of months yet and I will probably get another pass. I was a little set up by that little poem you sent in your last letter. It seemed very appropriate and speaks volumes for your thoughtfulness. I knew it was out of the firemen's magazine as soon as I saw it and it is stowed away in my pocketbook with that little letter from the kiddies that I got in Queen's Park. It will come in handy when I'm in the blues any time, as does that little letter and the photo. I often take a sly look at them and it sets me thinking of home right away. I don't think there is any chance of me going seriously wrong while I have those gentle reminders close to me all the time. I was just thinking of home as I was eating my supper tonight. I was sitting munching a chunk of bread about two inches thick streaked with margarine and a couple of spoonfuls of salmon and a canteen of tea with the British Navy in tea leaves floating on top. The thought came into my mind of what I would be having for Sunday night's supper at home. Well I was pretty near throwing it down in disgust but hunger compelled me to eat it. Well, dearie, I'm here and I've got to put up with it and bad and all as it is I don't think I would go back on what I have done if I could. I've started out and I'm going to finish but I'll be damned glad when it is finished and I can get back home to you and the kiddies.

Mrs. T. and Mrs. M. came up to say goodbye to us the night before we left England, and the Colonel and Major Butter, Capt. McKenzie, the adjutant, and a whole lot more of the officers shook hands with us and bade us God Speed, etc. You certainly had your nerve taking that gang up to the beach for ten cents. I'll tell you, my dear, if I had been there I wouldn't have owned you but I'd give a hundred dollars to have the privilege of riding with you (instead of sitting here listening to those darned guns dinning away day and night). This outfit I'm in now is delightfully lousy and I suppose I'll be as lousy as a cuckoo myself before long though I haven't discovered any on me as yet. I don't think much of the appearance of the Belgians or French. I'd heard a lot about the good looks of the French but I fail to see them myself. I've passed through a good part of France and a little of Belgium and to my mind even a passable good-looking woman is the exception more than the rule. Maybe they don't suit my taste but anyhow they have to show me where their good looks come in compared with the British or Canadians. This applies to both men and women....

So Lily is asking for Daddy, eh? Well she doesn't want her Daddy any more than her Daddy wants her and he won't lose any time getting back to you all just as soon as he gets a chance. It's a good job her tummy isn't bothering any more. I felt uneasy about her now that the fruit is in again and it would be just as well to watch her for it again this year as you can't be too careful in a case of that kind. Well, my dear, I've had my first crack in the trenches and I'll tell you it's wicked. The Germans shelled the tar out of us several times....

I received your dandy parcel yesterday and I'm afraid I made terribly short work of it. That tin box you sent this time was a good idea for though it was battered quite a bit the contents were in very good shape. There wasn't even a crumb knocked off the cake, which speaks well for the packing as well as the box. I think from the dents which showed in the tin that if it had been a cardboard box like the last, the cake and chocolate would have been in pretty bad shape whereas everything came out in as good condition as it was put in. The cake especially was fine as was also the lobster, in fact the whole lot was voted A1 both by myself and the others I invited to share it with me.

The dugouts and trenches are full of it [canned meat] and we can have it for breakfast, dinner, and supper if we want it. I've seen the bombers punch a hole in a can, stick a detonator in it, and throw it in the German trench where it explodes with a devil of a noise and scares the wits out of Fritz.

I think, my dear, you must be worrying too much and that is the cause of your headaches, for you never seemed to be bothered that way before and now you mention your head in almost every letter. There must be some cause for them and that is worry or ill health. If it is worry you can easily cure that yourself by ceasing to worry, which I suppose you will say is much more easily said than done. Well perhaps it is, but I think, old girl, if you just would try not to worry you would find it is much easier on your head and nerves. If it is your health get old Doc Haynes to give you a bottle or two, though it wouldn't be a bad idea to see him in either case for I suppose you have let yourself get thoroughly run down. You mention in this last letter how well Marty looks.... I'm tickled to hear the kiddies are so well but at the same time when I get home I want to see you looking just as well or better than them even. M. was shooting a little hot air when he said I was as fat as a pig because I'm not a bit different now than when I left. I may be a little stouter in the face and I'm wearing a dinky mustache as that seems to be the fashion in the Harmy and it saves quite a bit of time shaving in the morning but I'll push it off my face before I start for home as I don't want to scare the local population into hysterics. I intended sending the kiddies a couple of picture postcards this week but I don't believe there is such a thing as a picture postcard within miles....

I suppose by the time you get this letter the days at the beach will be numbered, much to the kiddies' disgust. G. told me in his letter that the crowd of you occupied one side of a streetcar one day and the number of tickets he gave the conductor would hardly pay for the sand the motorman would use on the rails. I suppose he would think it a huge joke and if the conductor was satisfied I guess Alec would be highly delighted. You can tell Alec there is a pond on a farm a little distance from where I am writing this that isn't any more than one hundred feet square, yet I've seen fish in it that would run three or four pounds apiece, but unfortunately I have neither the time or the tackle to go after them or else I should make a catch that would make him green with envy. Well, my dear,

it's getting so dark I can hardly see what I'm writing so I'll close. I'm still in good shape in spite of the rotten weather we are getting just now and I hope you and the kiddies are fit and not worrying too much.

*Dear Mrs. Giles: Will you kindly accept my sincere sympathy and condolence in the decease of that worthy citizen and heroic soldier, your husband, Private George Thomas Giles.*

*While one cannot too deeply mourn the loss of such a brave comrade, there is a consolation in knowing that he did his duty fearlessly and well, and gave his life for the cause of Liberty and the upbuilding of the Empire.*

*Again extending to you my heartfelt sympathy.*

*Faithfully,*
*Sam Hughes (signed)*
*Lieutenant-General,*
*Minister of Militia and Defence,*
*for Canada.*

# George Orwell

# A Hanging

A dreadful thing had happened – a dog,
come goodness knows whence, had appeared in the yard.

It was in Burma, a sodden morning of the rains. A sickly light, like yellow tin foil, was slanting over the high walls into the jail yard. We were waiting outside the condemned cells, a row of sheds fronted with double bars, like small animal cages. Each cell measured about ten feet by ten and was quite bare within except for a plank bed and a pot for drinking water. In

some of them brown, silent men were squatting at the inner bars, with their blankets draped round them. These were the condemned men, due to be hanged within the next week or two.

One prisoner had been brought out of his cell. He was a Hindu, a puny wisp of a man, with a shaven head and vague, liquid eyes. He had a thick, sprouting moustache, absurdly too big for his body, rather like the moustache of a comic man on the films. Six tall Indian warders were guarding him and

Reprinted by permission of Mrs. Sonia Brownell Orwell and Martin Secker & Warburg.

getting him ready for the gallows. Two of them stood by with rifles and fixed bayonets, while the others handcuffed him, passed a chain through his handcuffs and fixed it to their belts, and lashed his arms tight to his sides. They crowded very close about him, with their hands always on him in a careful, caressing grip, as though all the while feeling him to make sure he was there. It was like men handling a fish which is still alive and may jump back into the water. But he stood quite unresisting, yielding his arms limply to the ropes, as though he hardly noticed what was happening.

Eight o'clock struck and a bugle call, desolately thin in the wet air, floated from the distant barracks. The superintendent of the jail, who was standing apart from the rest of us, moodily prodding the gravel with his stick, raised his head at the sound. He was an army doctor, with a grey toothbrush moustache and a gruff voice. "For God's sake hurry up, Francis," he said irritably. "The man ought to have been dead by this time. Aren't you ready yet?"

Francis, the head jailer, a fat Dravidian in a white drill suit and gold spectacles, waved his black hand. "Yes sir, yes sir," he bubbled. "All iss satisfactorily prepared. The hangman iss waiting. We shall proceed."

"Well, quick march, then. The prisoners can't get their breakfast till this job's over."

We set out for the gallows. Two warders marched on either side of the prisoner, with their rifles at the slope; two others marched close against him, gripping him by arm and shoulder, as though at once pushing and sup-porting him. The rest of us, magistrates and the like, followed behind. Suddenly, when we had gone ten yards, the procession stopped short without any order or warning. A dreadful thing had happened – a dog, come goodness knows whence, had appeared in the yard. It came bounding among us with a loud volley of barks and leapt round us wagging its whole body, wild with glee at finding so many human beings together. It was a large woolly dog, half Airedale, half pariah. For a moment it pranced round us, and then, before anyone could stop it, it had made a dash for the prisoner and, jumping up, tried to lick his face. Everyone stood aghast, too taken aback even to grab at the dog.

"Who let that bloody brute in here?" said the superintendent angrily. "Catch it, some-one!"

A warder, detached from the escort, charged clumsily after the dog, but it danced and gambolled just out of his reach, taking everything as part of the game. A young Eurasian jailer picked up a handful of gravel and tried to stone the dog away, but it dodged the stones and came after us again. Its yaps echoed from the jail walls. The pris-oner, in the grasp of the two warders, looked on incuriously, as though this was another formality of the hanging. It was several min-utes before someone managed to catch the dog. Then we put my handkerchief through its collar and moved off once more, with the dog still straining and whimpering.

It was about forty yards to the gallows. I watched the bare brown back of the prisoner marching in front of me. He walked clumsily with his bound arms, but quite steadily, with that bobbing gait of the Indian who never straightens his knees. At each step his muscles slid neatly into place, the lock of hair on his scalp danced up and down, his feet printed themselves on the wet gravel. And once, in spite of the men who gripped him by each shoulder, he stepped slightly aside to avoid a puddle on the path.

It is curious, but till that moment I had never realized what it means to destroy a healthy, conscious man. When I saw the pris-oner step aside to avoid the puddle I saw the mystery, the unspeakable wrongness, of cutting a life short when it is in full tide. This man was not dying; he was alive just as we are alive. All the organs of his body were working – bowels digesting food, skin renewing itself, nails growing, tissues forming – all toiling away in solemn foolery. His nails would still be growing when he stood on the drop, when he was falling through the air with a tenth of a second to live. His eyes saw the yellow gravel and the grey walls, and his brain still remembered, foresaw, reasoned – reasoned even about puddles. He and we were a party of men walking together, seeing, hearing, feeling, understanding the same world; and in two minutes, with a sudden snap, one of us would be gone – one mind less, one world less.

The gallows stood in a small yard, separate from the main grounds of the prison, and overgrown with tall, prickly weeds. It was a brick erection like three sides of a shed, with planking on top, and above that two beams and a crossbar with the rope dangling. The hangman, a grey-haired convict in the white uniform of the prison, was waiting beside his machine. He greeted us with a servile crouch as we entered. At a word from Francis the two warders, gripping the prisoner more closely than ever, half led half pushed him to the gallows and helped him clumsily up the ladder. Then the hangman climbed up and fixed the rope round the prisoner's neck.

We stood waiting, five yards away. The warders had formed in a rough circle round the gallows. And then, when the noose was fixed, the prisoner began crying out to his god. It was a high, reiterated cry of "Ram! Ram! Ram! Ram!" not urgent and fearful like a prayer or cry for help, but steady, rhythmical, almost like the tolling of a bell. The dog answered the sound with a whine. The hangman, still standing on the gallows,

produced a small cotton bag like a flour bag and drew it down over the prisoner's face. But the sound, muffled by the cloth, still persisted, over and over again: "Ram! Ram! Ram! Ram! Ram!"

The hangman climbed down and stood ready, holding the lever. Minutes seemed to pass. The steady, muffled crying from the prisoner went on and on, "Ram! Ram! Ram!" never faltering for an instant. The superintendent, his head on his chest, was slowly poking the ground with his stick; perhaps he was counting the cries, allowing the prisoner a fixed number – fifty, perhaps, or a hundred. Everyone had changed color. The Indians had gone grey like bad coffee, and one or two of the bayonets were wavering. We looked at the lashed, hooded man on the drop, and listened to his cries – each cry another second of life; the same thought was in all our minds: oh, kill him quickly, get it over, stop that abominable noise!

Suddenly the superintendent made up his mind. Throwing up his head he made a swift motion with his stick. "Chalo!" he shouted almost fiercely.

There was a clanking noise, and then dead silence. The prisoner had vanished, and the rope was twisting on itself. I let go of the dog, and it galloped immediately to the back of the gallows; but when it got there it stopped short, barked, and then retreated into a corner of the yard, where it stood among the weeds, looking timorously out at us. We went round the gallows to inspect the prisoner's body. He was dangling with his toes pointed straight downwards, very slowly revolving, as dead as a stone.

The superintendent reached out with his stick and poked the bare brown body; it oscillated slightly. "*He's* all right," said the superintendent. He backed out from under the gallows, and blew out a deep breath. The moody look had gone out of his face quite suddenly. He glanced at his wristwatch. "Eight minutes past eight. Well, that's all for this morning, thank God."

The warders unfixed bayonets and marched away. The dog, sobered and conscious of having misbehaved itself, slipped after them. We walked out of the gallows yard, past the condemned cells with their waiting prisoners, into the big central yard of the prison. The convicts, under the command of warders armed with lathis, were already receiving their breakfast. They squatted in long rows, each man holding a tin pannikin, while two warders with buckets marched round ladling out rice; it seemed quite a homely, jolly scene after the hanging. An enormous relief had come upon us now that the job was done. One felt an impulse to sing, to break into a run, to snigger. All at once everyone began chattering gaily.

The Eurasian boy walking beside me nodded towards the way we had come, with a knowing smile: "Do you know sir, our friend [he meant the dead man] when he heard his appeal had been dismissed, he pissed on the floor of his cell. From fright. Kindly take one of my cigarettes, sir. Do you not admire my new silver case, sir? From the boxwallah, two rupees eight annas. Classy European style."

Several people laughed – at what, nobody seemed certain.

Francis was walking by the superintend-ent, talking garrulously: "Well, sir, all hass passed off with the utmost satisfactoriness. It was all finished – flick! like that. It iss not always so – oah, no! I have known cases where the doctor wass obliged to go beneath the gallows and pull the prissoner's legs to ensure decease. Most disagreeable!"

"Wriggling about, eh? That's bad," said the superintendent.

"Ach, sir, it iss worse when they become refractory! One man, I recall, clung to the bars of hiss cage when we went to take him out. You will scarcely credit, sir, that it took six warders to dislodge him, three pulling at each leg. We reasoned with him. 'My dear fellow,' we said, 'think of all the pain and trouble you are causing to us!' But no, he would not listen! Ach, he wass very trouble-some!"

I found that I was laughing quite loudly. Everyone was laughing. Even the superintendent grinned in a tolerant way. "You'd better all come out and have a drink," he said quite genially. "I've got a bottle of whisky in the car. We could do with it."

We went through the big double gates of the prison into the road. "Pulling at his legs!" exclaimed a Burmese magistrate suddenly, and burst into a loud chuckling. We all began laughing again. At that moment, Francis' anecdote seemed extraordinarily funny. We all had a drink together, native and European alike, quite amicably. The dead man was a hundred yards away.

Reginald Rose

# Thunder on Sycamore Street

"Do you know what a mob is like?
Do you know what they're capable of doing?"

*Characters*

FRANK MORRISON, a heavy man with a loud voice;
    about forty

CLARICE MORRISON, his wife

ROGER MORRISON, older son

CHRISTOPHER MORRISON, younger son

ARTHUR HAYES, a quiet man, between thirty-five
    and thirty-eight

PHYLLIS HAYES, his wife

MR. HARKNESS, Mrs. Hayes' father

JOSEPH BLAKE, a big, powerful man,
    in his late thirties

ANNA BLAKE, his wife

JUDY BLAKE, daughter

MRS. BLAKE, Joseph Blake's mother

CHARLIE DENTON, a neighbor

MRS. CARSON, a neighbor

*Setting: A residential street in an
    American suburb; the present.*

## Act One

*Fade in on a long shot of Sycamore Street in
the pleasant and tidy village of Eastmont. It is*

*6:40 P.M. and just getting dark. We see three
houses, modest but attractive, side by side,
each an exact replica of the other. Each has a
tiny front lawn and a tree or two in front of it.
Each has been lived in and cared for by people
who take pride in their own hard-won
respectability. The street is quiet. Walking
toward the houses now we see Arthur Hayes,
a quiet, bespectacled man between thirty-five
and thirty-eight years of age. He lives in the
second of the three houses. He walks slowly,
carrying a newspaper under his arm and
smoking a pipe. He stops in front of his house
and, almost in a daze, knocks the dottle out of
his pipe against his heel. As he is doing this,
we see Frank Morrison enter, also carrying a
newspaper. He is a heavy man, forceful and
aggressive, with a loud voice and a hearty
laugh. He is about forty years of age. Frank
Morrison lives right next door to Arthur in the
first of the three houses. He sees Arthur and
waves.*

FRANK: (*jovially*) Hey, Artie. How ya doin'?
(*Arthur is preoccupied. He doesn't register at
first. He looks blankly at Frank. Frank
laughs.*) Hey...wake up, boy. It's almost
time for supper.
*Arthur snaps out of it and forces a smile.*

ARTHUR: (*quietly*) Oh...hello, Frank. Sorry. I didn't see you.

FRANK: Didn't see me? Hey, wait till I tell Clarice. That diet she's got me on must be working. You have to look twice to see me! (*Laughing hard, Frank reaches for his keys*.) That's a hot one! (*Arthur smiles weakly*.) Say...isn't this late for you to be getting home?

ARTHUR: No, I don't think so. (*He looks at his watch*.) It's twenty to seven. I always get home about this time.

FRANK: Yeah. Well, I wouldn't want you to be late tonight. You know what tonight is, don't you?

ARTHUR: (*slowly*) Yes, I know what tonight is.

FRANK: (*a little hard*) Good.

*We hear footsteps and see a man walk by. He is Joseph Blake, a man in his late thirties, a big, powerful, but quiet man. Joseph Blake lives in the third house on the street. As he walks by them, they both look at him silently. Arthur turns away then, but Frank continues to stare at him. Camera moves in on Frank as he stares coldly at Joseph Blake. His face is hard, full of hatred. The footsteps recede.*

FRANK: (*low*) See you later, Artie.

*Frank turns and fits the key into the lock. There is utter silence. He fumbles with the lock, then silently swings the door open. He walks into the small foyer. The living room ahead is brightly lighted, but we see no one. Frank walks slowly, silently, into the living room. As he enters it, we hear a dozen pistol shots. Frank stiffens, clutches himself and falls to the floor as if dead. Then we hear a chorus of shrill screams and two small boys wearing cowboy hats and carrying pistols fling themselves upon Frank's body. Frank doesn't move as they clamber over him. One is Roger, age ten; the other is Christopher, age six. Christopher wears "Dr. Dentons."*

CHRISTOPHER: (*screaming*) I got him! I got him first.

ROGER: You did not!

CHRISTOPHER: I did so! Get offa him. I got him first. (*calling*) Hey, Mom...

ROGER: (*superior*) Boy, are you stupid! I got him three times before you even pulled the trigger.

CHRISTOPHER: (*squeaking*) What d'ya mean? I got him before you even...(*Roger tries to push Christopher off Frank's still motionless body*.) Before you even...(*Christopher grunts and fights back*.) Cut it out! Hey, Mom...

*Clarice, Frank's wife, a pleasant-looking woman in her early thirties, comes to living-room door from kitchen. She wears an apron. She calls out before she sees them.*

CLARICE: Now you boys stop that noise. (*She sees Roger pushing Christopher*.) Roger!

CHRISTOPHER: Cut it out, willya. I got him....

CLARICE: Roger! Stop that pushing....

CHRISTOPHER: I'm gonna sock you....

CLARICE: (*angrily*) Christopher, don't you dare! Frank! Will you do something... please!

ROGER: Go ahead. Sock me. You couldn't hurt a flea!

CHRISTOPHER: (*winding up*) Who says so?

ROGER: Boy, you must be deaf. I said so!

CLARICE: Frank!

*As Christopher swings at Roger, Frank suddenly comes to life with a tremendous roar. He rolls over, toppling both boys to the floor and with lightning swiftness he grabs both of their cap pistols. He stands up grinning. They both look at him, startled.*

FRANK: (*barking*) Get up! (*They both do, slowly*.) Get your hands up! (*They look at each other*.) Make it snappy if you don't want to draw lead. (*Christopher shrugs and raises his hands. To Roger*) You too, hombre!

ROGER: Aaaah, Dad...

FRANK: Last warning.

ROGER: (*disgusted*) Come on...(*Frank shoots*

46 *him with the cap pistol.*) What are you so
serious about?
*He walks away. Frank watches him, still not
giving up the cowboy pose.*
CLARICE: All right. Now that's enough
gunplay. All three of you can just settle
down. (*to Frank*) Hand 'em over.
*He grins and gives her the guns. Then he
bends over and kisses her.*
FRANK: Hello, honey.
*She kisses him dutifully, then speaks to
Roger, handing him the guns.*
CLARICE: Put these in your room and come
back with your hands washed. We're
sitting down to supper right now.
ROGER: (*desperately*) Right now? I gotta
watch *Range-busters*.
CLARICE: Not tonight. I told you we were
eating early.
ROGER: Ah, Mom...please...
CLARICE: Absolutely not. Come on, now.
Inside...
*Roger slumps off. Clarice turns to
Christopher as Frank begins to take off his
coat.*
CLARICE: And you're going to bed, mister.
CHRISTOPHER: No! I can't go to bed!
CLARICE: Christopher!
CHRISTOPHER: (*backing away*) I'm not tired
yet. Honest!
*Frank is hanging his coat up in the foyer.
Clarice advances toward Chris, who looks
for means of escape.*
CLARICE: I'm not going to argue with you.
CHRISTOPHER: Mom, fifteen minutes. Come
on. Please...
CLARICE: I'm going to start counting. One,
two...
CHRISTOPHER: (*fast*) Three four five six seven
eight nine ten.
*He runs away from her, but right into the
arms of Frank, who picks him up.*
FRANK: Trapped! Let's go, pal.
CHRISTOPHER: Aaah...

*Frank carries him past Clarice, who kisses
him on the way by. As they reach the door
which leads into bedroom, Roger comes out.
Christopher, in his father's arms, raps Roger
on the head with his knuckle.*
ROGER: Hey!
CHRISTOPHER: (*grinning*) Good night, Rog.
ROGER: Stupid!
FRANK: All right, now. That's enough out of
both of you. I don't want to hear another
peep.
*Frank takes Christopher into bedroom.
Camera follows Roger over to a dining table
set at one end of living room near a picture
window. This would probably be exactly the
same in all three houses. The only difference
in the three interior sets will be the way in
which they are decorated. There are dishes
on the table, glassware, etc. Roger slumps
into his chair and takes a piece of bread. He
munches on it as Clarice comes in from
kitchen carrying a steaming bowl of stew.
She sets it down and sits down.*
CLARICE: (*calling*) Frank!
FRANK: (*off*) O.K. I'll be right there.
ROGER: Hey, Mom, what are we eating so
early for?
CLARICE: (*serving*) Don't say "Hey, Mom."
ROGER: Well, what are we eating so early for?
CLARICE: Because we feel like eating early.
(*calling*) Frank!
*Frank walks in, loosening his tie.*
FRANK: What's for supper?
CLARICE: Beef stew.
ROGER: Look, if I could see the first five
minutes of *Range-busters*...
*Clarice ladles out the stew as Frank sits at
the table.*
CLARICE: Roger, I'm not going to tell you
again.
ROGER: (*anguished*) But, Mom, you don't
know what's happening. There's this
sneaky guy...
FRANK: Come on boy, dig into your dinner.

*Roger makes a face and gives up the battle.*

FRANK: (*to Clarice*) What time is the sitter coming?

CLARICE: Ten after seven. Do you know that's the third time today you've asked me.

FRANK: Just want to be sure.

CLARICE: I don't see why they have to make it so early anyway.

*Frank has a mouthful of food, so shrugs.*

ROGER: Make what so early, Dad?

CLARICE: Nothing. Eat your dinner.

FRANK: Good stew.

CLARICE: There's plenty more.

FRANK: (*chewing*) Mmmm. Hmmmm. Do anything special today, Rog?

ROGER: Nope. Just kinda hung around.

FRANK: Well, I don't know why you don't get out and do something. A boy your age . . .

ROGER: Some of the kids dumped garbage on the Blakes' lawn again.

FRANK: (*casually*) That so? What about you?

ROGER: Ah, what fun is that after you do it a couple of times?

FRANK: (*chewing*) Mmmm. Hey, how about eating your stew.

ROGER: I'm not hungry.

CLARICE: Frank, I wish you'd do something about that boy's eating. He's beginning to look like a scarecrow.

FRANK: He'll be all right. What time is it?

CLARICE: (*looking at watch*) Five of seven.

FRANK: We'd better snap it up.

CLARICE: Plenty of time. I'm leaving the dishes till later.

FRANK: Y'know. Clarry, this really ought to be something tonight.

*Roger starts to get up, but stops.*

ROGER: What ought to be something?

CLARICE: You just sit down and pay attention to your dinner. There's a glass of milk to be finished before you get up.

ROGER: (*grudgingly*) O.K. (*He sips the milk for a moment.*) Where you going tonight, Dad?

FRANK: We're going for a little walk.

ROGER: Well, what d'ya have to go out so early for?

FRANK: Just like that.

ROGER: (*aggressively*) Well, what the heck is the big secret, that's what I'd like to know. Everybody's acting so mysterious.

FRANK: (*sharply*) That's enough. Now I don't want to hear any more questions out of you. Your mother and I have some business to attend to, and that's it. You mind yours.

*Roger, stunned, looks at his father, then down at his plate. There is an awkward silence. Frank eats stolidly. They watch him.*

FRANK: (*to Clarice*) Where's that sitter?

CLARICE: It's not time yet. Take it easy, Frank.

*Frank gets up from the table, goes over to a box of cigars on top of the TV set and lights one. Clarice and Roger watch him silently.*

CLARICE: Aren't you going to have some dessert, Frank? There's some cherry pie left.

FRANK: I'll have it later.

*He puffs on the cigar.*

ROGER: (*low*) I'm sorry, Dad.

FRANK: (*turning*) Well, it's about time you learned some respect, d'you hear me? If I want you to know something I'll tell you.

ROGER: (*softly*) O.K. . . .

CLARICE: (*quickly*) Have some pie, honey. I heated it special.

*Frank goes to the table and sits down. He puts the cigar down and Clarice begins to cut him some pie.*

CLARICE: How late do you think we'll be, Frank?

FRANK: I don't know.

CLARICE: Do you think I ought to pack a thermos of coffee? It's going to be chilly.

FRANK: Might not be a bad idea.

*Frank now begins to show the first signs of being excited about the evening. He speaks, almost to himself.*

FRANK: Boy, I can't wait till I see his face. The

48

nerve of him. The absolute nerve. (*grinning*) What d'you think he'll do when we all ...

CLARICE: (*looking at Roger*) Frank ...

FRANK: (*as Roger stares*) Oh. Yeah. O.K., go ahead, Rog. You can turn on your program.

ROGER: Gee thanks, Dad.

*He jumps up, goes to the TV set, and turns it on. Frank and Clarice watch him get settled in front of TV set. We hear dialogue from set faintly. Roger watches in background, enraptured.*

FRANK: (*quietly*) What are they saying on the block?

CLARICE: I didn't speak to anyone. I was ironing all day.

FRANK: Charlie Denton called me at the office. I was right in the middle of taking an order from Martin Brothers for three A-81 tractors.

CLARICE: Three? Frank, that's wonderful.

FRANK: Not bad. Anyway, I made Mr. Martin wait while I spoke to Charlie. Charlie says it's gonna be one hundred percent. Every family on the block. He just called to tell me that.

CLARICE: Well, that's good. Everyone should be in on this.

FRANK: (*eating*) Clarry, I'm telling you this is going to be a job well done. It's how you have to do these things. Everybody getting together fast ... and boom, it's over. I can't wait till it's started. It's been long enough.

CLARICE: I saw her out the window today, hanging clothes in her yard like nothing was wrong. She didn't even look this way.

FRANK: What time is it?

CLARICE: Now you just asked me two minutes ago. It's about three minutes to seven. What's the matter with you? You'll be getting yourself an ulcer over this thing. Relax, Frank. Here, have some more pie.

FRANK: No. No more.

*He gets up and walks around nervously, slapping his fist into his palm. Roger is looking at him now. He is tense, excited, completely caught up in the impending event.*

FRANK: This is something big, you know that, Clarry? We're getting action without pussyfooting for once. That's it. That's the big part. There's too much pussyfooting going on all the time. Can't hurt anyone's feelings. Every time you turn around you're hurting some idiot's feelings. Well that's tough, I say. ...

CLARICE: (*indicating Roger*) Frank ...

FRANK: He can hear! He's old enough. You want something bad, you gotta go out and get it! That's how this world is. Boy, I like this, Clarry. You know what it makes me feel like? It makes me feel like a man! *He stalks up and down the room for a few moments as they watch him. Then he goes to the window and stands there looking out.*

CLARICE: (*quietly*) I think I'll just stack the dishes.

*She starts to do it. The doorbell rings. Roger jumps up.*

ROGER: I'll get it.

*He goes to the door and opens it. Arthur Hayes stands there a bit apologetically. He wears no overcoat, having just come from next door. He looks extremely upset.*

ARTHUR: Rog, is your dad in?

ROGER: Sure. Come in, Mr. Hayes.

*Arthur walks in slowly. Frank turns around, still excited. He goes over to Arthur.*

FRANK: (*loud*) Hey, Artie. Come on in.

ARTHUR: Hello, Frank ...

FRANK: (*laughing*) What can I do for you? (*Arthur looks hesitantly at Roger.*) Oh, sure. Rog, go help your mother.

*He walks off to dining table.*

FRANK: (*chuckling*) That's some kid, isn't he, Artie? How old is yours now?

ARTHUR: Twenty-one months.

FRANK: Yeah. Well that's still nothing but a crying machine. Wait a couple of years. He'll kill you.

ARTHUR: I guess so.

FRANK: And how! Sit down for a minute, Artie. What's on your mind?

ARTHUR: (*sitting, hesitantly*) Well, I don't know...I just...well...I just wanted...to talk.

FRANK: No kidding. Say, y'know you look a little green around the gills? What's the matter?

*Arthur Hayes takes off his eyeglasses and begins to polish them, a nervous habit in which he indulges when upset.*

ARTHUR: Nothing. I've had an upset stomach for a couple of days. Maybe that's it.

FRANK: (*nodding*) Yeah, that'll get you down all right. Probably a virus.

*Arthur nods and they look at each other awkwardly for a moment.*

FRANK: Well, what did you want to talk to me about?

*Arthur looks at the floor, trying to frame his answer carefully, afraid to offend. Finally he blurts it out.*

ARTHUR: What do you think about tonight?

FRANK: (*surprised*) What do you mean what do I think about it?

ARTHUR: Well, I've been kind of going over it all day, Frank. I talked with Phyllis before.

FRANK: (*a little hard*) And...

ARTHUR: Well, it was just talk. We were just talking it over to get clear on it, you know.

FRANK: Go ahead.

ARTHUR: And...well, look, Frank, it's a pretty hard thing. Supposing it were you?

FRANK: It's not.

ARTHUR: Well, I know that, but supposing it were?

*Frank stands up and goes over to Arthur.*

FRANK: Your glasses are clean. You wear 'em out, you have to buy a new pair. (*Arthur looks down at his glasses, then puts them on*

nervously.) Now what about it, Artie? What if I was the guy?

ARTHUR: Well, you know...how would you feel?

FRANK: How would I feel, huh? Now that's a good question, Artie. I'll answer it for you. It doesn't make any difference how I'd feel. Now let me ask you a question. Is he a lifelong buddy of yours?

ARTHUR: Well, now, you know he's not, Frank.

FRANK: Do you know him to say hello to?

ARTHUR: That's not the idea. He's...

FRANK: Artie...you don't even know the guy. What are you getting yourself all hot and bothered about? We all agreed, didn't we?

ARTHUR: Yes...everybody agreed...

FRANK: You. Me. The Dentons. The McAllisters. The Fredericks. The Schofields. Every family on Sycamore Street for that matter. We all agreed. That's how it is. The majority. Right?

ARTHUR: Well...I think we all ought to talk it over, maybe. Let it wait a few days.

*He takes off his glasses again and begins to wipe them.*

FRANK: Artie...we talked it over. (*Frank takes the handkerchief out of Arthur's hand and tucks in into his pocket.*) In about ten minutes we're starting. We expect to have a solid front, you know what I mean? Everybody. You included. You're my next door neighbor, boy. I don't want to hear people saying Artie Hayes wasn't there.

ARTHUR: (*hesitantly*) Well, I don't know, Frank. I thought...

*The phone rings. Frank goes toward it.*

FRANK: Go home, Artie. Don't worry about it. I'll see you in a few minutes. (*Frank goes to the phone and picks it up. Arthur stares at him.*) Hello...(*Arthur turns away and walks slowly to door.*) Speaking.

*Arthur goes out, dazed and frightened. Clarice comes into living room and stands waiting as Frank listens to phone.*

50

FRANK: (*angry*) What do you mean you can't get here? (*pause*) Well, this is a great time to call! (*pause*) I know. Yeah. (*He slams the phone down. To Clarice*) Our sitter can't get here. How d'you like that?

CLARICE: What's wrong with her?

FRANK: I don't know. She's got a cold, or something. Nice dependable girl you pick.

CLARICE: (*snapping*) Well, I didn't exactly arrange for her to get a cold, you know.

FRANK: Look. Clarry, we're going to this thing no matter what.

CLARICE: Well, I'm not leaving Chris with Roger. They'll claw each other to pieces.

FRANK: Then we'll take 'em with us.

CLARICE: You wouldn't...

FRANK: Who wouldn't? We're doing it for them as much as anyone else, aren't we? Well, they might as well see it.

CLARICE: Maybe I'd better stay home with them.

FRANK: No, sir. You've been in on this from the beginning. You're going. Come on, get Chris dressed. We haven't got much time.

CLARICE: Well...whatever you think, Frank...

FRANK: I'm telling you it's all right. Won't hurt 'em a bit. (*to Roger*) What d'you say, son? Want to come along?

ROGER: (*eagerly*) Oh boy! Really? (*Frank nods and grins. Roger leaps happily.*) Gee, Dad, you're the greatest guy in the whole world. *He runs over and hugs Frank.*

FRANK: (*grinning*) Go on, Clarry. Make it snappy.

*Clarice goes into the bedroom. Doorbell rings.*

ROGER: I'll get it, Dad.

*He runs to the door and opens it. Charlie Denton, forty years old and eager as a child, stands there. He comes in fast, excited.*

CHARLIE: Hiya, Rog. Frank, you all set?

FRANK: Hello, Charlie. Another minute or two. How's it look?

CHARLIE: Great. I'm checking house to house. Everybody's ready.

FRANK: Good. Any changes?

CHARLIE: Nope. It's gonna be fast and quiet. What time you got?

FRANK: (*calling*) Clarry, what time is it?

CLARICE: (*calling*) Twelve after.

CHARLIE: (*looking at watch*) Make it thirteen. At fifteen we go.

FRANK: Right. Hey, listen, you better look in on Artie Hayes next door. He's been acting a little peculiar.

CHARLIE: I spoke to him a little while ago on the street. I think he was coming over to see you. Don't worry about a thing. I'll be watching him. See you, Frank. Let's make this good.

FRANK: You bet we will. It looks like a beaut. Take off. (*Charlie goes out fast.*) Get on your coat, Rog. (*calling*) Clarry! *Roger goes to closet and begins to get his coat. Frank stalks nervously up and down.*

CLARICE: (*calling*) In a minute...

*Frank goes to the window and looks out. He watches and waits. We can see the excitement building within him. Roger, hat and coat on, joins him at window. Frank puts his arm on Roger's shoulder and talks, half to himself.*

FRANK: (*low*) How do you like that Artie Hayes? Maybe we ought to think it over! I could've belted him one. How do you like that guy!

ROGER: What do you mean, Dad?

FRANK: (*calling*) Clarry!

CLARICE: (*calling*) Here I am. Come on Chris. *Clarice walks into living room followed by a very sleepy Christopher. He is in his hat and coat. He wanders over to Frank.*

FRANK: What time is it?

CLARICE: Almost fourteen after.

FRANK: Almost fifteen. Put on your coat. *Clarice goes to the closet and does so. Frank follows her and gets his. He puts it on.*

*Clarice picks up a large thermos from the foyer table.*

CLARICE: (*low*) Frank...I'm busting with excitement.

FRANK: (*low*) Yeah. So'm I, honey. (*louder*) Come over here, boys. (*The two boys walk over to them.*) Stand here.

*They wait now behind the closed front door, all four of them tense, quiet, hardly able to stand the suspense. They wait for several seconds, and then, in the street, we begin to hear the heavy tread of marching feet.*

CHRISTOPHER: Hey, Daddy...where we going?

FRANK: Ssh. Be quiet, son.

*He bends over and picks Christopher up. The sound of marching feet grows louder and stronger. They wait till it reaches a crescendo. Frank speaks quietly now.*

FRANK: Let's go.

*He opens the front door and they walk into a mob of grimly advancing men and women. They join the mob and walk with them quietly, and the only sound we hear is the frightening noise of the tramping feet. Fade out.*

## Act Two

*Fade in on long shot of Sycamore Street. It is once again 6:40 P.M., the same night. We have gone backward in time and we now duplicate exactly the scene which opened Act One. Arthur Hayes walks on, stops in front of his house, knocks his pipe against his heel. Frank Morrison enters. Each of the movements they make, the attitudes they strike, and the inflections they use must be exact imitations of the Act One business. The audience must feel that this scene is a clip of film which we are rerunning.*

FRANK: (*jovially*) Hey, Artie. How ya doin'?

*Arthur is preoccupied. He doesn't register at first. He looks blankly at Frank.*

FRANK: (*laughing*) Hey...wake up, boy. It's almost time for supper.

*Arthur snaps out of it and forces a smile.*

ARTHUR: (*quietly*) Oh...hello, Frank. Sorry. I didn't see you.

FRANK: Didn't see me? Hey, wait till I tell Clarice. That diet she's got me on must be working. You have to look twice to see me! (*Laughing hard, Frank reaches for his keys.*) That's a hot one! (*Arthur smiles weakly.*) Say...isn't this late for you to be getting home?

ARTHUR: No, I don't think so. (*He looks at his watch.*) It's twenty to seven. I always get home about this time.

FRANK: Yeah. Well, I wouldn't want you to be late tonight. You know what tonight is, don't you?

ARTHUR: (*slowly*) Yes, I know what tonight is.

FRANK: (*a little hard*) Good.

*We hear footsteps and see a man walk by. He is Joseph Blake, a man in his late thirties, a big, powerful, but quiet man. Joseph Blake lives in the third house on the street. As he walks by them they both look at him silently. And now, for the first time, this scene moves in a different direction than did the scene at the beginning of Act One. Instead of coming in close on Frank, the camera comes in close on Arthur Hayes as he stands nervously in front of his door, afraid to look at either Joseph Blake or Frank Morrison. We hear Joseph's footsteps fade out. Arthur reaches for his keys.*

FRANK: (*low, off*) See you later, Artie.

*Arthur winces at this. We hear Frank's door opening and closing softly. Arthur turns now and looks off at Joseph Blake's house for a moment. Then he turns and opens his door. As he enters his foyer we hear dance music playing softly. The living room is lighted, and looking in from the foyer, we can see Mr. Harkness, Arthur's father-in-law, seated in an armchair, reading the newspaper. He is*

52

*perhaps sixty-five years old, and usually does nothing much more than sit reading the newspapers. He looks up as Arthur comes in.*

MR. HARKNESS: Hello, Arthur. (*calling off*) Here he is, Phyllis. (*to Arthur*) Little bit late, aren't you?

*Arthur is hanging up his coat. He is obviously worried. His face shows concern. His entire manner is subdued. He speaks quietly, even for Arthur.*

ARTHUR: No. Usual time.

*Mr. Harkness takes out a pocket watch, looks at it, shakes it.*

MR. HARKNESS: Mmm. Must be fast.

*He goes back to his newspaper. Arthur walks into the living room tiredly.*

ARTHUR: (*not caring*) How's your cough?

MR. HARKNESS: (*reading*) Still got it. I guess I must've swigged enough cough syrup to float a rowboat today. Waste of time and money!

*Phyllis enters from kitchen as Arthur goes over to phonograph from which the dance music is blasting. He is just ready to turn it off as she enters.*

MR. HARKNESS: Cough'll go away by itself like it always does.

PHYLLIS: (*brightly*) Hello, darling. Ah…don't turn it off.

*He turns as she walks over to him. She kisses him possessively and leads him away from the phonograph. The music continues.*

PHYLLIS: How did it go today, dear?

ARTHUR: All right. Nothing special.

PHYLLIS: What about the Franklin closing?

ARTHUR: It's called off till tomorrow.

PHYLLIS: How come?

ARTHUR: I didn't ask them.

PHYLLIS: Well, you'd think they'd at least give you a reason. You should've asked. I don't like it when people push you around like that.

*Arthur goes over to a chair without answering. A pipe is on an end table next to*

the chair. He begins to fill it. Phyllis goes to a small bar on which is a cocktail shaker and one glass. She picks up the shaker.

ARTHUR: What's that?

PHYLLIS: I made you a drink.

ARTHUR: No. No thanks. I don't want a drink now.

PHYLLIS: Oh, Artie! I made it specially for you. You look tired. Come on, it'll do you good. (*She begins to pour the drink.*) Sit down, dear. I'll bring it over to you.

*Arthur sits down. Phyllis finishes pouring the drink and brings it to him. He takes it. She waits, smiling, for him to drink it.*

ARTHUR: How come you made me a drink tonight?

PHYLLIS: Just for luck. Taste it. (*She sits on the arm of the chair. He tastes it slowly. She puts her arm around him.*) Good?

ARTHUR: (*slowly*) It's good.

PHYLLIS: I though you'd like it.

ARTHUR: Where's Billy?

PHYLLIS: Asleep.

ARTHUR: Isn't it kind of early?

PHYLLIS: He didn't get much of a nap today. The poor baby couldn't keep his eyes open. Artie, he's getting to be such a devil. You should've seen him this afternoon. He got into my bag and took my lipstick. If I only could've taken a picture of his face. He walked into the kitchen and I swear I almost screamed. You never saw anything so red in your life. Drink your drink, darling. It took me ten minutes to scrub it off.

*Obediently, Arthur sips his drink.*

ARTHUR: (*mildly*) I'd like to have seen him before he went to bed.

PHYLLIS: Now you know I had to get finished early tonight, Artie. (*She gets up and goes toward the kitchen.*) We're eating in a few minutes. I'm just making melted cheese sandwiches. We can have a snack later if you're hungry.

ARTHUR: Later?

PHYLLIS: (*looking at him oddly*) Yes, later. When we get back.

*Arthur puts his drink down. All of his movements are slow, almost mechanical, as if he has that day aged twenty years. Phyllis goes into kitchen. He takes off his glasses and begins polishing them.*

MR. HARKNESS: Melted cheese sandwiches.

ARTHUR: (*not hearing*) What?

MR. HARKNESS: I said melted cheese sandwiches. That gluey cheese. Do you like it?

ARTHUR: No.

MR. HARKNESS: Me neither. Never did.

*He goes back to his paper. Arthur gets up and goes to phonograph. He stands over it, listening. Phyllis comes in carrying a tray on which are three glasses of tomato juice. She gives it to Arthur.*

PHYLLIS: Put these on the table like a good boy. (*He takes it and looks at her strangely.*) What's the matter with you, Artie? You've hardly said a word since you got home... and you keep looking at me. Are you sick, or something?

ARTHUR: No. I'm not sick.

PHYLLIS: Here, let me feel your head. (*She does so.*) No, you feel all right? What is it?

ARTHUR: Nothing. I'm just tired, I guess.

PHYLLIS: Well, I hope you perk up a little.

*She goes off into kitchen. Arthur goes slowly to dining table which is set in the same spot as the Morrison dining table. He puts the glasses on it, and sets the tray on the end table. He takes a sip of his drink. Phyllis comes in from the kitchen carrying a platter of melted cheese sandwiches. She goes to the table, puts it down.*

PHYLLIS: Dinner. Come on, Dad, while they're hot. Artie...

ARTHUR: You go ahead. I'm not hungry.

PHYLLIS: Oh, now, let's not start that. You have to eat. Try one. They're nice and runny.

ARTHUR: Really, I'm not hungry.

PHYLLIS: Well, you can at least sit with us. I haven't seen you since half past eight this morning.

*Arthur goes slowly over to the table and sits down. Mr. Harkness ambles over.*

MR. HARKNESS: Well, I'm good and hungry. Tell you that. Got any pickles?

PHYLLIS: No pickles. You know they give you heartburn.

MR. HARKNESS: Haven't had heartburn in a long time. Wouldn't mind a slight case if it came from pickles.

*They are all seated now, Phyllis facing the window. Arthur sits quietly. Mr. Harkness busies himself drinking water while Phyllis serves the sandwiches, potato salad, etc.*

PHYLLIS: Artie...potato salad?

ARTHUR: No. Look, Phyllis...

PHYLLIS: Just a little.

*She puts a spoonful on a heavily loaded plate and passes it to him. He takes it. Now she serves her father.*

PHYLLIS: Potato salad, Dad?

MR. HARKNESS: I'll help myself.

*She puts the bowl down and helps herself as does Mr. Harkness.*

PHYLLIS: (*brightly*) What happened at the office, dear? Anything new?

ARTHUR: No. It was quiet.

PHYLLIS: Did you hear about the Walkers wanting to sell their house?

ARTHUR: No.

PHYLLIS: You know, for a real-estate man you hear less about real estate than anyone I ever saw. I spoke to Margie Walker this morning. I just got to her in time. You're going to handle the sale. She told me she hadn't even thought of you till I called. Why is that, dear?

ARTHUR: I don't know why it is.

PHYLLIS: Well, anyway, she's expecting you to call her tomorrow. It ought to be a very nice sale for you, dear.

*Arthur nods and looks down at his plate. There is silence for a moment.*

MR. HARKNESS: (*chewing*)This stuff gets under my teeth.

PHYLLIS: Dad!

MR. HARKNESS: Well, I can't help it, can I?

*They eat for a moment and then Phyllis, looking out the window, sees movement in the house next door, the Blake house. She can no longer hold back the topic she's been trying not to discuss in front of Arthur.*

PHYLLIS: Look at them. Every shade in the house is down. (*She looks at her watch.*) There isn't much more time. I wonder if they know. Do you think they do, Artie?

ARTHUR: (*tired*) I don't know.

PHYLLIS: They must. You can't keep a thing like this secret. I wonder how they feel. (*She looks at Arthur.*) Artie, aren't you going to eat your dinner?

ARTHUR: (*slowly*) How can you talk about them and my dinner in the same breath?

PHYLLIS: For Heaven's sakes...I don't know what's the matter with you tonight.

ARTHUR: (*quietly*) You don't, do you?

*He gets up from the table and walks over to the phonograph. He stands there holding it with both hands, listening to the slick dance music. Then abruptly, he turns it off. Phyllis looks as if she is about to protest, but then decides not to.*

MR. HARKNESS: What d'you suppose is gonna happen over there? Boy, wouldn't I like to go along tonight.

PHYLLIS: (*looking at Arthur*) Dad, will you please stop.

MR. HARKNESS: Well, I would! How do you think it feels to be sixty-two years old and baby-sitting when there's real action going on right under your nose? Something a man wants to get into.

ARTHUR: (*turning*) Be quiet!

MR. HARKNESS: Now listen here....

ARTHUR: I said be quiet!

*He takes off his glasses and walks over to the table.*

PHYLLIS: Artie, stop it! There's no need for you to raise your voice like that.

*Arthur speaks more quietly now, feeling perhaps that he has gone too far.*

ARTHUR: Then tell your father to keep his ideas to himself!

MR. HARKNESS: (*angrily*) Wait a minute!

*Phyllis, in the ensuing argument, is quiet, calm, convincing, never losing her temper, always trying to soothe Arthur, to sweeten the ugly things she says by saying them gently.*

PHYLLIS: Dad, be quiet. Listen, Artie, I know you're tired, darling, but there's something we might as well face. In about fifteen or twenty minutes you and I and a group of our friends and neighbors are going to be marching on that house next door. Maybe it's not such a pleasant thing to look forward to, but something has to be done. You know that, Artie. You agreed to it with all the others.

ARTHUR: I didn't agree to anything. You agreed for the Hayes household. Remember?

PHYLLIS: All right, I agreed. I didn't hear you disagreeing. Oh, what's the difference, darling? You've been acting like there's a ten-ton weight on your back ever since you heard about it. And there's no point to it. It's all decided.

ARTHUR: All decided. What right have we got to decide?

PHYLLIS: It's not a question of right, Artie. Don't you see? It's something we have to do, right or wrong. Do you want them to live next door to you? Do you really want them?

ARTHUR: I always thought a man was supposed to be able to live anywhere he chooses no matter what anyone else wants.

PHYLLIS: But, dear, this isn't anywhere. This

is Sycamore Street. It's not some back alley in a slum! This is a respectable neighborhood. Artie, let's be realistic. That's one of the few things we can really say we have. We're respectable. Do you remember how hard we worked to get that way?

ARTHUR: Respectable! Phyllis, for Heaven's sakes. We're talking about throwing a man out of his own home. What is the man? He's not a monster. He's a quiet guy who minds his own business. How does that destroy our respectability?

PHYLLIS: (*hard*) He got out of prison two months ago. He's a common hoodlum.

ARTHUR: We don't know for sure.

PHYLLIS: We know. Charlie Denton doesn't lie. He saw the man's picture in the Rockville papers just fifty miles from here the day he got out. Tell me, what does he do for a living? Where did he get the money to buy that house?

ARTHUR: I don't think that's any of your business.

PHYLLIS: But, Artie, the man was in jail for four years. That's our business! How do you know what he did? How do you know he won't do it again?

ARTHUR: We have police.

PHYLLIS: Police! Will the police stop his child from playing with Billy? What kind of a child must that be? Think about it. Her father is an ex-convict. That's a lovely thing to tell our friends. Why yes...you know Billy's little friend Judy. Of course you do. Her father spent a great deal of time in prison. Charming people. It's beautiful for the neighborhood, isn't it, Artie? It makes real-estate prices just skyrocket up. Tell me, who do you think'll be moving in next...and where'll we go? *Arthur doesn't answer. He sits down in a chair, troubled, trying to find an argument. Phyllis watches him closely.*

MR. HARKNESS: Listen, Artie....

*But Phyllis puts her hand on his arm to shut him up. Arthur is thinking and she wants to see if her argument has worked.*

ARTHUR: Look, Phyllis, this is a mob we're getting together. We're going to order this man out of his house...or we're going to throw him out. What right have we got to do it? Maybe most of us'd rather not have him as a neighbor, but, Phyllis, the man is a human being, not an old dog. This is an ugly thing we're doing....

PHYLLIS: We've got to do something to keep our homes decent. There's no other way. Somebody's always got to lose, Artie. Why should it be all of us when there's only one of him?

ARTHUR: I...I don't know.

*Arthur suddenly gets up and goes toward the front door as if going out. He buttons his jacket. Phyllis gets up, concerned.*

PHYLLIS: Where are you going?

ARTHUR: I'm going to talk to Frank Morrison.

PHYLLIS: All right. Maybe Frank'll make sense to you. (*calling*) Wear your coat. *But Arthur has opened the door and intends to go out without it. Phyllis looks at her watch.*

PHYLLIS: Arthur, it's freezing out! (*He is outside the door now.*) You'll catch cold. (*The door closes. She stands watching after him, obviously upset. Her father resumes his eating. She looks at the door for a long time. Then, without looking around*) Dad...

MR. HARKNESS: Mmmm?

PHYLLIS: What do you think he'll do?

MR. HARKNESS: Well...I don't know. You got any more of these melted cheese businesses? I'm hungry.

PHYLLIS: No.

*She goes to the window and looks out.*

MR. HARKNESS: Why don't you sit down, Phyl? He'll be all right.

PHYLLIS: What do you mean all right? Look at him. He's standing in front of Frank's house afraid to ring the bell.

MR. HARKNESS: He'll calm down. Come away from that window and sit down. Have some coffee.

*She moves away from the window and sits at table.*

PHYLLIS: I've never seen him like this before.

MR. HARKNESS: Well, what are you worried about? Tell you what. I'll go along with you. Boy, wouldn't I like to be in on a thing like this once. Let Artie stay home and mind the baby if that's how he feels.

*Phyllis turns on her father violently and for the first time we see how much Arthur's decision means to her.*

PHYLLIS: (*fiercely*) He's got to go! Don't you understand?

MR. HARKNESS: What the dickens is eating you? No, I don't understand. (*Phyllis gets up and goes to the window. She looks out tensely.*) Would you mind telling me what you're talking about?

PHYLLIS: (*startled*) Oh no!

*She turns and runs to the front door. She starts to open it and run out. As she gets it half open we hear a low voice calling, Charlie Denton's voice.*

CHARLIE: (*low*) Artie! Hey, Artie!

*She closes the door silently and stands against it, frightened. Cut to street in front of Frank's house. Arthur stands there, having just been hailed by Charlie. He turns, and then we see Charlie hurrying down the street toward him. Charlie gets to him, takes him by the arm.*

CHARLIE: (*low*) What are you doing out here now?

ARTHUR: (*guiltily*) Nothing. I was...well, I was getting some air, that's all.

CHARLIE: Look, boy, this thing has got to be timed on the button. Everybody's supposed to be in his house right now. Nobody's supposed to be wandering around the streets. What time've you got?

ARTHUR: (*with an effort*) Listen, Charlie, I want to talk to you about tonight.

CHARLIE: I haven't got time to talk.

ARTHUR: Please. It's important.

CHARLIE: (*tough*) What the heck's the matter with you?

ARTHUR: Nothing. Nothing, Charlie...

CHARLIE: What time've you got? (*He grabs Arthur's wrist and holds it up in the light. He holds his own wrist next to it and compares the watches.*) You're three minutes *slow*.

ARTHUR: I know. This watch...it runs slow, Charlie....

CHARLIE: Well, fix it, will ya? The timing's the most important part.

ARTHUR: I will. Look, about this thing tonight...

CHARLIE: Listen, if you're gonna start in with me about the plan, take it up with the committee, will ya, please? All of a sudden everybody's an expert on how to run the show. If you want the organizing job I'll be glad to give it to you.

ARTHUR: No, it's not that. It's organized very well. There's something else.

CHARLIE: Are you gonna fix that watch?

ARTHUR: I will. I've been meaning to set it all day. Listen...these people...the Blakes. They've got a kid....

CHARLIE: So has my mother. Here, gimme this. (*He grabs Arthur's wrist and sets his watch.*) There. At seven-fifteen on the nose we go. Now get back into your house.

*He walks off fast.*

ARTHUR: Charlie...

*But Charlie keeps going. Arthur watches him. Then he goes up to Frank Morrison's front door and rings the bell. From inside we hear Roger calling.*

ROGER: (*off*) I'll get it.

*Roger opens the front door, and now again, Roger's and Arthur's movements must be exactly as they were in the first act, except that now the camera catches them from outside the house.*

ARTHUR: Rog, is your Dad in?

ROGER: Sure. Come on in, Mr. Hayes.

*Arthur walks in slowly. The door closes.
Fade out.*

*Fade in on the living room of Arthur's
house. Phyllis sits tensely waiting for him.
The dining table is cleared. Mr. Harkness is
back in his easy chair reading the papers. We
hear a key in the lock, the door opens and
Arthur enters. He walks slowly, despising
himself for not having been stronger with
Frank or Charlie. Phyllis gets up as he comes
in. He doesn't look at her but walks over to
the window and stands there. She comes up
behind him. He doesn't turn around.*

PHYLLIS: Artie...Artie, are you all right?

*He turns around slowly, speaks heavily.*

ARTHUR: Yeah, I'm fine.

PHYLLIS: What happened? What'd you say to
them?

ARTHUR: I said nothing.

PHYLLIS: (*hopefully*) Well, what do you mean
you said nothing. Didn't you talk about it?

ARTHUR: No, I didn't talk about it. I didn't
talk about anything. Will you leave me
alone?

*She backs away, alarmed. Then she looks at
her watch.*

PHYLLIS: (*softly*) We only have a couple of
minutes, dear.

ARTHUR: I'm not going out there.

PHYLLIS: I'd better get our coats.

ARTHUR: Did you hear what I just said?

PHYLLIS: We'll have to bundle up. It's only
about twenty degrees out.Did you know
that?

ARTHUR: I said I'm not going.

*Phyllis backs away from him. He turns to
the window. We can see that she is hugely
upset, almost desperate. She looks at him
fiercely. Mr. Harkness gets up quietly with
his paper and goes into the next room. We
hear the door close. Arthur doesn't move.*

PHYLLIS: (*strongly*) I want to tell you
something. I'm going to get our coats now,
and we're going to put them on, and we're
going to stand in the doorway of our house

until it's seven-fifteen.

ARTHUR: (*turning*) Stop it.

PHYLLIS: And then we're going to walk out
into the gutter, you and me, the Hayes
family, and we're going to be just like
everybody else on Sycamore Street!

ARTHUR: (*shouting*) Phyllis! I've told you...
I'm not going to be a part of this thing!

*Phyllis studies him for a long moment.*

PHYLLIS: Listen to me, Artie. Listen to me
good. I didn't think you needed to hear this
before. But you're going to hear it now.
We're going out there. Do you want to
know why? Because we're not going to be
next!

ARTHUR: You're out of your mind!

PHYLLIS: (*roaring*) Sure I am! I'm out of my
mind all right. I'm crazy with fear because
I don't want to be different. I don't want
my neighbors looking at us and wondering
why we're not like them.

ARTHUR: (*amazed*) Phyllis...you're making
this up! They won't think that.

PHYLLIS: They will think that! We'll be the
only ones, the odd ones who wanted to let
an ex-convict live with us. They'll look the
other way when we walk the streets.
They'll become cold and nasty...and all of
a sudden we won't have any neighbors.
(*pointing at the Blake's house*) We'll be like
them!

*Arthur stands looking at her and it begins to
sink in. She knows it and goes after him.*

PHYLLIS: We can't be different! We can't
afford it! We live on the good will of these
people. Your business is in this town. Your
neighbors buy us the bread we eat! Do you
want them to stop?

ARTHUR: I don't know...Phyllis...I don't
know what to think...I...can't...throw a
stone at this man.

PHYLLIS: (*strong*) You can! You've got to, or
we're finished here.

*He stares at her, not knowing what to say
next. She has almost won and knows it. She*

58 *looks at her watch.*

PHYLLIS: Now just...wait...just stand there....

*She runs to the closet and takes out their overcoats. She throws hers on and brings his to him, holds it for him.*

PHYLLIS: Put it on!

ARTHUR: I...can't. They're people. It's their home.

PHYLLIS: (*shouting*) We're people too! I don't care what happens to them. I care what happens to us. We belong here. We've got to live here. Artie, for the love of God, we don't even know them. What's the difference what happens to them? What about us?

*He has no answer. She begins to put his coat on. He stands there, beaten, wrecked, moving his arms automatically, no longer knowing the woman who is putting on his coat. She talks as she helps him.*

PHYLLIS: There. It won't be long. I promise you. It won't be long. That's my Artie. That's my darling. Let's button up, dear. It's cold. We'll be back in an hour, and it'll be over. There. Now put on your gloves, darling.

*She takes him by the arm and he stands there letting her do as she wills. He puts on his gloves without knowing he is doing it, and they wait together, there in the doorway. She looks at him, trying to read him, as we begin to hear the cold and chilling sound of the tramping feet. Mr. Harkness comes out of the bedroom and stands there looking at them. Phyllis looks at her watch. The tramping grows louder. They wait in silence. Then she opens the door. We see the crowd, grimly marching, and the Morrisons are at the head of it. No one looks at the Hayes. The dull thud of the tramping feet is sickening to hear. Arthur closes his eyes. Slowly now Phyllis pushes him forward. He steps out of the house and moves ahead to join the others, as if in a dream. Phyllis follows, catches up, and takes his arm as they join the marching mob. Fade out.*

## Act Three

*Fade in on a long shot of Sycamore Street. It is once again 6:40 P.M., same night. We have gone backward in time, and again we duplicate the scene which opened Acts One and Two. Arthur Hayes walks on, stops in front of his house, knocks his pipe against his heel. Frank Morrison enters. Again, each of the movements must be exact imitations of the movements in Acts One and Two. It is as if we are starting the play again.*

FRANK: (*jovially*) Hey, Artie. How ya doin'? *Arthur is preoccupied. He doesn't register at first. He looks blankly at Frank.*

FRANK: (*laughing*) Hey...wake up, boy. It's almost time for supper. *Arthur snaps out of it and forces a smile.*

ARTHUR: (*quietly*) Oh...hello, Frank. Sorry. I didn't see you.

FRANK: Didn't see me? Hey, wait till I tell Clarice. That diet she's got me on must be working. You have to look twice to see me! (*Laughing hard, Frank reaches for his keys.*) That's a hot one! (*Arthur smiles weakly.*) Say...isn't this late for you to be getting home?

ARTHUR: No, I don't think so. (*He looks at his watch.*) It's twenty to seven. I always get home about this time.

FRANK: Yeah. Well, I wouldn't want you to be late tonight. You know what tonight is, don't you?

ARTHUR: (*slowly*) Yes, I know what tonight is.

FRANK: (*a little hard*) Good.

*We hear footsteps and see a man walk by. He is Joseph Blake. They both look at him silently. Camera now follows him as he walks silently toward his house, the third of the three houses we see. As he walks, we hear faintly in background:*

FRANK: (*off*) See you later, Artie.

*We hear Frank's door open and close. Then we hear Arthur's door open, and for an instant, we hear the same dance music coming from Arthur's house that we heard in Act Two. Then Arthur's door closes. By this time Joseph Blake is in front of his door. He looks off silently at the other two houses. Then he opens his front door and enters his house. As he closes the door we hear running feet, and then we see Judy, Joe's six-year-old daughter, in a bathrobe and slippers, running at him.*

JUDY: (*calling*) Daddy Daddy Daddy Daddy.

*She runs into his arms. He lifts her up and hugs her.*

JOE: Mmm. You smell sweet.

JUDY: (*excited*) I had a hairwash with Mommy's special shampoo. It smells like gar . . . gar . . .

JOE: Gardenias. Did anyone ever tell you you smelled like gardenias even without Mommy's shampoo?

JUDY: (*grinning*) You're silly.

*He tickles her and she giggles.*

ANNA: (*calling*) Judy!

JUDY: (*importantly*) We've got company.

JOE: Oh? Who is it, darling?

JUDY: A lady.

ANNA: (*calling*) Judy!

*Joe puts her down. She runs inside. Joe takes off his coat, puts it into the closet and walks into the living room. Joe's wife, Anna, stands near a chair. Anna, in her early thirties, is a quiet, small woman who has obviously been through a great deal of suffering in the past five years. She looks extremely nervous and upset now. Seated at the far end of the room in a rocking chair is Joe's mother, Mrs. Blake. She is quite old, quite spry for her years, and inclined to be snappish. Also seated in the room is a middle-aged woman, a neighborhood busybody named Mrs. Carson. She wears an odd, old-fashioned hat and sits stiffly, not at home, quite*

uncomfortable, but determined to do what she has come to do. The living room again is an exact duplicate of the Morrison and Hayes living rooms. It is furnished sparsely and not well. It is obvious that the Blakes have not been living there long. As Joe gets into the room, Anna comes toward him.

ANNA: Joe, this is Mrs. Carson.

JOE: (*politely*) Mrs. Carson.

*He turns to her for a moment. She nods curtly. Then he turns back to Anna and kisses her gently.*

JOE: Hello, darling.

ANNA: Joe . . .

*But he walks away from her and goes to his mother. He bends over and kisses her on the forehead.*

MRS. BLAKE: Your face is cold.

JOE: (*smiling*) It's freezing out. How do you feel?

MRS. BLAKE: Just fine, Joe.

*He pats her cheek and turns to find Judy behind him, holding a piece of drawing paper and a crayon. On the paper is a childish scribble that looks vaguely like a boat. Anna, a tortured expression on her face, wants to say something, but Joe looks at the drawing, grinning.*

JUDY: Daddy . . .

JOE: The *Queen Mary*! Now that is what I call beautiful.

JUDY: It is not! It's just s'posed to be a sailboat. How do you draw a sail?

ANNA: (*shakily*) Joe . . . Mrs. Carson . . .

JOE: Well, let's see . . . . (*He takes the crayon and paper and studies it.*) I suppose you think it's easy to draw a sail.

JUDY: (*serious*) No. I don't.

ANNA: (*sharply*) Joe. (*She comes over and snatches the paper away from him. He looks at her.*) Judy, go into your room.

JOE: Wait a minute, Anna. Take it easy.

ANNA: (*near tears*) Judy, did you hear me?

JOE: Darling, what's the matter with you?

ANNA: Joe . . .

JUDY: Mommy, do I have to?

JOE: (*gently*) Maybe you'd better go inside for a few minutes, baby.

*Judy unhappily goes into her room. Anna waits till we hear the door close. Joe puts his arms around her.*

JOE: Tell me. What's wrong, Anna?

ANNA: (*almost sobbing*) Joe! I don't understand it! Mrs. Carson says....She...

JOE: (*gently*)Mrs. Carson says what?

ANNA: (*breaking down*) She says...Joe... they're going to throw us out of our house. Tonight! Right now! What are we going to do?

JOE: (*softly*) Well, I don't know. Who's going to throw us out of our house?

*But Anna can't answer. Joe grips her tightly, then releases her and walks to Mrs. Carson who sits stolidly, waiting.*

JOE: Who's going to throw us out, Mrs. Carson? Do you know?

MRS. CARSON: Well, like I told Mrs. Blake there, I suppose it's none of my business, but I'm just not the kind that thinks a thing like this ought to happen to people without them getting at least a...well, a warning. Know what I mean?

JOE: No, I don't know what you mean, Mrs. Carson. Did someone send you here?

MRS. CARSON: (*indignantly*) Well, I should say not! If my husband knew I was here he'd drag me out by the hair. No, I sneaked in here, if you please, Mr. Blake. I felt it was my Christian duty. A man ought to have the right to run away, I say.

JOE: What do you mean run away, Mrs. Carson?

MRS. CARSON: Well, you know what I mean.

JOE: Who's going to throw us out?

MRS. CARSON: Well, everybody. The people on Sycamore Street. You know. They don't feel you ought to live here, because...Now I don't suppose I have to go into that.

JOE: (*understanding*) I see.

ANNA: (*breaking in*) Joe, I've been waiting

and waiting for you to come home. I've been sitting here...and waiting. Listen....

JOE: (*quietly*) Hold it, Anna. (*to Mrs. Carson*) What time are they coming, Mrs. Carson?

MRS. CARSON: Quarter after seven. That's the plan. (*She looks at her watch and gets up.*) It's near seven now. They're very angry people, Mr. Blake. I don't think it'd be right for anyone to get hurt. That's why I'm here. If you take my advice, you'll just put some stuff together in a hurry and get out. I don't think there's any point in your calling the police either. There's only two of 'em in Eastmount and I don't think they'd do much good against a crowd like this.

JOE: Thank you, Mrs. Carson.

MRS. CARSON: Oh, don't thank me. It's like I said. I don't know you people, but there's no need for anyone getting hurt long as you move out like everybody wants. No, sir. I don't want no part nor parcel to any violence where it's not necessary. Know what I mean?

JOE: Yes. I know what you mean.

MRS. CARSON: I don't know why a thing like this has to start up anyway. It's none of my business, but a man like you ought to know better than to come pushing in here...a fine old neighborhood like this! After all, right is right.

JOE: (*controlled*) Get out, Mrs. Carson.

MRS. CARSON: What? Well I never! You don't seem to know what I've done for you, Mr. Blake.

ANNA: Joe...

JOE: Get out of this house.

*He goes to a chair in which lies Mrs. Carson's coat. He picks it up and thrusts it at her. She takes it, indignant and a bit frightened. Joe turns from her. She begins to put her coat on.*

MRS. CARSON: Well, I should think you'd at least have the decency to thank me. I

might've expected this though. People like
you!

ANNA: Mrs. Carson, please...

JOE: Anna, stop it!

*He strides to the door and holds it open. Mrs.
Carson walks out.*

MRS. CARSON: I think maybe you'll be getting
what you deserve, Mr. Blake. Good night.
*She goes out. Joe slams the door.*

ANNA: It's true. I can't believe it! Joe! Did you
hear what she said? (*She goes to Joe, who
still stands at the door, shocked.*) Well, what
are you standing there for?

JOE: (*amazed*) I don't know.

ANNA: Joe, I'm scared. I'm so scared, I'm sick
to my stomach. What are we going to do?
*Joe puts his arms around her as she begins
to sob. He holds her close till she quiets
down. Then he walks her slowly over to his
mother.*

JOE: (*to his mother*) Will you read to Judy for
a few minutes, Mother? It's time for her
story. (*Mrs. Blake starts to get up.*) Winnie
the Pooh. She'll tell you what page.
*Mrs. Blake nods and gets up and goes into
Judy's room.*

ANNA: What are you doing, Joe? We've only
got fifteen minutes....Don't you
understand?

JOE: (*quietly*) What do you want me to do? I
can't stop them from coming here.
*She goes to him and looks up at him,
pleading now.*

ANNA: (*whispering*) Joe. Let's get out. We've
got time. We can throw some things into
the car....

JOE: Isn't it a remarkable thing? A quiet
street like this and people with thunder in
their hearts.

ANNA: Listen to me, Joe—please. We can get
most of our clothes in the car. We can stop
at a motel. I don't care where we go.
Anywhere. Joe, you're not listening. (*loud*)
What's the matter with you?

JOE: We're staying.

ANNA: (*frightened*) No!

JOE: Anna, this is our home and we're
staying in it. No one can make us get out of
our home. No one. That's a guarantee I
happen to have since I'm born.

ANNA: (*sobbing*) Joe, you can't! Do you know
what a mob is like? Do you know what
they're capable of doing?

JOE: It's something I've never thought of
before...a mob. I guess they're capable of
doing ugly things.

ANNA: Joe, your talking and talking and the
clock is ticking so fast. Please...please...
Joe. We can run. We can go somewhere
else to live. It's not so hard.

JOE: It's very hard. Anna, when it's not your
own choice.

ANNA: (*sobbing*) What are you talking about?
What else've we got to do? Stand here and
fight them? We're not an army. We're one
man and one woman and an old lady and
a baby.

JOE: And the floor we stand on belongs to us.
Not to anyone else.

ANNA: They don't care about things like that.
Joe, listen to me, please. You're not making
sense. Listen...Judy's inside. She's six
years old now and she's only really known
you for a few weeks. We waited four years
for you, and she didn't remember you
when you picked her up and kissed her
hello, but, Joe, she was so happy. What are
you gonna tell her when they set fire to her
new house?

JOE: I'm gonna tell her that her father fought
like a tiger to stop them.

ANNA: (*crying*) Oh, no! No! No! What good
will that do? Joe...please...please...

JOE: (*thundering*) Stop it! (*Anna turns away
from him and covers her face. After a long
pause, quietly.*) It's this way, Anna. We have
a few things we own. We have this house
we've just bought with money left from
before...money you could have used
many times. We have a mortgage and a

very old car and a few pieces of furniture. We have my job.

ANNA: (*bitterly*) Selling pots and pans at kitchen doors.

JOE: (*patiently*) We have my job. And we have each other and that's what we have. Except there's one more thing. We have the right to live where we please and how we please. We're keeping all of those things, Anna. They belong to us.

*He comes up behind her and puts his hands on her shoulders. She sinks down in a chair, turned away from him, and sobs. He stands over her. She continues to sob. He holds her and tries to quiet her. The bedroom door opens and Judy bounces into the room. Joe gets up and goes to her as Anna tries to dry her tears.*

JUDY: Grandma says I'm supposed to go to bed now. Do I have to, Daddy?

JOE: (*smiling*) It's time, honey.

JUDY: (*disappointed*) Gee whiz. Some night, I'm gonna stay up until four o'clock in the morning!

JOE: Some night, you can. (*He kisses her.*) Good night, baby. Give Mommy a kiss.

*Judy goes to Anna and speaks as she is kissing her.*

JUDY: Really? I really can stay up until four o'clock?

JOE: Really.

JUDY: Night, Mommy.

ANNA: Good night, darling.

*Judy runs off gleefully to the bedroom.*

JUDY: Oh boy! (*calling*) Grandma . . .

*The door closes. Anna gets up and goes to window. She is still terrified, but a bit calmer now. She looks out and then turns to Joe. He watches her.*

ANNA: What've we done to hurt them? What've we done? I don't understand.

JOE: (*softly*) Well, I guess maybe they think we've destroyed the dignity of their neighborhood, darling. That's why they've thrown garbage on our lawn.

ANNA: Dignity! Throwing garbage. Getting together a mob. Those are dignified things to do. Joe, how can you want to stay? How can you want to live on the same street with them? Don't you see what they are?

JOE: They're people, Anna. And I guess they're afraid, just like we are. That's why they've become a mob. It's why people always do.

*The bedroom door opens and Joe's mother enters. She goes to her rocker and sits in it and begins to rock.*

ANNA: What are they afraid of?

JOE: Living next door to someone they think is beneath them. An ex-convict. Me.

*Anna runs to Joe and grips him excitedly.*

ANNA: What do they think you did? They must think you're a thief or a murderer.

JOE: Maybe they do.

ANNA: Well, they can't. You'll tell them. You'll tell them, Joe.

JOE: Anna, listen. . . .

ANNA: It could've happened to any one of them. Tell them you're not a common criminal. You were in an accident, and that's all it was. An accident. Joe, they'll listen. I know they will.

JOE: No, Anna. . . .

ANNA: (*eagerly*) All you have to do is tell them and they'll go away. It's not like you committed a crime or anything. You were speeding. Everybody speeds. You hit an old man, and he died. He walked right in front . . .

ANNA: (*pleading*) Joe, please. Look at me. I'm so frightened. . . . You have to tell them.

JOE: Anna, we have our freedom. If we beg for it, then it's gone. Don't you see that?

ANNA: (*shouting*) No!

*He comes to her and grips her, and speaks to her with his face inches from hers.*

JOE: How can I tell it to you? Listen, Anna, we're only little people, but we have certain rights. Judy's gonna learn about them in school in a couple of years . . . and

they'll tell her that no one can take them away from her. She's got to be able to believe that. They include the right to be different. Well, a group of neighbors have decided that we have to get out of here because they think we're different. They think we're not nice. (*strongly*) Do we have to smile in their faces and tell them we are nice? We don't have to win the right to be free! It's the same as running away, Anna. It's staying on their terms, and if we can't stay here on our terms, then there are no more places to stay anywhere. For you— for me—for Judy—for anyone, Anna.
*She sees it now and she almost smiles, but the tears are running down her cheeks and it's difficult to smile. Joe kisses her forehead.*

JOE: (*quietly*) Now we'll wait for them.
*Anna goes slowly to a chair and sits in it. Mrs. Blake rocks rhythmically on her rocking chair. Joe stands firm at one side of the room and they wait in silence. Suddenly the ticking of the clock on the mantelpiece thunders in our ears and the monotonous beat of it is all we hear. They wait. Anna looks at Joe and then speaks softly.*

ANNA: Joe. My hands are shaking. I don't want them to shake.
*Joe walks over to her, stands over her strongly and clasps both her hands together. Then he hold them in his till they are still. The clock ticks on, and now we cut to it. It reads ten after seven. Dissolve to a duplicate of the clock which now reads quarter after seven. Cut to long shot of room as we begin to hear the tramping of the feet down the street. They wait. The rocker rocks. The clock ticks. The tramping grows louder. Joe stands in the centre of the room, hard and firm. Then he turns to his mother and speaks gently and softly.*

JOE: Go inside, Mother.

MRS. BLAKE: (*slowly*) No, Joe. I'm staying here. I want to watch you. I want to hear you. I want to be proud.

*She continues to rock and now the tramping noise reaches a crescendo and then stops. For a moment there is silence, absolute silence, and then we hear a single angry voice.*

CHARLIE DENTON: (*shouting*) Joseph Blake! (*There is a chorus of shouts and a swelling of noise.*) Joseph Blake . . . come out here! *The noise from outside grows in volume. Inside only the rocking chair moves.*

FIRST MAN: (*shouting*) Come out of that house! *The noise, the yelling of the crowd, continues to grow. Inside the room no one gives a signal that they have heard.*

SECOND MAN: (*shouting*) We want you, Joseph Blake!

FRANK MORRISON: (*shouting*) Come out—or we'll drag you out!
*The yelling continues, grows louder. Still the Blakes do not move. Then suddenly a rock smashes through the window. Glass sprays the floor. The pitch of the noise outside rises even more. Joe begins to walk firmly to the door.*

ANNA: (*softly*) Joe . . .
*But he doesn't hear her. He gets to the door and flings it open violently and steps outside. As he does, the shouting, which has reached its highest pitch, stops instantly and from deafening noise we plunge into absolute silence, broken only by the steady creaking of the rocking chair inside. Joe stands there in front of his house like a rock. Now for the first time we see the crowd. The camera plays over the silent faces watching him—the faces of the men and women and children. The Morrisons are directly in front, Charlie Denton is further back. Mrs. Carson is there. And far to the rear we see Arthur Hayes and Phyllis. Still the silence holds. Then, little by little, the people begin to speak. At first we only hear single voices from different parts of the crowd.*

FIRST MAN: (*shouting*) Look at him, standing there like he owns the block!

64

*There is a chorus of ad-lib approvals.*

SECOND MAN: (*shouting*) Who do you think you are busting in where decent people live?

*Another chorus of approvals. Joe stands like a fierce and powerful statue.*

FIRST WOMAN: (*shouting*) Why don't you go live with your own kind...in a gutter somewhere?

*Another chorus of approvals. The camera moves about catching the eagerness, the mounting temper of the crowd, then the shame and anguish of Arthur Hayes, then the giant strength of Joe.*

FIRST MAN: (*shouting*) Your limousine is waiting, Mr. Blake. You're taking a one-way trip!

*There are a few laughs at this, and now the crowd, although not moving forward, is a shouting mass again. Joe still waits quietly.*

CHARLIE DENTON: (*shouting*) Well, what are we waiting for? Let's get him!

*The intensity of the noise grows and the mob begins to move forward. Then, with a tremendous roar, Frank Morrison stops them.*

FRANK: (*roaring*) Quiet! Everybody shut up.

*The noise dies down gradually.*

FRANK: (*to crowd*) Now listen to me! This whole thing is gonna be handled the way we planned at the meeting.

*Roger, standing next to Frank, looks at him adoringly. Chris holds Clarice's hand and looks around calmly.*

CLARICE: (*loud*) That's right! It's what we agreed on.

FRANK: (*shouting*) This man here is gonna be asked politely and quietly to pack his things and get his family out of here. We don't have to tell him why. He knows that. He's gonna be given a chance to leave right now. If he's got any brains in his head he'll be out in one hour—and nobody'll touch him or his house. If he hasn't...

*There is a low-throated, ominous murmur from the crowd.*

FRANK: Right! This thing is gonna be done fair and square. (*turning to Joe*) What d'ya say, Mr. Blake?

*Joe looks at him for a long time. The crowd waits silently. Arthur Hayes lowers his head and clenches his fists, and looks as if he wants to be sick. The crowd waits. When Joe speaks, it is with a controlled fury that these people have never heard before. He speaks directly to Frank.*

JOE: I spit on your fairness! (*The crowd gasps. Joe waits, then he thunders out.*) I own this house and God gave me the right to live in it. The man who tries to take it away from me is going to have to climb over a pile of my bones to do it. You good people of Sycamore Street are going to have to kill me tonight! Are you ready, Mr. Morrison? Don't bother to be fair. You're the head man here. Be first!

*The crowd, rocked back on its heels, doesn't know what to do. Behind Joe, in the house, we see framed in the doorway the rocking chair moving steadily, and Anna standing next to it. Frank is stunned by this outburst. He calls for action. But not with the force he displayed earlier.*

FRANK: You heard him, everybody....Let's get him.

JOE: I asked for you first, Mr. Morrison!

FRANK: (*shouting*) Listen to me! Let's go, men!

*But the crowd is no longer moving as a whole. Some of them are still strongly with Frank, including Charlie, the first man, the second man, and several of the others. But others are not so sure of themselves now.*

CHARLIE: (*roaring*) Don't let him throw you, Frank! He asked for it. Let's give it to him!

*Joe looks only at Frank. Waits calmly for him.*

FRANK: (*roaring*) Come on!

*He takes a step forward, but the people behind him don't follow. He turns to them.*

FRANK: What's the matter with you people?

JOE: They're waiting for you, Mr. Morrison.
*Frank whirls and faces him and they look long and hard at each other. Cut to Charlie Denton at rear of crowd. He has a stone in his hand.*

CHARLIE: (*shouting*) Let's start it off, Frankie boy.
*He flings the stone. We hear it hit and drop to the ground. The crowd gasps. Cut to Joe. There is blood running down the side of this head. He stands there firmly. Cut to Arthur Hayes. He looks up in horror, and then a transformation comes over him. He seems to grow taller and broader. His face sets strongly and he begins to stride forward, elbowing people aside. Phyllis knows. She clings to him, trying to pull him back.*

PHYLLIS: (*screaming*) Artie...Artie...don't...
*But he breaks loose from her and pushes forward. Whoever is in his way is knocked aside, and finally he reaches Joe. He looks up at Joe. Then he turns and stands next to him. He takes off his eyeglasses and flings them into the crowd.*

ARTHUR: (*strong*) Throw the next stone at me, neighbors. I live here too!
*Now the crowd is uncertain as the two men stand together and the blood runs down Joe's face. Frank tries to rally them. During his next lines we shoot through the open door into the living room. Mrs. Blake gets up from her rocking chair and takes Anna's hand. Together they walk to the front door, come outside and stand proudly beside Joe and Arthur.*

FRANK: Listen to me! Pay attention, you people. Let's remember what we came here to do...and why! This man is garbage. He's cluttering up our street. He's wrecking our neighborhood. We don't want him here. We agreed, every last man and woman of us...we agreed to throw him out! Are we gonna let him stop us? If we do—you know what'll happen.
*Mrs. Blake and Anna are out of the house now. They wait, along with Joe and Arthur. The crowd listens. Frank shouts on, running from person to person as the crowd begins ashamedly to drift away. Christopher clings to Frank's jacket, and begins to sob.*

FRANK: You know what Sycamore Street'll be like. I don't have to tell you. How do we know who we'll be rubbing elbows with next? Listen, where are you going? We're all together in this! What about our kids? Listen to me, people. Our kids'll be playing and going to school with his. How do you like that, neighbors? Makes you a little sick, doesn't it? Come back here! I'm telling you we've got to do this! Come back here!
*But the crowd continues to drift away. Finally only the Morrisons and Phyllis Hayes are left in the street. Joe and his family, and Arthur, watch them proudly. Roger looks at his bewildered father and then he turns away, takes Clarice's hand, and his father is no longer the greatest guy in the world. Frank looks down at the sobbing Christopher, and picks him up and walks slowly off. Clarice and Roger follow. The Blakes turn and go into their house, leaving Arthur on the porch. And standing alone, starkly in the middle of the street, is Phyllis. Arthur looks at her as she stands, heartbreakingly alone, for a long time.*

ARTHUR: (*sadly*) Well, what are you standing there for? My neighbor's head is bleeding! *And then, slowly, knowing that Arthur is no longer a grown-up child, Phyllis moves forward into Joseph Blake's house.*

*Fade out.*

Kurt Vonnegut, Jr.

# Harrison Bergeron

"I am the Emperor!" cried Harrison.
"Do you hear?
I am the Emperor!
Everybody must do what I say at once!"

The year was 2081, and everybody was finally equal. They weren't only equal before God and the law. They were equal every which way. Nobody was smarter than anybody else. Nobody was better looking than anybody else. Nobody was stronger or quicker than anybody else. All this equality was due to the 211th, 212th, and 213th Amendments to the Constitution, and to the unceasing vigilance of agents of the United States Handicapper General.

Some things about living still weren't quite right, though. April, for instance, still drove people crazy by not being springtime. And it was in that clammy month that the H-G men took George and Hazel Bergeron's fourteen-year-old son, Harrison, away.

It was tragic, all right, but George and Hazel couldn't think about it very hard. Hazel had a perfectly average intelligence, which meant she couldn't think about anything except in short bursts. And George, while his intelligence was way above normal, had a little mental handicap radio in his ear. He was required by law to wear it at all times. It was tuned to a government transmitter. Every twenty seconds or so, the transmitter would send out some sharp noise to keep people like George from taking unfair advantage of their brains.

George and Hazel were watching television. There were tears on Hazel's cheeks, but she'd forgotten for the moment what they were about.

On the television screen were ballerinas.

A buzzer sounded in George's head. His thoughts fled in panic, like bandits from a burglar alarm.

"That was a real pretty dance, that dance they just did," said Hazel.

"Huh?" said George.

"That dance – it was nice," said Hazel.

"Yup," said George. He tried to think a little about the ballerinas. They weren't really very good – no better than anybody else would have been, anyway. They were burdened with sashweights and bags of birdshot, and their faces were masked, so that no one, seeing a free and graceful gesture or a pretty face, would feel like something the cat dragged in. George was toying with the vague notion that maybe dancers shouldn't be handicapped. But he didn't get very far with it before another noise in his ear radio scattered his thoughts.

George winced. So did two out of the eight ballerinas.

Hazel saw him wince. Having no mental handicap herself, she had to ask George what the latest sound had been.

"Sounded like somebody hitting a milk bottle with a ball peen hammer," said George.

"I'd think it would be real interesting, hearing all the different sounds," said Hazel, a little envious. "All the things they think up."

"Um," said George.

"Only, if I was Handicapper General, you know what I would do?" said Hazel. Hazel, as a matter of fact, bore a strong resemblance to the Handicapper General, a woman named Diana Moon Glampers. "If I was Diana Moon Glampers," said Hazel, "I'd have chimes on Sunday – just chimes. Kind of in honor of religion."

"I could think, if it was just chimes," said George.

"Well – maybe make 'em real loud," said Hazel. "I think I'd make a good Handicapper General."

"Good as anybody else," said George.

"Who knows better'n I do what normal is?" said Hazel.

"Right," said George. He began to think glimmeringly about his abnormal son who was now in jail, about Harrison, but a twenty-one-gun salute in his head stopped that.

"Boy!" said Hazel, "that was a doozy, wasn't it?"

It was such a doozy that George was white and trembling, and tears stood on the rims of his red eyes. Two of the eight ballerinas had collapsed to the studio floor, were holding their temples.

"All of a sudden you look so tired," said Hazel. "Why don't you stretch out on the sofa, so's you can rest your handicap bag on the pillows, honeybunch." She was referring to the forty-seven pounds of birdshot in a canvas bag, which was padlocked around George's neck. "Go on and rest the bag for a little while," she said. "I don't care if you're not equal to me for a while."

George weighed the bag with his hands. "I don't mind it," he said. "I don't notice it any more. It's just a part of me."

"You been so tired lately – kind of wore out," said Hazel. "If there was just some way we could make a little hole in the bottom of the bag, and just take out a few of them lead balls. Just a few."

"Two years in prison and two thousand dollars' fine for every ball I took out," said George. "I don't call that a bargain."

"If you could just take a few out when you came home from work," said Hazel. "I mean – you don't compete with anybody around here. You just set around."

"If I tried to get away with it," said George, "then other people'd get away with it – and pretty soon we'd be right back to the dark ages again, with everybody competing against everybody else. You wouldn't like that, would you?"

"I'd hate it," said Hazel.

"There you are," said George. "The min- ute people start cheating on laws, what do you think happens to society?"

If Hazel hadn't been able to come up with an answer to this question, George couldn't have supplied one. A siren was going off in his head.

"Reckon it'd fall all apart," said Hazel.

"What would?" said George blankly.

"Society," said Hazel uncertainly. "Wasn't that what you just said?"

"Who knows?" said George.

The television program was suddenly interrupted for a news bulletin. It wasn't clear at first as to what the bulletin was about, since the announcer, like all announcers, had a serious speech impediment. For about half a minute, and in a state of high excitement, the announcer tried to say, "Ladies and gentlemen . . ."

He finally gave up, handed the bulletin to a ballerina to read.

"That's all right . . ." Hazel said of the announcer, "he tried. That's the big thing. He tried to do the best he could with what God gave him. He should get a nice raise for trying so hard."

"Ladies and gentlemen . . ." said the ballerina, reading the bulletin. She must have been extraordinarily beautiful, because the mask she wore was hideous. And it was easy to see that she was the strongest and most graceful of all the dancers, for her handicap bags were as big as those worn by two-hundred-pound men.

And she had to apologize at once for her voice, which was a very unfair voice for a woman to use. Her voice was a warm, luminous, timeless melody. "Excuse me . . ." she said, and she began again, making her voice absolutely uncompetitive.

"Harrison Bergeron, age fourteen," she said in a grackle squawk, "has just escaped from jail, where he was held on suspicion of plotting to overthrow the government. He is a genius and an athlete, is under-handicapped, and should be regarded as extremely dangerous."

A police photograph of Harrison Berge-ron was flashed on the screen upside down, then sideways, upside down again, then right side up. The picture showed the full length of Harrison against a background calibrated in feet and inches. He was exactly seven feet tall.

The rest of Harrison's appearance was Halloween and hardware. Nobody had ever borne heavier handicaps. He had outgrown hindrances faster than the H-G men could think them up. Instead of a little ear radio for a mental handicap, he wore a tremendous pair of earphones, and spectacles with thick, wavy lenses. The spectacles were intended to make him not only half blind, but to give him whanging headaches besides.

Scrap metal was hung all over him. Ordi-narily, there was a certain symmetry, a mili-tary neatness, to the handicaps issued to strong people, but Harrison looked like a walking junkyard. In the race of life, Harri-son carried three hundred pounds.

And to offset his good looks, the H-G men required that he wear at all times a red rubber ball for a nose, keep his eyebrows shaved off, and cover his even white teeth with black caps at snaggle-tooth random.

"If you see this boy," said the ballerina, "do not – I repeat, do not – try to reason with him."

There was the shriek of a door being torn from its hinges.

Screams and barking cries of consterna-tion came from the television set. The photo-graph of Harrison Bergeron on the screen jumped again and again, as though dancing to the tune of an earthquake.

George Bergeron correctly identified the earthquake, and well he might have – for many was the time his own home had

danced to the same crashing tune. "My God..." said George, "that must be Harri-son!"

The realization was blasted from his mind instantly by the sound of an auto-mobile collision in his head.

When George could open his eyes again, the photograph of Harrison was gone. A liv-ing, breathing Harrison filled the screen.

Clanking, clownish, and huge, Harrison stood in the centre of the studio. The knob of the uprooted studio door was still in his hand. Ballerinas, technicians, musicians, and announcers cowered on their knees before him, expecting to die.

"I am the Emperor!" cried Harrison. "Do you hear? I am the Emperor! Everybody must do what I say at once!" He stamped his foot and the studio shook.

"Even as I stand here..." he bellowed, "crippled, hobbled, sickened ... I am a greater ruler than any man who ever lived! Now watch me become what I *can* become!"

Harrison tore the straps of his handicap harness like wet tissue paper, tore straps guaranteed to support five thousand pounds.

Harrison's scrap-iron handicaps crashed to the floor.

Harrison thrust his thumbs under the bar of the padlock that secured his head har-ness. The bar snapped like celery. Harrison smashed his headphones and spectacles against the wall.

He flung away his rubber-ball nose, revealed a man that would have awed Thor, the god of thunder.

"I shall now select my Empress!" he said, looking down on the cowering people. "Let the first woman who dares rise to her feet claim her mate and her throne!"

A moment passed, and then a ballerina arose, swaying like a willow.

Harrison plucked the mental handicap from her ear, snapped off her physical handi-

70 caps with marvellous delicacy. Last of all, he removed her mask.

She was blindingly beautiful.

"Now ..." said Harrison, taking her hand, "shall we show the people the meaning of the word dance? Music!" he commanded.

The musicians scrambled back into their chairs, and Harrison stripped them of their handicaps, too. "Play your best," he told them, "and I'll make you barons and dukes and earls."

The music began. It was normal at first – cheap, silly, false. But Harrison snatched two musicians from their chairs, waved them like batons as he sang the music as he wanted it played. He slammed them back into their chairs.

The music began again and was much improved.

Harrison and his Empress merely listened to the music for a while – listened gravely, as though synchronizing their heartbeats with it.

They shifted their weights to their toes.

Harrison placed his big hands on the girl's tiny waist, letting her sense the weightlessness that would soon be hers.

And then, in an explosion of joy and grace, into the air they sprang!

Not only were the laws of the land abandoned, but the law of gravity and the laws of motion as well.

They reeled, whirled, swivelled, flounced, capered, gambolled, and spun.

They leaped like deer on the moon.

The studio ceiling was thirty feet high, but each leap brought the dancers nearer to it.

It became their obvious intention to kiss the ceiling.

They kissed it.

And then, neutralizing gravity with love and pure will, they remained suspended in air inches below the ceiling, and they kissed each other for a long, long time.

It was then that Diana Moon Glampers, the Handicapper General, came into the studio with a double-barrelled ten-gauge shotgun. She fired twice, and the Emperor and the Empress were dead before they hit the floor.

Diana Moon Glampers loaded the gun again. She aimed it at the musicians and told them they had ten seconds to get their handicaps back on.

It was then that the Bergerons' television tube burned out.

Hazel turned to comment about the blackout to George. But George had gone out into the kitchen for a can of beer.

George came back in with the beer, paused while a handicap signal shook him up. And then he sat down again. "You been crying?" he said to Hazel.

"Yup," she said.

"What about?" he said.

"I forget," she said. "Something real sad on television."

"What was it?" he said.

"It's all kind of mixed up in my mind," said Hazel.

"Forget sad things," said George.

"I always do," said Hazel.

"That's my girl," said George. He winced. There was the sound of a riveting gun in his head.

"Gee – I could tell that one was a doozy," said Hazel.

"You can say that again," said George.

"Gee ..." said Hazel, "I could tell that one was a doozy."

# Here
# Comes
# the
# Future!

## B.F. Skinner

# "Education in Walden Two

"I can't believe you can really get spontaneity and freedom through a system of tyrannical control."

We assembled for an early breakfast, leaving our work clothes in our rooms for a later change. Castle had discovered himself in his coveralls in a mirror in one of the lavatories and refused to appear in public so attired unless he could carry a sign reading "Man at Work!" As it happened, we had no need for work clothes. Frazier appeared just as we were finishing breakfast and announced that we were to spend the morning visiting the schools, and that we would pick up a labor-credit or two during the afternoon.

He led the way outdoors and we skirted the flower beds in a long arc which brought us to the small picnic tables where we had rested on our first day at Walden Two. Large sheets of paper were thumbtacked to the tables, and several students, most of them ten or twelve years old but two or three certainly no older than eight, were drawing what looked like Euclidian constructions with heavy black pencils. Other children were driving pegs into the ground and running strings from one peg to another. Two surveyor's transits and a steel measuring tape were in use. So far as I could see, Euclid was getting a firsthand experimental check. Or it might have been trigonometry, I was not sure. Frazier seemed to know no more about it than the rest of us. He shrugged off Rodge's hesitant inquiry and pressed forward toward the nearest wing of the children's building. Perhaps he merely wanted to take things in order, for this proved to be the nursery.

A young woman in a white uniform met us in a small waiting room near the entrance. Frazier addressed her as Mrs. Nash.

"I hope Mr. Frazier has warned you," she said with a smile, "that we're going to be rather impolite and give you only a glimpse of our babies. We try to protect them from infection during the first year. It's especially important when they are cared for as a group."

"What about the parents?" said Castle at once. "Don't parents see their babies?"

"Oh, yes, so long as they are in good health. Some parents work in the nursery. Others come around every day or so, for at least a few minutes. They take the baby out for some sunshine, or play with it in a play-room." Mrs. Nash smiled at Frazier. "That's the way we build up the baby's resistance," she added.

She opened a door and allowed us to look into a small room, three walls of which were lined with cubicles, each with a large glass window. Behind the windows we could see babies of various ages. None of them wore more than a diaper, and there were no bedclothes. In one cubicle a small, red new-born was asleep on its stomach. Some of the older babies were awake and playing with toys. Near the door a baby on all fours pressed its nose against the glass and smiled at us.

"Looks like an aquarium," said Castle.

"And very precious fish they are," said Mrs. Nash, as if the comparison were not unfamiliar.

"Which is yours?" asked Frazier.

"Over there asleep," said Mrs. Nash, pointing to a far corner. "Almost ready to graduate, too. He'll be a year old next month." She drew the door gently shut before we had satisfied our curiosity.

"I can show you one of the units in the isolation room, which isn't being used," she said, leading the way along the corridor. She opened another door and we entered. Two of the cubicles stood against the wall.

"This is a much more efficient way of keeping a baby warm than the usual practice of wrapping it in several layers of cloth," said Mrs. Nash, opening a safety-glass window to permit Barbara and Mary to look inside. "The newborn baby needs moist air at about 88 or 90 degrees. At six months, 80 is about right."

"How do you know that?" said Castle, rather belligerently.

"The baby tells us," said Mrs. Nash pleasantly, as if the question were also familiar.

"You know the story about the bath water, don't you, Mr. Castle?" Frazier interrupted. "The temperature's all right if the baby doesn't turn red or blue."

"But I hope..." Castle began.

"It's only a matter of a degree or two," said Mrs. Nash quickly. "If the baby's too warm, it does turn rather pinkish, and it usually cries. It always stops crying when we lower the temperature." She twisted the dial of a thermostat on the front of a cubicle.

"And I suppose if frost forms around the nose it's too cold," said Castle, getting himself under control.

"The baby turns rather pale," said Mrs. Nash laughing, "and takes a curious posture with its arms along its sides or slightly curled up. With a little practice we can tell at a glance whether the temperature is right or not."

"But why don't you put clothes on them?" said Barbara.

"What for? It would mean laundry for us and discomfort for the child. It's the same with sheets and blankets. Our babies lie on a stretched plastic cloth which doesn't soak up moisture and can be wiped clean in a moment."

"It looks terribly comfortable," I said. "Why don't you all sleep that way?"

"We're working on that," said Frazier, apparently quite seriously. "It would save no end of laundry, and, as you say, it would be comfortable."

"Clothing and blankets are really a great nuisance," said Mrs. Nash. "They keep the baby from exercising, they force it into uncomfortable postures...."

"When a baby graduates from our Lower Nursery," Frazier broke in, "it knows nothing of frustration, anxiety, or fear. It never cries except when sick, which is very seldom, and it has a lively interest in everything."

"But is it prepared for life?" said Castle. "Surely you can't continue to protect it from frustration or frightening situations forever."

"Of course not. But it can be prepared for them. We can build a tolerance for frustration by introducing obstacles gradually as the baby grows strong enough to handle them. But I'm getting ahead of our story. Have you any other point to make, Mrs. Nash?"

"I suppose you'd like to have them know how much work is saved. Since the air is filtered, we only bathe the babies once a week, and we never need to clean their nostrils or eyes. There are no beds to make, of course. And it's easy to prevent infection. The compartments are soundproofed, and the babies sleep well and don't disturb each other. We can keep them on different schedules, so the nursery runs smoothly. Let me see, is there anything else?"

"I think that's quite enough," said Frazier. "We have a lot of ground to cover this morning."

"Not so fast, if you please," said Castle. "I'm not satisfied yet. Aren't you raising a lot of very inadequate organisms? Controlled temperature, noiseless sleep – aren't these babies going to be completely at the mercy of a normal environment? Can you go on coddling them forever?"

"I can answer that, Mrs. Nash," said Frazier. "The answer is *no*. Our babies are

especially resistant. It's true that a constant annoyance may develop a tolerance, but the commoner result is that the baby is worn down or enervated. We introduce annoyances slowly, according to the ability of the baby to take them. It's very much like inoculation."

"Another thing," said Castle. "What about mother love?"

Frazier and Mrs. Nash looked at each other and laughed.

"Are you speaking of mother love as an essence, Mr. Castle?" said Frazier.

"I am not!" said Castle, bristling. "I'm speaking of a concrete thing. I mean the love which the mother gives her baby – the affection – well, to be really concrete, the kisses, the fondling, and so on, I suppose you'd say. You can't expect me to give you the physical dimensions of mother love!" He was confused and flushed. "It's real enough to the baby, I'll bet!" he added blackly.

"Very real," said Frazier quietly. "And we supply it in liberal doses. But we don't limit it to mothers. We go in for father love, too – for everybody's love – community love, if you wish. Our children are treated with affection by everyone – and thoughtful affection too, which isn't marred by fits of temper due to overwork or careless handling due to ignorance."

"But the personal relation between the mother and the child – isn't there some sort of patterning? I thought the whole personality could be shaped in that way?" Castle appealed to me for professional support, but I failed him.

"Can you come to the Upper Nursery, Mrs. Nash?" said Frazier.

"Let me check my staff," said Mrs. Nash. She disappeared into the "aquarium," returned almost immediately, and led us to another wing.

The quarters for children from one to three

consisted of several small playrooms with Lilliputian furniture, a child's lavatory, and a dressing and locker room. Several small sleeping rooms were operated on the same principle as the baby-cubicles. The temperature and the humidity were controlled so that clothes or bedclothing were not needed. The cots were double-decker arrangements of the plastic mattresses we had seen in the cubicles. The children slept unclothed, except for diapers. There were more beds than necessary, so that the children could be grouped according to developmental age or exposure to contagious diseases or need for supervision, or for educational purposes.

We followed Mrs. Nash to a large screened porch on the south side of the building, where several children were playing in sandboxes and on swings and climbing apparatuses. A few wore "training pants"; the rest were naked. Beyond the porch was a grassy play yard enclosed by closely trimmed hedges, where other children, similarly undressed, were at play. Some kind of marching game was in progress.

As we returned, we met two women carrying food hampers. They spoke to Mrs. Nash and followed her to the porch. In a moment five or six children came running into the playrooms and were soon using the lavatory and dressing themselves. Mrs. Nash explained that they were being taken on a picnic.

"What about the children who don't go?" said Castle. "What do you do about the green-eyed monster?"

Mrs. Nash was puzzled.

"Jealousy. Envy," Castle elaborated. "Don't the children who stay home ever feel unhappy about it?"

"I don't understand," said Mrs. Nash.

"And I hope you won't try," said Frazier, with a smile. "I'm afraid we must be moving along."

We said goodbye, and I made an effort to thank Mrs. Nash, but she seemed to be puzzled by that too, and Frazier frowned as if I had committed some breach of good taste.

"I think Mrs. Nash's puzzlement," said Frazier, as we left the building, "is proof enough that our children are seldom envious or jealous. Mrs. Nash was twelve years old when Walden Two was founded. It was a little late to undo her early training, but I think we were successful. She's a good example of the Walden Two project. She could probably recall the experience of jealousy, but it's not part of her present life."

"Surely that's going too far!" said Castle. "You can't be so godlike as all that! You must be assailed by emotions just as much as the rest of us!"

"We can discuss the question of godlikeness later, if you wish," replied Frazier. "As to emotions — we aren't free of them all, nor should we like to be. But the meaner and more annoying — the emotions which breed unhappiness — are almost unknown here, like unhappiness itself. We don't need them any longer in our struggle for existence, and it's easier on our circulatory system, and certainly pleasanter, to dispense with them."

"If you've discovered how to do that, you are indeed a genius," said Castle. He seemed almost stunned as Frazier nodded assent. "We all know that emotions are useless and bad for our peace of mind and our blood pressure," he went on. "But how arrange things otherwise?"

"We arrange them otherwise here," said Frazier. He was showing a mildness of manner which I was coming to recognize as a sign of confidence.

"But emotions are — fun!" said Barbara. "Life wouldn't be worth living without them."

"Some of them, yes," said Frazier. "The productive and strengthening emotions — joy and love. But sorrow and hate — and the high-voltage excitements of anger, fear, and rage – are out of proportion with the needs of modern life, and they're wasteful and dangerous. Mr. Castle has mentioned jealousy – a minor form of anger, I think we may call it. Naturally we avoid it. It has served its purpose in the evolution of man; we've no further use for it. If we allowed it to persist, it would only sap the life out of us. In a co-operative society there's no jealousy because there's no need for jealousy."

"Each of us," Frazier began, "is engaged in a pitched battle with the rest of mankind."

"A curious premise for a Utopia," said Castle. "Even a pessimist like myself takes a more hopeful view than that."

"You do, you do," said Frazier. "But let's be realistic. Each of us has interests which conflict with the interests of everybody else. That's our original sin, and it can't be helped. Now, 'everybody else' we call 'society.' It's a powerful opponent, and it always wins. Oh, here and there an individual prevails for a while and gets what he wants. Sometimes he storms the culture of a society and changes it slightly to his own advantage. But society wins in the long run, for it has the advantage of numbers and of age. Many prevail against one, and men against a baby. Society attacks early, when the individual is helpless. It enslaves him almost before he has tasted freedom.

"Considering how long society has been at it, you'd expect a better job. But the campaigns have been badly planned and the victory has never been secure. The behavior of the individual has been shaped according to revelations of 'good conduct,' never as the result of experimental study. But why not experiment? The questions are simple enough. What's the best behavior for the individual so far as the group is concerned? And how can the individual be induced to behave in that way? Why not explore these questions in a scientific spirit?

"We could do just that in Walden Two. We had already worked out a code of conduct – subject, of course, to experimental modification. The code would keep things running smoothly if everybody lived up to it. Our job was to see that everybody did. Now, you can't get people to follow a useful code by making them into so many jacks-in-the-box. You can't foresee all future circumstances, and you can't specify adequate future conduct. You don't know what will be required. Instead you have to set up certain behavioral processes which will lead the individual to design his own 'good' conduct when the time comes. We call that sort of thing 'self-control.'

"Take the principle of 'Get thee behind me, Satan,' for example," Frazier continued. "It's a special case of self-control by altering the environment. Subclass A3, I believe. We give each child a lollipop which has been dipped in powdered sugar so that a single touch of the tongue can be detected. We tell him he may eat the lollipop later in the day, provided it hasn't already been licked. Since the child is only three or four, it is a fairly diff–"

"Three or four!" Castle exclaimed.

"All our ethical training is completed by the age of six," said Frazier quietly. "A simple principle like putting temptation out of sight would be acquired before four. But at such an early age the problem of not licking the lollipop isn't easy. Now, what would you do, Mr. Castle, in a similar situation?"

"Put the lollipop out of sight as quickly as possible."

"Exactly. I can see you've been well trained. Or perhaps you discovered the principle for yourself. We're in favor of original inquiry wherever possible, but in this case we have a more important goal and we don't hesitate to give verbal help. First of all, the children are urged to examine their own behavior while looking at the lollipops. This helps them to recognize the need for self-control. Then the lollipops are concealed, and the children are asked to notice any gain in happiness or any reduction in tension. Then a strong distraction is arranged – say, an interesting game. Later the children are reminded of the candy and encouraged to examine their reaction. The value of the distraction is generally obvious. Well, need I go on? When the experiment is repeated a day or so later, the children all run with the lollipops to their lockers and do exactly what Mr. Castle would do – a sufficient indication of the success of our training."

"I wish to report an objective observation of my reaction to your story," said Castle, controlling his voice with great precision. "I find myself revolted by this display of sadistic tyranny."

"I don't wish to deny you the exercise of an emotion which you seem to find enjoyable," said Frazier. "So let me go on. Concealing a tempting but forbidden object is a crude solution. For one thing, it's not always feasible. We want a sort of psychological concealment – covering up the candy by paying no attention. In a later experiment the children wear their lollipops like crucifixes for a few hours."

"'Instead of the cross, the lollipop,/About my neck was hung,'" said Castle.

"I wish somebody had taught me that, though," said Rodge, with a glance at Barbara.

"Don't we all?" said Frazier. "Some of us learn control, more or less by accident. The rest of us go all our lives not even understanding how it is possible, and blaming our failure on being born the wrong way."

"How do you build up a tolerance to an annoying situation?" I said.

"Oh, for example, by having the children 'take' a more and more painful shock, or drink cocoa with less and less sugar in it until a bitter concoction can be savored without a bitter face."

"But jealousy or envy – you can't administer them in graded doses," I said.

"And why not? Remember, we control the social environment, too, at this age. That's why we get our ethical training in early. Take this case. A group of children arrive home after a long walk tired and hungry. They're expecting supper; they find, instead, that it's time for a lesson in self-control: they must stand for five minutes in front of steaming bowls of soup.

"The assignment is accepted like a problem in arithmetic. Any groaning or complaining is a wrong answer. Instead, the children begin at once to work upon themselves to avoid any unhappiness during the delay. One of them may make a joke of it. We encourage a sense of humor as a good way of not taking an annoyance seriously. The joke won't be much, according to adult standards – perhaps the child will simply pretend to empty the bowl of soup into his upturned mouth. Another may start a song with many verses. The rest join in at once, for they've learned that it's a good way to make time pass."

The living quarters and daily schedules of the older children furnished a particularly good example of behavioral engineering. At first sight they seemed wholly casual, almost haphazard, but as Frazier pointed out their significant features and the consequences of each, I began to make out a comprehensive, almost Machiavellian design.

The children passed smoothly from one age group to another, following a natural process of growth and avoiding the abrupt changes of the home-and-school system. The arrangements were such that each child emulated children slightly older than himself and hence derived motives and patterns for much of his early education without adult aid.

The control of the physical and social environment, of which Frazier had made so much, was progressively relaxed – or, to be more exact, the control was transferred from the authorities to the child himself and to the other members of his group. After spending most of the first year in an air-conditioned cubicle, and the second and third mainly in an air-conditioned room with a minimum of clothing and bedding, the three- or four-year-old was introduced to regular clothes and given the care of a small standard cot in a dormitory. The beds of the five- and six-year-olds were grouped by threes and fours in a series of alcoves furnished like rooms and treated as such by the children. Groups of three or four seven-year-olds occupied small rooms together, and this practice was continued, with frequent change of roommates, until the children were about thirteen, at which time they took temporary rooms in the adult building, usually in pairs. At marriage, or whenever the individual chose, he could participate in building a larger room for himself or refurnishing an old room which might be available.

A similar withdrawal of supervision, proceeding as rapidly as the child acquired control of himself, could be seen in the dining arrangements. From three through six, the children ate in a small dining room of their own. The older children, as we had observed on our first day at Walden Two, took their meals at specified times in the adult quarters. At thirteen all supervision was abandoned, and the young member was free to eat when and where he pleased.

We visited some of the workshops, laboratories, studies, and reading rooms used in lieu of classrooms. They were occupied, but it was not entirely clear that the children were actually in school. I supposed that the few adults to be seen about the building were teachers, but many of them were men, contrary to my conception of schoolteachers at that age level, and more often than not they were busy with some private business. Since Frazier had requested that we avoid questions or discussions in the presence of the children, we proceeded from one room to another in growing puzzlement. I had to admit that an enormous amount of learning was probably going on, but I had never seen a school like it before.

We inspected a well-equipped gymnasium, a small assembly room, and other facilities. The building was made of rammed earth and very simply decorated, but there was a pleasant "non-institutional" character about it. The doors and many of the windows stood open, and a fair share of the schoolwork, or whatever it was, took place outside. Children were constantly passing in and out. Although there was an obvious excitement about the place, there was little of the boisterous confusion which develops in the ordinary school when discipline is momentarily relaxed. Everyone seemed to be enjoying extraordinary freedom, but the efficiency and comfort of the whole group were preserved.

Frazier said, "We don't have to worry about standardization in order to permit pupils to transfer from one school to another, or to appraise or control the work of particular schools. We don't need 'grades.' Everyone knows that talents and abilities don't develop at the same rate in different children. A fourth-grade reader may be a sixth-grade mathematician. The grade is an administrative device which does violence to the nature of the developmental process. Here the child advances as rapidly as he likes in any field. No time is wasted in forcing him to participate in, or be bored by, activities he has outgrown. And the backward child can be handled more efficiently too.

"We also don't require all our children to develop the same abilities or skills. We don't insist upon a certain set of courses. I don't suppose we have a single child who has had a 'secondary school education,' whatever that means. But they've all developed as rapidly as advisable, and they're well educated in many useful respects. By the same token we don't waste time in teaching the unteachable. The fixed education represented by a diploma is a bit of conspicuous waste which has no place in Walden Two. We don't attach an economic or honorific value to education. It has its own value or none at all.

"Since our children remain happy, energetic, and curious, we don't need to teach 'subjects' at all. We teach only the techniques of learning and thinking. As for geography, literature, the sciences – we give our children opportunity and guidance, and they learn them for themselves. In that way we dispense with half the teachers required under the old system, and the education is incomparably better. Our children aren't neglected, but they're seldom, if ever, *taught* anything.

"Education in Walden Two is part of the life of the community. We don't need to resort to trumped-up life experiences. Our children begin to work at a very early age. It's no hardship; it's accepted as readily as sport or play. And a good share of our education goes on in workshops, laboratories, and fields. It's part of the Walden Two Code to encourage children in all the arts and crafts. We're glad to spend time in instructing them, for we know it's important for the future of Walden Two and our own security.

"Our laboratories are good because they are real. Our workshops are really small engineering laboratories, and anyone with a genuine bent can go farther in them than the college student. We teach anatomy in the slaughterhouse, botany in the field, genetics in the dairy and poultry house, chemistry in the medical building and in the kitchen and dairy laboratory. What more can you ask?"

The schoolwork in the area near the building had gradually come to an end, and the migration toward the dining room had taken place. Frazier stood up and straightened his knees with care. The rest of us also got up – except Castle, who stayed stubbornly in his place.

"I can't believe," he began, looking at the ground and apparently not caring whether he was heard or not, "I can't believe you can really get spontaneity and freedom through a system of tyrannical control. Where does initiative come in? When does the child begin to think of himself as a free agent? What is freedom, anyway, under such a plan?"

"Freedom, freedom," said Frazier, stretching his arms and neck and almost singing the words, as if he were uttering them through a yawn. "Freedom is a question, isn't it? But let's not answer it now. Let's let it ring, shall we? Let's let it ring."

Isaac Asimov

# Tomorrow's Tool Is Changing Our Lives Today

If the computers stop, will we then find ourselves unable to survive?

*Nothing that was worthy in the past departs;*
*no truth or goodness realized by man ever*
*dies...but is still here and...lives and*
*works through endless changes.*
THOMAS CARLYLE

A generation ago, during the Second World War, the Electronic Numerical Integrator and Computer (ENIAC) was built at the University of Pennsylvania in Philadelphia.

It was the wonder of the world – the first fully electronic computer, an "artificial brain." It weighed thirty tons and took up fifteen hundred square feet of floor space. It

contained nineteen thousand vacuum tubes, used up as much energy as a locomotive, cost three million dollars, and solved at enormous speed problems too complicated for human beings.

Now, one generation has passed: one generation, a little over thirty years. The rickety, unreliable, energy-guzzling vacuum tubes are gone – replaced by solid-state transistors which, over the years, have been made smaller and smaller and smaller. Finally, tiny chips of silicon, a quarter-inch square, as thin as paper, daintily touched with traces of other substances here and there, are made into compact little intricacies that are fitted with tiny aluminum wires and joined to make microcomputers.

For three hundred dollars, from any mail-order house, at almost any corner store, one can now get a computer that consumes no more energy than a light bulb, is small enough to be held in the hand, and can do far more than ENIAC – twenty times faster and thousands of times more reliably.

Still, from year to year, these microcomputers grow more flexible, more versatile, and cheaper. Almost anything can now be computerized, permitting changing environmental conditions to be taken into account and the workings of a device adjusted instanteously to suit. Watches, vending machines, pinball games, traffic signals, and automobile engines can be outfitted to observe, remember, and respond in a way that will maximize efficiency and adjust to changing conditions.

In the home, microcomputers will be able to respond to ready-made programs that are being devised in ever-greater quantity and versatility. Program a microcomputer properly and it will update your Christmas list, do the billing, organize a tax return, or run the heating and lighting of a house in as complex a pattern as one wishes, judging for itself temperatures and light intensities and adjusting matters to suit. It will water the lawn or turn on the TV, adjusting focus and switching stations in a pre-set pattern.

To put it briefly, the microcomputer will do anything that is simple and repetitive. It can sense and respond more delicately and quickly than can any human being. It doesn't get tired, annoyed, or bored. And, properly programmed, it does not make mistakes.

It's catching on, too. Just as North Americans became TV-saturated in the 1950's, it seems we will be microcomputersaturated in the 1980's.

Will we become too dependent on our computers, though, while they continue technology's task of bringing comfort to us all? If the computers stop, will we then find ourselves unable to survive?

We'll become dependent, of course, and we will find survival difficult. The nation's armed forces would find themselves helpless, scientific research would limp, and, worst of all, the government itself would be paralysed if only because the tax people would be instantly out of business. And don't say, "Good riddance." A government can survive the death of its leader or any disaster you can name short of a thermonuclear war. But, make it impossible for the nation to collect its taxes and process its payments, and we'll have uncorrectable chaos in a surprisingly short time.

But, can we voluntarily go back? Think about it; all through history, human beings have turned away from simplicity – from the horse to the car, from the letter to the telephone – and adopted complexity whenever they could. They chose those dependencies that, while they lasted, made life richer and more comfortable. And they turned against those which, even while they lasted – tilling soil behind a team of oxen, say – broke backs and wore out bodies.

In line with this, it appears certain that the world will continue to put the computer to work just about everywhere – from outer space to the supermarket, from the corporate office to the farm, from the factory assembly line to the nursery.

The coming of the computer will see still further shifts.

Unskilled *mental* labor is on the way out.

More and more, the dull processes of shuffling and adjusting and checking and listing and all the other things that first irritate and then stultify the brain will be done by computer.

And what will be left? Leisure. Amusement. Creation.

Computers can be programmed, for instance, to play chess. If a person learns the rules of the moves, he or she can begin to play at once and, of course, be soundly trounced by the computer. The human player can, however, learn from his own mistakes (that's the beauty of the complex programming of the human brain) and improve his game. And he will learn more effectively than against a human adversary.

To be sure, a streak of puritanism would lead many of us to disdain this sort of thing as "playing" or "fooling around." There is the fear that dependence on the computer for our amusement will cause our own mental abilities and self-reliance to go slack and rot.

That, however, may be precisely the wrong way of looking at it. For it is the unrewarding and repetitive rote work of today – occupying, as it does, only the surface of the mind – that rots our mental abilities; and it is the creative "play" that can enhance and stimulate them.

Until now we have labored merely to maintain our social and economic structure. There's been very little time and energy left over to advance it. Upon full computerization, the world will run itself with only minimal human supervision, and the major part of human thought and energy can be put to extending the social and cultural aspects of daily living.

Then, too, a leisure culture may, in itself, lower the birth rate overall, as has been the case all along with the upper classes, which invariably have had a lower birth rate. Computerization may therefore be an important step toward solving the population problem (though it probably won't work quickly enough for us to be able to depend on it alone in this respect).

Furthermore, it is a small step from computers that play games to computers that educate. If we can learn to play chess by playing a computer, could we not do the same were the computer to make other information available? Might not a computer possibly have the knowledge of humanity at its disposal?

The computerized library and teaching machine will make it easier for anyone at any age to investigate anything...to go as far as he or she likes in any intellectual direction, whether deeply or trivially, either intensely or dilettantishly.

A world could result in which the general level of intellectual curiosity and liveliness will be greatly enhanced and in which people of any age will have the mental sprightliness we tend to associate now with only the young.

# Ben Wicks

**"Which one is yours?"**

From *Wicks* by Ben Wicks. Reprinted by permission of The Canadian Publishers, McClelland and Stewart Limited, Toronto.

Susan Carson

# New Origin of Species

Bizarre combinations of species aren't new.

Bizarre combinations of species aren't new. Ancient Greek literature teems with a wild assortment of part-human, part-animal creatures. The Egyptians endowed their goddesses with the heads of frogs, cats, and snakes, and the patron saint of Hindu shopkeepers was a god with four arms and an elephant's head.

But such creatures aren't real. There are no winged commuters in business suits because men and birds can't breed with each other. The future of each species has always been determined by which male sperm will unite with which female egg to produce offspring – and that means fish sperm with fish eggs and human sperm with human eggs.

However, just five years ago in California a group of biochemists broke through this natural barrier with a genetic trick to mix one species with another. The new substance, which they called "recombinant DNA," made it immediately possible to create new life forms, albeit modest in capability, but ones that had never existed before. Science had found a way to distort evolution.

Already in the U.S. 150 labs are engaged in recombinant DNA research. Within a year there may be close to twelve projects in Canada. Since just one accident could cause a disaster, it is obvious that some kind of legislation is necessary to ensure that everyone obeys the rules. Yet if we legislate the scientist's function, we risk stifling scientific creativity and missing out on something great. Frustrating or not, this is the kind of situation the Canadian public is increasingly going to be called upon to deal with in the coming years. Here's some information to help you make *your* decision.

"New Origin of Species" by Susan Carson, as it appeared in *The Canadian*, July 2, 1977. Reprinted by permission of the author.

## How It Works

Simply put, you take a cell from some plant or animal and extract the chemical (DNA) that governs all the physical and mental characteristics of the whole being. Do the same with another, totally different, plant or animal. Graft the two together. Presto! Shake hands with an orange that quacks, with a flower that can eat you for breakfast – or even with the Flying Nun.

Well, not quite yet, although all that is now possible in theory. Meanwhile, scientists are working with much simpler and less sophisticated forms of life.

## The Good News

Scientists think that most diseases – over two thousand, in fact – have a genetic base. For victims of these diseases future applications of recombinant DNA techniques could mean life itself.

Take diabetes, for example. It's on the increase, though no one really knows why. The insulin supply for its treatment, which is extracted from cattle and pigs, can't keep pace with demand. Soon there may not be enough. There's almost no chance that we could manufacture it synthetically; it's just too expensive. But the DNA responsible for the manufacture of human insulin could be inserted in bacteria and allowed to reproduce a million times over, setting up cheap, fast, miniature insulin factories. Similar techniques might be used in the future to stimulate growth hormones, cure infertility, and prevent embolisms and blood clots.

Even the commonest cold, or for that matter anything else caused by a virus, could benefit from recombinant DNA. At the moment there's virtually no effective drug against viruses. Vaccination is expensive;

since the patient's body must manufacture its own antibodies – and not everyone makes antibodies equally well – there's always the danger he'll die before the antibodies can work. With the new technique, large amounts of antibodies could be quickly grown and administered as soon as the patient caught the disease.

The great dream is one day to be able to cure genetic diseases by surgically implanting a corrective gene that would function for the defective one. The technique could eventually be applied to unborn babies with hemophilia. The genes responsible for producing the missing enzyme (which allows the body to function normally) could be injected through the placenta, allowing the fetus to produce the enzyme on its own.

Certain plants possess the ability to make their own fertilizer. If this ability could be transferred to food crops such as wheat and rice, it would drastically reduce the need for scarce and expensive fertilizers, and increase food production.

A few years ago a bacterium was developed that, under lab conditions, would eat some of the chemical constituents of oil slicks. Now new, more efficient bacteria that eat The Whole Thing have been patented by General Electric in the U.S. By using recombinant DNA these bacteria could multiply and devour whole oil spills.

Traces of uranium and platinum exist in abandoned mines but it's too expensive to recover them by traditional methods. With recombinant DNA, however, bacteria specifically bred to eat such rare elements could be unleashed, allowed to graze, then collected and whirled in a centrifuge that would extract the precious metal.

## The Bad News

The chances for the creation of some

Godzilla-like creature that would burst from the lab to torment an unsuspecting planet are just about nil. But some scientists do worry that a new Andromeda-type virus, for which there would be no known immunization, might accidentally be developed, escape, and spread a deadly plague.

The risks are intensified because the crossbreeding is usually done with *E. coli*, a bacterium that abounds in the human intestine, as well as in animals, fish, and sewage. Scientists chose it because they know more about it than any other living thing. If anything nasty did escape from the lab, however, it would find temporary quarters in the first human intestine it met.

Even specially weakened *E. coli*, designed to live only under lab conditions, might still pass on dangerous recombinant genes to healthier bacteria, points out Dr. Liebe F. Cavalieri, of the Sloan-Kettering Institute for Cancer Research in Rye, New York. Writing in the *New York Times*, he suggested that if weakened *E. coli* containing DNA from cancer viruses were accidentally poured down a lab sink and came into contact with normal *E. coli* in the sewage, the cancer, normally not infectious, could be spread in epidemic proportions by normally harmless bacteria.

It is the irreversibility of what might escape that is so frightening. In a letter to *Science* magazine, Columbia University professor emeritus Erwin Chargaff wrote: "You can stop splitting the atom; you can stop visiting the moon; you can stop using aerosols; you may even decide not to kill entire populations by the use of a few bombs. But you cannot recall a new form of life...."

Then there's the black side of the potential benefits. Take insulin, for example. Some have worried that if bacteria given the ability to produce insulin found their way into a human intestine (via the ubiquitous *E.*

*coli*), the body would overproduce the hormone and the victim would probably die. (Others feel that the amounts would be negligible compared with the body's own production of insulin.) Oil-eating bacteria might attack essential oil reserves deep in the ground as well as in storage tanks. Even the possibility of giving crops like wheat and rice the ability to make their own fertilizer isn't perfect. If the crop were to take on the toughness and resistance of weeds, plus the ability to grow almost anywhere, the result might wipe out other vegetation – as well as the wildlife that fed on it.

And if we're being really negative, we can't ignore the possibility of biological warfare. *E. coli*, or other bacteria that normally live in man and animals, could be given the ability to produce deadly toxins, such as botulism. In such a case, protection by immunization would be out of the question.

## The Time Zone

Insulin by the recombination process is nearest on the horizon. It may be a couple of years away. It may be here by the time this article appears. It all depends on the luck of the draw. One expert has estimated that the surgical implantation of normal genes may be common practice in a generation. (Others think it may take several generations.) Self-fertilization of food crops could take decades.

No one can say when science will actually achieve all the predicted benefits. But things are moving faster than anyone expected. As recently as 1965, most scientists pointed to the impossibility of isolating a single gene and claimed that such developments were at least decades off. In fact, they were just four years away.

## DNA and the Law

The U.S. will probably legislate recombinant DNA standards. The Carter administration has asked Congress to impose unprecedented federal controls in the area. In Canada, an interdepartmental government committee is investigating the possibility of either introducing new legislation or making use of existing laws. A report to the government is expected shortly. Aware that this will not be the only occasion when such questions will arise, the government has little choice but to see that society is protected by the law.

Time is short. In the U.S. and Britain researchers are beginning to pull out all the stops. If Canada delays legislation, we're likely to find our country has become research heaven for companies from around the world anxious to work unfettered by expensive safety checks. Under such circumstances, Columbia University professor emeritus Erwin Chargaff may yet be right when he says of recombinant DNA: "The future will curse us for it."

# Charles Panati

# Breakthroughs

Some exciting breakthroughs promise
a better future for us all. . . .

## Eat and Grow Thin

Imagine indulging in your favorite foods and not gaining an ounce. Maybe even losing weight. This is not the goal of obesity research being conducted at the University of Illinois, but it could become one of its spin-offs – and very soon.

If you're seriously overweight, your doctor most likely has prescribed diet and exercise. You may have tried both, with only minimal success, and, like many heavy people, simply given up. Well, help is on the way – in the form of the most perfect slenderizing treatment imaginable. Dr. Sarfer Niazi, an Illinois pharmacologist, has found a thinning compound, perfluorooctyl bromide, that coats your gastrointestinal tract, temporarily blocking the absorption of food. The darkest chocolates, richest creams and pastries pass through your body without depositing a single calorie. After performing this miracle, the chemical, too, is eliminated, unchanged and unabsorbed. The perfluorooctyl bromide molecule is too large to enter the stomach lining or intestines. The drug has been tailor-made for those sixty million seriously overweight Americans whose lives are threatened by obesity, but it

will be difficult to keep the drug away from all those obsessed with slender figures.

In one study, Niazi allowed rats a liberal diet, weighing them and their food intake every day. Rats not fed the chemical responded with weight gains of eight percent a week; those fed the coating substance before each meal registered a one percent *decline* in weight. Niazi figures this result is the equivalent of a person losing eight pounds a week, regardless of his or her diet. The rats showed no adverse effects to the drug, and the wastes they excreted were normal, if rich in nutrients. Tests with rabbits and guinea pigs are running smoothly. Next, Niazi will try the slenderizing drug on chimpanzees. If it works, he'll schedule tests for people who are dangerously overweight.

The drug is expensive – about fifty dollars a quart. But mass production could reduce the cost to a few pennies a dose. Niazi says that a dieter would have to take about 1.5 ounces before each meal. He emphasizes that the coating chemical should be used in tandem with a supervised regimen of diet and exercise, and that the slenderizer should not be viewed as a green light for indulging in food orgies. The Food and Drug Administration intends to doublecheck Niazi's findings to ensure that the drug does not enter the blood stream or accumulate in body tissues. If all goes well, perfluorooctyl bromide could be on the market – under a more appetizing name – by 1982. However, if Niazi has his way, you'll have to enter a hospital to get the drug. Otherwise, he feels, the temptation to gulp a few spoonfuls before every meal could be too great to resist. Unwittingly, people might diet themselves to death.

## Spray Bandage

In the 1980's you'll be able to spray on a clear, thin bandage that has magic properties: it permits air and medications to pass through, while protecting against bacteria. It will be a convenience for many of us, but for those who suffer burns over much of their bodies, the spray bandage is a breakthrough that's truly a blessing.

A major burn is the maximum trauma that the human body can suffer and survive. To prevent infection, severe burns are now dressed with pigskin. It's effective, but the dressing must be changed two or three times a day. Also, pigskin bandage must be removed if medication has to be applied to the injured area, or if a doctor needs to check on the progress of recovery – all intensely painful procedures for a patient.

The new dressing – called a Hydron Burn Bandage – is the culmination of two decades of research and has already been tested at the Burns Institute of Shriners Hospital in Cincinnati, to the mutual satisfaction of doctors and patients. The bandage is formed by spraying a clear chemical solution over a wound, then sprinkling the area with a fine powdered polymer. The result is a biomaterial that "breathes" and stretches with the skin; it's invisible and porous, with the consistency of a soft contact lens. (Individual Hydron bandages have protected several burn patients for as long as twenty-seven days.) Since it is transparent, doctors

can visually monitor healing, and the porous matrix of the bandage allows antibiotics to flow through. A good soaking in water and the Hydron bandage painlessly lifts off.

The Hydron Burn Bandage is undergoing tests at various burn centres around the country. Once it's approved by the FDA, the dressing could be sold in a spray can with an accompanying can of polymer powder. During the early 1980's it will be used exclusively in hospitals and burn centres, but before the end of the decade it could be stocked on drugstore shelves. You will be able to bandage, without pain, any burn, cut, or bruise that requires a few days of sterile environment.

## Recapture Youth's Fitness

When young and in your healthy prime you'll bank some of your body cells as an investment in your future. Bottles of your white blood cells will be frozen, to be thawed decades later and injected into your body to fight infections and to ward off the diseases of old age. Periodic shots of your cells may even delay old age itself. It sounds like science fiction, but this youth bank of tomorrow could be made possible from advances in the 1980's in the burgeoning field of cryobiology.

Cryobiology is the tricky science of freezing cells. Tricky because if a cell is frozen too fast, ice crystals form inside and puncture the cell's walls. If a cell is frozen too slowly, salts build up and destroy it. The freezing process is further complicated by the fact that each different kind of cell in your body has its own optimum rate of freezing and thawing. However, several breakthroughs in cryobiology have already occurred. Today, red blood cells are routinely frozen at temperatures between $-80°$ C to $-196°$ C, and 200 000 units of frozen red cells are thawed each year for transfusions in the United States.

In a few years cryobiologists at the Oak Ridge National Laboratory predict they'll be able to freeze your more fragile white blood cells, which are the soldiers that fight disease. This technique should promote a host of new medical treatments. By 1985, freezing white blood cells could be a lifesaving technique for leukemia victims. The Oak Ridge scientists claim that a leukemia patient whose disease is in remission could gradually build a reserve of frozen healthy cells that he could donate to himself if his condition worsened. A child with a genetically high risk of developing leukemia could start a healthy cell savings account that would support him in later life if he developed the disease.

All of us stand to benefit from frozen white blood cells. The scientists speculate that white and red blood cells donated and frozen when you're in your teens, and periodically injected into your body after you reach forty, could bolster your immune system, which naturally deteriorates with age. The red blood cells may improve the oxygen-carrying potential of your blood, increasing your stamina and lessening fatigue to such an extent that you would get a second wind in your sixties. Your young white blood cells might teach your older cells tricks they'd forgotten for fighting colds and other infections.

No respectable cryobiologist claims that weekly or monthly shots of young blood cells will turn your bald head hairy or smooth out laugh lines and crow's-feet. Such treatments could, though, significantly strengthen your defences against such degenerative diseases of old age as diabetes, renal failure and kidney stones, arthritis, cancer (at least those kinds that may be caused by viruses or environmental antagonists), and certain heart problems. If transfusions of youthful cells really perform as cryobiologists anticipate, they will have effectively slowed down the aging process itself.

## Growing New Limbs

By applying gentle, steady, and very weak electric currents, doctors in just one decade may be able to help the body regrow damaged or diseased joints and bones, and straighten deformed spines. A few decades beyond lies the very real possibility for the regeneration of lost fingers and toes, entire arms and legs.

Any scientist who has watched a newt produce a missing arm or leg has wondered if the process could be duplicated in humans. If limb regeneration could be forced to occur in animals more evolved than the newt, then certainly it could be possible for us, too. With that belief as their lodestar, biologists in the mid-1970's achieved major breakthroughs in regeneration with animals. Using continuous electric currents, they succeeded in inducing frogs to grow back severed toes, then entire legs. Rat amputees regrew arms from the shoulder to the elbow – with cartilage, bone, nerves, and muscles in perfect anatomical precision. Biologists discovered that the healing currents always had to be *pulled out* of the stump in order to coax regrowth; inward-flowing current actually caused degeneration. So successful were these experiments that the research challenge for the 1980's is to understand why some animals spontaneously regrow limbs while others need external currents to accomplish regrowth. This will be the first step toward achieving the regeneration of lost human limbs.

Various clues are already emerging.

Recently three biologists at Purdue University found that amphibians spontaneously grow new limbs through the use of electric currents that naturally travel along the surface of the animal's skin. These skin currents course along the limbs of newts, increasing fiftyfold along the stump of amputated limbs. As the limb begins to regenerate spontaneously, the skin currents gradually weaken, and by the time the limb has fully regrown the currents have returned to their normal values.

What is the source of these natural, miraculous currents?

Until a few years ago biologists thought these currents were generated by nerve cells and that they peaked when nerves were shocked by injury or amputation. Now they know that the newts' natural regeneration currents spring from concentrations of sodium in the skin covering a stump. By alternately increasing and decreasing sodium concentrations, biologists have measured a sort of yo-yo acceleration and deceleration of limb growth.

## A Nasal Spray to Enhance

## Your Memory

Forgotten where you parked your car? Can't remember where you left your best dress to be altered? Sniff vasopressin and you'll remember.

Vasopressin is a hormone located in the cherry-sized pituitary gland, at the base of the brain. Scientists working with vasopressin have found that a few whiffs of the chemical can stimulate memory, even in the severest cases of amnesia and senility. What's more, the results are lasting. Vasopressin must be inhaled rather than taken orally because it is a member of the peptide family of organic compounds, which decompose in the digestive tract.

Recently, at the University of Liège in Belgium, vasopressin experiments were conducted on a group of males between the ages of fifty and sixty-five. After receiving three doses of vasopressin for three consecutive days, the men registered significant improvement on memory and learning tests. In fact, one man who had remembered nothing for three months, from the time an auto accident left him in a fifteen-day coma, regained his full recall faculties on the seventh day of vasopressin treatment. In another experiment at Madrid's Hospital Clínico de San Carlos, doctors had similar success with the spray. Four amnesia patients, three suffering memory loss from car accidents and one from alcoholism, were treated with vasopressin, and within five days their amnesia disappeared.

Specifically how vasopressin works remains a mystery. First synthesized in 1968, the substance was initially known to help regulate the body's water content. The idea that vasopressin might affect memory was proposed by Dr. D. de Wied, a Dutch scientist at the University of Utrecht. Dr. de Wied discovered that by removing the pituitary gland in rats he could impair their memory and interfere with their learning ability. Identification of the hormone, and follow-up work with more rats, confirmed the link between vasopressin and memory: rats that sniffed vasopressin not only learned faster, but better remembered the paths through intricate mazes.

Vasopressin does produce mild side effects; namely, more rapid heartbeat and higher blood pressure, both of which can be potential problems, particularly for the elderly. But researchers assert that any undesirable effects may be eliminated without reducing vasopressin's effectiveness if the drug is administered in very small doses over longer periods of time. Sandoz, the company that synthesized the chemical, predicts it could market a completely safe version of vasopressin by 1985.

Thus far the hormone has been tested only on short-term memory – the ability to recall events of the recent past. But tests are underway to determine if vasopressin can also activate childhood memories, or possibly even help a person regain the facility with a foreign language learned earlier in life. Since vasopressin has already been prescribed in the treatment of diabetes, rigorous testing on people to document its effects on long-term memory should not take long. For the moment, though, vasopressin will be used primarily to treat amnesia victims. But in the near future, vasopressin may help you sharpen your memory and enhance your learning ability. The regular use of vasopressin may even sustain your brain's memory mechanism so that you could be spared the forgetfulness which usually accompanies old age.

## Increasing Your Attention Span

The degree to which you can concentrate on a task may make the difference between success or failure. Some of us seem to be plagued by frustratingly short attention spans, which cause us to be easily distracted. If that's the problem, a shot of ACTH/MSH may offer a solution.

Amphetamines, the popular pep pills, speed up the mind, but they don't give it focused direction. There is, however, a natural brain protein that does both. It's present in two hormones located in the pituitary gland. One of these chemicals, ACTH (adrenocorticotropic hormone), is known to stimulate the secretion of sex hormones; the other, MSH (melanocyte-stimulating hormone), regulates the amount of dark brown pigment (melanin) in your skin. This "sex-tanning" compound may prove to be a chemical wonder.

In 1971, studies on rats showed that the ACTH/MSH protein improved memory. More recently, work by endocrinologist Dr. Abba Kastin of the Tulane University School of Medicine reveals that the protein produces a dual effect in people: it improves visual retention and heightens their powers of concentration. Students injected with the compound were better able to remember geometrical figures flashed before them, as well as to concentrate more effectively on their studies, and for longer periods of time. When the students' concentration was tested by a series of monotonous, repetitious tasks, those who received the brain protein scored higher than those injected with a placebo. It's possible that if you're one of those fortunate people who can concentrate despite the most tempting distractions, your body may naturally produce a generous amount of ACTH/MSH.

Perhaps the most significant discovery concerning ACTH/MSH is that it appears to be the only significant drug for the mentally retarded. Retarded patients given injections of the protein have been able to comprehend tasks more rapidly and demonstrate clearer thinking. This fact may indicate that some forms of retardation are caused by lack of a "concentration" compound. Also, Dr. Kastin has begun testing his hypothesis that ACTH/MSH may be effective in treating senile patients and hyperactive children. Certain forms of learning disabilities and senility may prove to be due to nothing more than the loss or congenital lack of sufficient amounts of the concentration hormone.

# Spider Robinson

# No Renewal

...the bottom line of his birth certificate says,
simply and blessedly, "...expiry date: May 12, 2049."

Douglas Bent, Jr., sits in his kitchen, waiting for his tea to heat. It is May 12, his birthday, and he has prepared wintergreen tea. Douglas allows himself this extravagance because he knows he will receive no birthday present from anyone but himself. By a trick of Time and timing, he has outlived all his friends, all his relatives. The concept of neighborliness, too, has predeceased him; not because he has none, but because he has too many.

His may be, for all he knows, the last small farm in Nova Scotia, and it is bordered on three sides by vast mined-out clay pits, gaping concentric cavities whose insides were scraped out and eaten long ago, their husk thrown away to rot. On the remaining perimeter is an apartment-hive, packed with ant-like swarms of people. Douglas knows none of them as individuals; at times, he doubts the trick is possible.

Once Douglas's family owned hundreds of acres along what was then called simply The Shore Road; once the Bent spread ran from the Bay of Fundy itself back over the peak of the great North Mountain, included a sawmill, rushing streams, hundreds of thousands of trees, and acre after acre of pasture and hay and rich farmland; once the Bents were one of the best-known families from Annapolis Royal to Bridgetown, their livestock the envy of the entire Annapolis Valley.

Then the petrochemical industry died of thirst. With it, of course, went the plastics industry. Clay suddenly became an essential substitute – and the Annapolis Valley is mostly clay.

Now the Shore Road is the Fundy Trail, six lanes of high-speed traffic; the Bent spread is fourteen acres on the most inaccessible part of the Mountain; the sawmill has been replaced by the industrial park that ate

Reprinted by permission of Kirby McCauley Ltd.

the clay; the pasture and the streams and the farmland have been disembowelled or paved over; all the Bents save Douglas Jr. are dead or moved to the cities; and no one now living in the Valley has ever seen a live cow, pig, duck, goat, or chicken, let alone envied them. Agribusiness has destroyed agriculture, and synthoprotein feeds (some of) the world. Douglas grows only what crops replenish themselves, feeds only himself.

He sits waiting for the water to boil, curses for the millionth time the solar-powered electric stove that supplanted the family's woodburner when firewood became impossible to obtain. Electric stoves take too long to heat, call for no tending, perform their task with impersonal callousness. They do not warm a room.

Douglas's gnarled fingers idly sort through the wintergreen he picked this morning, spurn the jar of sugar that stands nearby. All his life, Douglas has made wintergreen tea from fresh maple sap, which requires no sweetening. But this spring he journeyed with drill and hammer and tap and bucket to his only remaining maple tree, and found it dead. He has bought maple-flavored sugar for this birthday tea, but he knows it will not be the same. Then again, next spring he may find no wintergreen.

So *many* old familiar friends have failed to reappear in their season lately – the deer moss has gone wherever the hell the deer went to, crows no longer raid the compost heap, even the lupins have decreased in number and in brilliance. The soil, perhaps made self-conscious by its conspicuous isolation, no longer bursts with life.

Douglas realizes that his own sap no longer runs in the spring, that the walls of his house ring with no voice save his own. If a farm surrounded by wasteland cannot survive, how then shall a man? *It is my birthday*, he thinks, *how old am I today?*

He cannot remember.

He looks up at the electric clock (the family's two-hundred-year-old cuckoo clock, being wood, did not survive the Panic Winter of '94), reads the date from its face (there are no longer trees to spare for fripperies like paper calendars), sits back with a grunt. *2049, like I thought, but when was I born?*

So many things have changed in Douglas's lifetime, so many of Life's familiar immutable aspects gone forever. The Danielses to the east died childless: their land now holds a sewage treatment plant.

On the west the creeping border of Annapolis Royal has eaten the land up, excreting concrete and steel and far too many people as it went. Annapolis is now as choked as New York City was in Douglas's father's day. Economic helplessness has driven Douglas back up the North Mountain, step by inexorable step, and the profits (he winces at the word) that he reaped from selling off his land parcel by parcel (as, in his youth, he bought it from his ancestors) have been eaten away by the rising cost of living. Here, on his last fourteen acres, in the two-storey house he built with his own hands, Douglas Bent, Jr., has made his last stand.

He questions his body as his father taught him to do, is told in reply that he has at least ten or twenty more years of life left. *How old am I?* he wonders again, *forty-five? Fifty? More?* He has simply lost track, for the years do not mean what they did. It matters little; though he may have vitality for twenty years more, he has money for no more than five. Less, if the new tax laws penalizing old age are pushed through in Halifax.

The water has begun to boil. Douglas places wintergreen and sugar in the earthenware mug his mother made (back when clay was dug out of the backyard with a shovel), removes the pot from the stove, and pours. His nostrils test the aroma; to his dismay, the fake smells genuine. Sighing from his belly, he moves to the rocking chair by the kitchen window, places the mug on the sill, and sits down to watch another sunset. From here Douglas can see the Bay, when the wind is right and the smoke from the industrial park does not come between. Even then, he can no longer see the far shores of New Brunswick, for the air is thicker than when Douglas was a child.

The clock hums, the mug steams. The winds are from the north – a cold night is coming, and tomorrow may be one of the improbable "bay-steamer" days with which Nova Scotia salts its spring. It does not matter to Douglas: his solar heating is far too efficient. His gaze wanders down the access road which leads to the highway; it curves downhill and left and disappears behind the birch and alders and pine that line it for a half-mile from the house. If Douglas looks at the road right, he can sometimes convince himself that around the bend are not strip-mining shells and brick apartment-hives but arable land, waving grain, and the world he once knew. Fields and yaller dogs and grazing goats and spring mud and tractors and barns and goat-berries like stockpiles of B-B shot....

Douglas's mind wanders a lot these days. It has been a long time since he enjoyed thinking, and so he has lost the habit. It has been a long time since he had anyone with whom to share his thoughts, and so he has lost the inclination. It has been a long time since he understood the world well enough to think about it, and so he has lost the ability.

Douglas sits and rocks and sips his tea, spilling it down the front of his beard and failing to notice. *How old am I?* he thinks for the third time, and summons enough will to try and find out. Rising from the rocker with an effort, he walks on weary wiry legs to the living room, climbs the stairs to the attic, pausing halfway to rest.

*My father was sixty-one* he recalls as he sits, wheezing, on the stair *when he accepted euthanasia. Surely I am not that old. What keeps me alive?*

He has no answer.

When he reaches the attic, Douglas spends fifteen minutes in locating the ancient trunk in which Bent family records are kept. They are minutes well-spent: Douglas is cheered by many of the antiques he must shift to get at the trunk. Here is the potter's wheel his mother worked; there the head of the axe with which he once took off his right big toe; over in the corner a battered peavey from the long-gone sawmill days. They remind him of a childhood when life still made sense, and bring a smile to his grizzled features. It does not stay long.

Opening the trunk presents difficulties – it is locked, and Douglas cannot remember where he put the key. He has not seen it for many years, or the trunk for that matter. Finally he gives up, smashes the old lock with the peavey, and levers up the lid (the Bents have always learned leverage as they got old, working efficiently long after strength has gone). It opens with a shriek, hinges protesting their shattered sleep.

The past leaps out at him like the woes of the world from Pandora's Box. On top of the pile is a picture of Douglas's parents, Douglas Sr. and Sarah, smiling on their wedding day, Grandfather Lester behind them near an enormous barn, grazing cattle visible in the background.

Beneath the picture he finds a collection of receipts for paid grain-bills, remembers the days when food was cheap enough to feed animals, and there were animals to be fed. Digging deeper, he comes across cancelled cheques, insurance policies, tax records, a collection of report cards, and letters wrapped in ribbon. Douglas pulls up short at the handmade rosary he gave his mother for her fifteenth anniversary, and wonders if either of them still believed in God even then. Again, it is hard to remember.

At last he locates his birth certificate. He stands, groaning with the ache in his calves and knees, and threads his way through the crowded attic to the west window, where the light from the setting sun is sufficient to read the fading document. He seats himself on the shell of a television that has not worked since he was a boy, holds the paper close to his face, and squints.

"May 12, 1989," reads the date at the top.

*Why, I'm fifty years old* he tells himself in wonderment. *Fifty; I'll be damned.*

There is something about that number that rings a bell in Douglas's tired old mind, something he can't quite recall about what it means to be fifty years old. He squints at the birth certificate again.

And there on the last line, he sees it, sees what he had almost forgotten, and realizes that he was wrong – he will be getting a birthday present today after all.

For the bottom line of his birth certificate says, simply and blessedly, "...expiry date: May 12, 2049."

Downstairs, for the first time in years, there is a knock at the door.

# Arthur Hoppe

# I Love You – This Is a Recording

## It was the telephone company that preserved civilization.

Herewith is another unwritten chapter from that unpublished text, *A History of the World, 1950 to 1999.* Its title: "Ma Bell Saves the Day."

By the early 1970's, the old morality had crumbled. The old certitudes had vanished. Wars, riots, and revolutions flourished. Neighbor mistrusted neighbor. People no longer touched each other. Conversations were icily polite.

And from the look in the eyes of mankind, it was clear that the human race was on the brink.

It was the telephone company that preserved civilization.

With people retreating inward on themselves, the number of telephone calls placed daily had dropped alarmingly. To stimulate business, it was suggested that the company provide another recorded message as a public service.

"We already give our subscribers the time and the weather," said the Board Chairman irritably. "What else do people need these days?"

"Sympathy?" suggested a vice-president, half jokingly.

The new service was an instant success. At first people were hesitant to dial "S-Y-M-P-A-T-H-Y." "That's silly," they'd say, shaking their heads. Then, when they were sure no one was listening, they'd pick up the phone in embarrassed secretiveness.

"Poor dear," the recording began in a gentle voice of sweet consolation. "I'm so terribly sorry for you. Oh, the pain you must be suffering! But how brave you are not to show it. How very proud of you I am. Poor dear."

After one month, studies showed each subscriber was making an average of 3.4 calls to the number daily. The company immediately announced plans for new recorder services. Next came, "I-L-O-V-E-Y-O-U":

"Oh, dearest, how deeply I love you – with my whole soul, my whole being. You are everything on earth to me – my sun, my moon, my stars...."

This was quickly followed by "F-R-I-E-N-D-S-H-I-P" ("Hi, there, old buddy..."), "C-O-N-F-I-D-E-N-C-E" ("Gosh, you're just about the greatest..."), and "S-E-C-U-R-I-T-Y" ("There, now, there's absolutely nothing to worry about as long as we have each other").

Special messages were added for those with special needs, such as "M-O-T-H-E-R" ("Oh, it's so good to hear your voice, son. Are you getting enough to eat? Are you wearing your galoshes? Are you...").

Surprisingly, one of the most popular was "A-U-T-H-O-R-I-T-Y" ("When you hear the signal, you will have sixty seconds to state your dilemma." After sixty seconds, a stern voice came on to thunder: "You know what's right. Now, by God, do it!").

Thus humanity came to have everything that man had always wanted from his fellow man – sympathy, love, friendship, confidence, security, and authority. And yet, oddly enough, deep down people were still uneasy.

Further studies were made. And at last the telephone company came up with the solution: "U-L-T-I-M-A-T-E-N-E-E-D."

"You are a singular human being, unique among all living creatures, different from all other men. You are that God-created miracle: you are, above all else, an individual.

"This is a recording."

# Ray Bradbury

# Marionettes, Inc.

Duplicate self or friends;
new humanoid plastic 1990 models,
guaranteed against all physical wear.

They walked slowly down the street at about ten in the evening, talking calmly. They were both about thirty-five, both eminently sober.

"But why so early?" said Smith.

"Because," said Braling.

"Your first night out in years and you go home at ten o'clock."

"Nerves, I suppose."

"What I wonder is how you ever managed it. I've been trying to get you out for ten years for a quiet drink. And now, on the one night, you insist on turning in early."

"Mustn't crowd my luck," said Braling.

"What did you do, put sleeping powder in your wife's coffee?"

"No, that would be unethical. You'll see soon enough."

They turned a corner. "Honestly, Braling, I hate to say this, but you *have* been patient with her. You may not admit it to me, but marriage has been awful for you, hasn't it?"

"I wouldn't say that."

"It's got around, anyway, here and there, how she got you to marry her. That time back in 1979 when you were going to Rio . . ."

"Dear Rio. I never *did* see it after all my plans."

"And how she tore her clothes and rumpled her hair and threatened to call the police unless you married her."

"She always was nervous, Smith, understand."

"It was more than unfair. You didn't love her. You told her as much, didn't you?"

"I recall that I was quite firm on the subject."

"But you married her anyhow."

"I had my business to think of, as well as my mother and father. A thing like that would have killed them."

"And it's been ten years."

"Yes," said Braling, his grey eyes steady. "But I think perhaps it might change now. I think what I've waited for has come about. Look here."

He drew forth a long blue ticket.

"Why, it's a ticket for Rio on the Thursday rocket!"

"Yes, I'm finally going to make it."

"But how wonderful! You *do* deserve it! But won't *she* object? Cause trouble?"

Braling smiled nervously. "She won't know I'm gone. I'll be back in a month and no one the wiser, except you."

Smith sighed. "I wish I were going with you."

"Poor Smith, your marriage hasn't exactly been roses, has it?"

"Not exactly, married to a woman who overdoes it. I mean, after all, when you've been married ten years, you don't expect a woman to sit on your lap for two hours every evening, call you at work twelve times a day, and talk baby talk. And it seems to me that in the last month she's gotten worse. I wonder if perhaps she isn't a little simple-minded?"

"Ah, Smith, always the conservative. Well, here's my house. Now, would you like to know my secret? How I made it out this evening?"

"Will you really tell?"

"Look up there!" said Braling.

They both stared up through the dark air.

In the window above them, on the second floor, a shade was raised. A man about thirty-five years old, with a touch of grey at either temple, sad grey eyes, and a small, thin mustache, looked down at them.

"Why, that's *you*!" cried Smith. "Sh-h-h, not so loud!" Braling waved upward. The man in the window gestured significantly and vanished. "I must be insane," said Smith.

"Hold on a moment."

They waited.

The street door of the apartment opened and the tall, spare gentleman with the mustache and the grieved eyes came out to meet them.

"Hello, Braling," he said.

"Hello, Braling," said Braling.

They were identical.

Smith stared. "Is this your twin brother? I never knew...."

"No, no," said Braling quietly. "Bend close. Put your ear to Braling Two's chest."

Smith hesitated and then leaned forward to place his head against the uncomplaining ribs.

*Tick-tick-tick-tick-tick-tick-tick-tick.*

"Oh no! It *can't* be!"

"It is."

"Let me listen again."

*Tick-tick-tick-tick-tick-tick-tick-tick.*

Smith staggered back and fluttered his eyelids, appalled. He reached out and touched the warm hands and the cheeks of the thing.

"Where'd you get him?"

"Isn't he excellently fashioned?"

"Incredible. Where?"

"Give the man your card, Braling Two."

Braling Two did a magic trick and produced a white card:

## MARIONETTES, INC.

*Duplicate self or friends; new humanoid plastic 1990 models, guaranteed against all physical wear. From $7600 to our $15 000 de luxe model.*

"No," said Smith.

"Yes," said Braling.

"Naturally," said Braling Two.

"How long has this gone on?"

"I've had him for a month. I keep him in the cellar in a toolbox. My wife never goes downstairs, and I have the only lock and key to that box. Tonight I said I wished to take a walk to buy a cigar. I went down cellar and took Braling Two out of his box and sent him back up to sit with my wife while I came on out to see you, Smith."

"Wonderful! He even *smells* like you: Bond Street and Melachrinos!"

"It may be splitting hairs, but I think it highly ethical. After all, what my wife wants most of all is *me*. This marionette *is* me to the hairiest detail. I've been home all evening. I shall be home with her for the next month. In the meantime another gentleman will be in Rio after ten years of waiting. When I return from Rio, Braling Two here will go back in his box."

Smith thought that over a minute or two. "Will he walk around without sustenance for a month?" he finally asked.

"For six months if necessary. And he's built to do everything – eat, sleep, perspire – everything, natural as natural is. You'll take good care of my wife, won't you, Braling Two?"

"Your wife is rather nice," said Braling Two. "I've grown rather fond of her."

Smith was beginning to tremble. "How long has Marionettes, Inc., been in business?"

"Secretly, for two years."

"Could I – I mean, is there a possibility..." Smith took his friend's elbow earnestly. "Can you tell me where I can get one, a robot, a marionette, for myself? You *will* give me the address, won't you?"

"Here you are."

Smith took the card and turned it round and round. "Thank you," he said. "You don't know what this means. Just a little respite. A night or so, once a month even. My wife loves me so much she can't bear to have me gone an hour. I love her dearly, you know, but remember the old poem: 'Love will fly if held too lightly, love will die if held too tightly.' I just want her to relax her grip a little bit."

"You're lucky, at least, that your wife loves you. Hate's my problem. Not so easy."

"Oh, Nettie loves me madly. It will be my task to make her love me comfortably."

"Good luck to you, Smith. Do drop around while I'm in Rio. It will seem strange, if you suddenly stop calling by, to my wife. You're to treat Braling Two, here, just like me."

"Right! Goodbye. And thank you."

Smith went smiling down the street. Braling and Braling Two turned and walked into the apartment hall.

On the crosstown bus Smith whistled softly, turning the white card in his fingers:

*Clients must be pledged to secrecy, for while an act is pending in Congress to legalize Marionettes, Inc., it is still a felony, if caught, to use one.*

"Well," said Smith.

*Clients must have a mold made of their body and a color index check of their eyes, lips, hair, skin, etc. Clients must expect to wait for two months until their model is finished.*

Not so long, thought Smith. Two months

from now my ribs will have a chance to mend from the crushing they've taken. Two months from now my hand will heal from being so constantly held. Two months from now my bruised underlip will begin to reshape itself. I don't mean to sound ungrateful....He flipped the card over.

*Marionettes, Inc., is two years old and has a fine record of satisfied customers behind it. Our motto is "No Strings Attached." Address: 43 South Wesley Drive.*

The bus pulled to his stop; he alighted, and while humming up the stairs he thought, Nettie and I have fifteen thousand in our joint bank account. I'll just slip eight thousand out as a business venture, you might say. The marionette will probably pay back my money, with interest, in many ways. Nettie needn't know. He unlocked the door and in a minute was in the bedroom. There lay Nettie, pale, huge, and piously asleep.

"Dear Nettie." He was almost overwhelmed with remorse at her innocent face there in the semidarkness. "If you were awake you would smother me with kisses and coo in my ear. Really, you make me feel like a criminal. You have been such a good, loving wife. Sometimes it is impossible for me to believe you married me instead of that Bud Chapman you once liked. It seems that in the last month you have loved me more wildly than *ever* before."

Tears came to his eyes. Suddenly he wished to kiss her, confess his love, tear up the card, forget the whole business. But as he moved to do this, his hand ached and his ribs cracked and groaned. He stopped, with a pained look in his eyes, and turned away. He moved out into the hall and through the dark rooms. Humming, he opened the kidney desk in the library and filched the bank book.

"Just take eight thousand dollars is all." he said. "No more than that." He stopped. "Wait a minute."

He rechecked the bank book frantically. "Hold on here!" he cried. "Ten thousand dollars is missing!" He leaped up. "There's only five thousand left! What's she done? What's Nettie done with it? More hats, more clothes, more perfume! Or, wait – I know! She bought that little house on the Hudson she's been talking about for months, without so much as a by your leave!"

He stormed into the bedroom, righteous and indignant. What did she mean, taking their money like this? He bent over her. "Nettie!" he shouted. "Nettie, wake up!"

She did not stir. "What've you done with my money!" he bellowed.

She stirred fitfully. The light from the street flushed over her beautiful cheeks.

There was something about her. His heart throbbed violently. His tongue dried. He shivered. His knees suddenly turned to water. He collapsed. "Nettie, Nettie!" he cried. "What've you done with my money!"

And then, the horrid thought. And then the terror and the loneliness engulfed him. And then the fever and disillusionment. For, without desiring to do so, he bent forward and yet forward again until his fevered ear was resting firmly and irrevocably upon her round pink bosom. "Nettie!" he cried.

*Tick-tick-tick-tick-tick-tick-tick-tick.*

As Smith walked away down the avenue in the night, Braling and Braling Two turned in at the door to the apartment. "I'm glad he'll be happy too," said Braling.

"Yes," said Braling Two abstractedly.

"Well, it's the cellar box for you, B-Two." Braling guided the other creature's elbow down the stairs to the cellar.

"That's what I want to talk to you about," said Braling Two, as they reached the concrete floor and walked across it. "The cellar, I don't like it. I don't like that toolbox."

"I'll try and fix up something more comfortable."

"Marionettes are made to move, not lie still. How would you like to lie in a box most of the time?"

"Well..."

"You wouldn't like it at all. I keep running. There's no way to shut me off. I'm perfectly alive and I have feelings."

"It'll only be a few days now. I'll be off to Rio and you won't have to stay in the box. You can live upstairs."

Braling Two gestured irritably. "And when you come back from having a good time, back in the box I go."

Braling said, "They didn't tell me at the marionette shop that I'd get a difficult specimen."

"There's a lot they don't know about us," said Braling Two. "We're pretty new. And we're sensitive. I hate the idea of you going off and laughing and lying in the sun in Rio while we're stuck here in the cold."

"But I've wanted that trip all my life," said Braling quietly.

He squinted his eyes and could see the sea and the mountains and the yellow sand. The sound of the waves was good to his inward mind. The sun was fine on his bared shoulders. The wine was most excellent.

"*I'll* never get to go to Rio," said the other man. "Have you thought of that?"

"No, I..."

"And another thing. Your wife."

"What about her?" asked Braling, beginning to edge toward the door.

"I've grown quite fond of her."

"I'm glad you're enjoying your employment." Braling licked his lips nervously.

"I'm afraid you don't understand. I think...I'm in love with her."

Braling took another step and froze.

"You're *what*?"

"And I've been thinking." said Braling Two, "how nice it is in Rio and how I'll never get there, and I've thought about your wife and...I think we could be very happy."

"Th-that's nice." Braling strolled as casually as he could to the cellar door. "You won't mind waiting a moment, will you? I have to make a phone call."

"To whom?" Braling Two frowned.

"No one important."

"To Marionettes, Incorporated? To tell them to come get me?"

"No, no – nothing like that!" He tried to rush out the door.

A metal-firm grip seized his wrists. "Don't run!"

"Take your hands off!"

"No."

"Did my wife put you up to this?"

"No."

"Did she guess? Did she talk to you? Does she know? Is *that* it?" He screamed. A hand clapped over his mouth.

"You'll never know, will you?" Braling Two smiled delicately. "You'll never know."

Braling struggled. "She *must* have guessed; she *must* have affected you!"

Braling Two said, "I'm going to put you in the box, lock it, and lose the key. Then I'll buy another Rio ticket for your wife."

"Now, now, wait a minute. Hold on. Don't be rash. Let's talk this over!"

"Goodbye, Braling."

Braling stiffened. "What do you mean, 'goodbye'?"

Ten minutes later Mrs. Braling awoke. She put her hand to her cheek. Someone had just kissed it. She shivered and looked up. "Why...you haven't done that in years," she murmured.

"We'll see what we can do about that," someone said.

# Nelson Bond

# Vital Factor

"My name is Wilkins.
I can power
the ship you want."

Wayne Crowder called himself a forceful man. Those who knew him best (none knew him really well) substituted adjectives somewhat less flattering. He was, they said, a cold and ruthless man; a man of iron will and icy determination; a man with a heart to match his granite jaw. Not cunning, dishonest, or unfair. Just hard. A man who wanted his own way – and got it.

In an era that sees more fortunes lost than gained, Crowder proved his ability and acumen by getting rich. Even in these days of exaggerated material and labor costs this can be done by a bold, determined man who admits no obstacles. Wayne Crowder did it. He patented a simple household product needed by everyone, sold it at a penny profit that crushed all would-be competition, and made himself a multimillionaire despite the staggering levies of the Department of Internal Revenue. He built himself a towering structure and placed his private office at its peak. He dwelt in the clouds, both figuratively and literally. In sense and essence, those whom he employed were his underlings.

A man of ice and stone and ink and steel, they called him. And in the main, their judgment was correct.

But he surprised them.

One afternoon he said to his secretary, "Get me my engineers."

The engineers sat deferentially before his massive desk. Wayne Crowder told them crisply, "Gentlemen – I want you to build me a spaceship."

The engineers eyed him, and then each other, a bit apprehensively. Their spokesman cleared his throat.

"A spaceship, sir?"

"I have decided," said Crowder, "to be the man who gives space flight to mankind."

One of the experts said, "We can design you such a ship, sir. That part is not too hard. The fundamental blueprint has been in existence for many years; the submarine is its basis. But..."

"Yes?"

"But the motor that will power such a ship," said the engineer frankly, "we cannot provide. Men have searched it for decades, but the answer is not yet found. In other words, we can build you a ship, but we can't lift that ship from Earth's surface."

"Design the ship," said Crowder, "and I will find the motor you need."

The chief engineer asked, "Where?"

Crowder answered, "A fair question. And my answer is: I do not know. But somewhere in this world is a man who does know the secret – and will reveal it if I provide the money to convert his theory to fact. I'll be that man."

"You'll be besieged by crackpots."

"I know it. You men must help me separate the wheat from the chaff. But anyone who shows up with a promising idea, however fantastic it may sound, shall have a chance to show what he can do."

"You mean you'll subsidize their experiments? It will cost a fortune!"

"I have a fortune," said Crowder succinctly. "Now get to work. Build me the ship, and I will make it fly."

Wayne Crowder summoned the newsmen. Their stories were spectacular, amusing. Press syndicates took jeering delight in offering the world the magnate's offer of one hundred thousand dollars in cold cash to the man who would make it possible for a vessel to rise from this planet. But the stories circulated to the distant corners of the globe; the offer was transmitted in a dozen tongues.

The prediction of the engineers was verified. The Crowder office building became a mecca and a haven for the lunatic fringe of humanity; their blueprints and scale models clogged its corridors, their letters were an inky deluge that threatened to engulf the expanded staff of clerks employed to sort, examine, scrutinize each scheme. Crowder himself saw only those few who passed the winnowing screen of the corps. Most of these he eventually turned away, but some he placed on a retaining wage and set to work. He poured a prince's ransom into the construction of new laboratories. His wide proving grounds became the bedlam workshop for upward of a score of would-be conquistadors of space.

The weeks rolled by; the spaceship

designed by the engineers left the blueprint stage and went into construction. But still no subsidized inventor had made good his boast that his pet engine – of steam or explosive, gas or atomic, or whatever fuel – would lift the metal monster from Earth's surface. Many tests were made. Some were comic, some tragic. But all were failures.

Still Crowder did not swerve.

"He will come," he said. "Money and determination will buy anything. One day he will appear."

And he was right. One day there came to his office a stranger. He was a small man. He looked even smaller in that tremendous room. He was an unusual visitor in that he carried no briefcase fat with blueprints, schematics, or formulae. He was unusual in that he neither blustered, cowered, nor deferred to his host. He was a pleasant little stranger, birdlike of eye and movement.

He said, "My name is Wilkins. I can power the ship you want."

"So?" said Crowder.

"But it will be unlike that meaningless huge bullet your engineers are building. Rockets are a foolish waste of time. My motor requires a different sort of vessel."

"Where are your plans?" asked Crowder.

"Here," and he tapped his head.

Crowder said impassively, "I am supporting a score of others who claim the same. None has been successful. What makes you think your idea will work?"

"The flying disks," replied the little man.

"Eh?"

"I've solved their secret. My idea is based on the principle that lets them fly. Electromagnetism. Utilization of the force of gravity. Or its opposite: counter-gravity."

"Thank you very much," said Crowder. "Now if you'll excuse me . . ."

"Wait!" bade the little man. "There is one thing more. There is this."

He drew from his pocket a metal object the size and shape of an ashtray. He suspended it over Crowder's desk – and took his hand away. It hung there in midair. Crowder touched it. A gentle tingling stirred his fingertips, but the object did not fall. Crowder sat down again slowly.

"Enough," he said. "What do you want?"

"For my services," said Wilkins, "you have already set a fair price. Three other things. A workshop in which to build a pilot model. Expert assistance. And an answer."

Crowder's brows lifted. "An answer?"

"An answer to one question. Why do you want so much to build this ship?"

"Because," said Crowder frankly, "I love power. Because I am ambitious. I would be the first to conquer space because to do so will make me greater, richer, stronger than any other man. I would be the master, not merely of one world, but of worlds."

"An honest answer," said Wilkins, "if a strange one."

"What other could there be?"

"There could be mine," said the little man thoughtfully. "I would leave this planet and go elsewhere – to Mars, perhaps – because there are strange beauties yet to find. Because there will be scarlet sunsets over barren wastes, and in the star-strewn night the thin, cold air of a dying world stirring in restless sighs across the valleys of the dry canals. Because my soul yearns to set foot on another world as yet untrod by man."

Crowder said brusquely, "You are a sentimentalist. I am a man of logic. No matter. We can work together. Your workshop will be ready in the morning."

Four months later, in the smoky haze of an October sunset, the two men sat together again. But not this time in Crowder's tower office. This time they crouched within the cubicle of a small, disk-shaped machine made by Crowder's engineers on plans designed by Wilkins. Outside, great crowds were gathered to witness the test flight. They stirred and murmured, waiting restlessly, as inside the control room of the craft Wilkins installed the final secret part he had not revealed to those who built his driving apparatus.

The little man secured a wire here, made a minute adjustment in another place. Crowder growled impatiently.

"Well, Wilkins? What's holding us up?"

"Nothing now." Wilkins laid down his tools, moved to the outer rim of the curiously shaped craft, and raised a metal screen which allowed him to look out upon the proving grounds. "Or – sentiment, perhaps. A wish to look once more on Earth's familiar scenes."

"You are a maudlin fool," sniffed Crowder, "or else you are afraid. Perhaps you have decided your invention won't work, after all?"

"It will work."

"Then turn on your motor. Let me hear its roar and feel the tug as we cut free of Earth's gravity and fly outward into space."

The little man lowered the port and moved back to the controls. He touched a lever and depressed a key. His hands moved dreamily across the board. Said Crowder fretfully, "I'm beginning to distrust you, Wilkins. If this is all a hoax ... When are going to take off? You said at five sharp, and" – he glanced at his watch – "it is now five-oh-two. Well ... Do we move?"

"We are already moving," said Wilkins.

Once more he lifted the screen that covered the port. Crowder saw the purple-black of space, cream-splattered with myriad stars. Behind them, receding Earth was a toy balloon ... a dime ... a firefly.

"By Gad!" cried Crowder, stumbling to his feet. "By Gad, you've done it, Wilkins!"

Wilkins smiled.

A great elation tore at Crowder's breast. He knew emotion at last, this cold, hard man. He cried triumphantly, "Then I was right! There is nothing money and determination cannot buy. I swore to be the man to conquer space, and I've made good. It's a triumph of power and ambition."

"And sentiment," said Wilkins.

"What! Your dreaming would have died aborning, but for me. I made this possible, Wilkins; don't ever forget that. My capital, my forcefulness, my will."

He stared at distant Earth through glowing eyes.

"This is but the beginning," he said. "We'll build a larger model. One great enough to hold a hundred men. We'll launch the first invasion of a world. I'll forge a new empire – on Mars. Turn back now, Wilkins."

"No," said Wilkins. "I think not."

"What? We've proven this ship can fly. Now we'll go back and prepare for greater flights."

"Not so," said the little man. "We will go on."

"What's this?" roared Crowder. "You defy me? Are you mad?"

"No," said Wilkins. "Sentimental."

He took off his coat. He took off his necktie and his shirt, slipped off his trousers and his shoes. Beneath his clothing shone another garb, a strange apparel totally unlike anything Crowder had ever seen before. A gleaming, tight-knit cloth of golden hue, curiously outlining the quite unhuman aspects of his small physique. He smiled at Crowder, and it was a friendly smile. But it was not the smile of a creature born on Earth.

"Your money and ambition paved the way," said the man from Mars, "but sentiment was the vital factor that sent me to you. You see – I wanted to go home."

# Mary Ellen Solt

# elegy
# for three
# astronauts

```
          astronaut
          satronau
          starona
          staron
          staro
          star
          stars
          starsa
          starsai
          starsail
          starsailo
          starsailor
```

```
   w w w
    i i i
   d d d
a s t r        n a u t
a s t r   O    n a u t
a s t r        n a u t
   w w w
    i i i
   d d d
   o o o
   w w w
```

```
          astronaut
          satronau
          starona
          staron
          staro
          star
          stars
          starsa
          starsai
          starsail
          starsailo
          starsailor
```

```
          starsailor
          satrsailo
          astrsao
          astrso
          astro
          astron
          astrona
          astonau
          astronaut
```

# May Swenson

# Southbound on the Freeway

A tourist came in from Orbitville,
parked in the air, and said:

The creatures of this star
are made of metal and glass.

Through the transparent parts
you can see their guts.

Their feet are round and roll
on diagrams – or long

measuring tapes – dark
with white lines.

They have four eyes.
The two in the back are red.

Sometimes you can see a 5-eyed
one, with a red eye turning

on the top of his head.
He must be special –

the others respect him,
and go slow,

when he passes, winding
among them from behind.

They all hiss as they glide,
like inches, down the marked

tapes. Those soft shapes,
shadowy inside

the hard bodies – are they
their guts or their brains?

From *New & Selected Things Taking Place* by May Swenson. Copyright © 1963 by May Swenson. First appeared in *The New Yorker*. By permission of Little, Brown and Company in association with the Atlantic Monthly Press.

# Gore Vidal

# Visit to a Small Planet

"This *is* the wrong costume, isn't it?"

*Characters*
KRETON

ROGER SPELDING

ELLEN SPELDING

MRS. SPELDING

JOHN RANDOLPH

GENERAL POWERS

AIDE

PAUL LAURENT

SECOND VISITOR

PRESIDENT OF PARAGUAY

## Act One

*Stock shot: The night sky, stars. Then slowly a luminous object arcs into view. As it is almost upon us, dissolve to the living room of the Spelding house in Maryland.*

*Superimpose card:* "THE TIME: THE DAY AFTER TOMORROW"

*The room is comfortably balanced between the expensively decorated and the homely. Roger Spelding is concluding his TV broadcast. He is middle-aged, unctuous, resonant. His wife, bored and vague, knits passively while he talks at his desk. Two technicians are on hand, operating the equipment. His daughter, Ellen, a lively girl of twenty, fidgets as she listens.*

SPELDING: (*into microphone*)...and so, according to General Powers...who should know if anyone does...the flying object which has given rise to so much irresponsible conjecture is nothing more than a meteor passing through the earth's orbit. It is not, as many believe, a secret weapon of this country. Nor is it a space ship as certain lunatic elements have suggested. General Powers has assured me that it is highly doubtful there is any form of life on other planets capable of building a spaceship. "If any travelling is to be done in space, we will do it first." And those are his exact words.... Which winds up another week of news. (*Crosses to pose with wife and daughter.*) This is Roger Spelding, saying good night to Mother and Father America, from my old homestead in Silver Glen, Maryland, close to the warm pulse-beat of the nation.

TECHNICIAN: Good show tonight, Mr. Spelding.

SPELDING: Thank you.

TECHNICIAN: Yes sir, you were right on time.

*Spelding nods wearily, his mechanical smile and heartiness suddenly gone.*

MRS. SPELDING: Very nice, dear. Very nice.

TECHNICIAN: See you next week, Mrs. Spelding.

SPELDING: Thank you, boys.

*Technicians go.*

SPELDING: Did you like the broadcast, Ellen?

ELLEN: Of course I did, Daddy.

SPELDING: Then what did I say?

ELLEN: Oh, that's not fair.

SPELDING: It's not very flattering when one's own daughter won't listen to what one says while millions of people...

ELLEN: I always listen, Daddy, you know that.

MRS. SPELDING: We love your broadcasts, dear. I don't know what we'd do without them.

SPELDING: Starve.

ELLEN: I wonder what's keeping John?

SPELDING: Certainly not work.

ELLEN: Oh, Daddy, stop it! John works very hard and you know it.

MRS. SPELDING: Yes, he's a perfectly nice boy, Roger. I like him.

SPELDING: I know. I know: he has every virtue except the most important one: he has no get-up-and-go.

ELLEN: (*precisely*) He doesn't want to get up and he doesn't want to go because he's already where he wants to be on his own farm which is exactly where *I'm* going to be when we're married.

SPELDING: More thankless than a serpent's tooth is an ungrateful child.

ELLEN: I don't think that's right. Isn't it "more deadly..."

SPELDING: Whatever the exact quotation is, I stand by the sentiment.

MRS. SPELDING: Please don't quarrel. It always gives me a headache.

SPELDING: I never quarrel. I merely reason, in my simple way, with Miss Know-it-all here.

ELLEN: Oh, Daddy! Next you'll tell me I should marry for money.

SPELDING: There is nothing wrong with marrying a wealthy man. The horror of it has always eluded me. However, my only wish is that you marry someone hard-working, ambitious, a man who'll make his mark in the world. Not a boy who plans to sit on a farm all his life, growing peanuts.

ELLEN: English walnuts.

SPELDING: Will you stop correcting me?

ELLEN: But, Daddy, John grows walnuts....

*John enters, breathlessly.*

JOHN: Come out! Quickly. It's coming this way. It's going to land right here!

SPELDING: *What's* going to land?

JOHN: The space ship. Look!

SPELDING: Apparently you didn't hear my broadcast. The flying object in question is a meteor, not a space ship.

*John has gone out with Ellen. Spelding and Mrs. Spelding follow.*

MRS. SPELDING: Oh, my! Look! Something *is* falling! Roger, you don't think it's going to hit the house, do you?

SPELDING: The odds against being hit by a falling object that size are, I should say, roughly, ten million to one.

JOHN: Ten million to one or not it's going to land right here and it's *not* falling.

SPELDING: I'm sure it's a meteor.

MRS. SPELDING: Shouldn't we go down to the cellar?

SPELDING: If it's not a meteor, it's an optical illusion...mass hysteria.

ELLEN: Daddy, it's a real space ship. I'm sure it is.

SPELDING: Or maybe a weather balloon. Yes, that's what it is. General Powers said only yesterday...

JOHN: It's landing!

SPELDING: I'm going to call the police...the army! (*Bolts inside.*)

ELLEN: Oh look how it shines!

JOHN: Here it comes!

MRS. SPELDING: Right in my rose garden!

ELLEN: Maybe it's a balloon.

JOHN: No, it's a space ship and right in your own backyard.

ELLEN: What makes it shine so?

JOHN: I don't know but I'm going to find out. (*Runs off toward the light.*)

ELLEN: Oh, darling, don't! John, please! John, John come back!

*Spelding, wide-eyed, returns.*

MRS. SPELDING: Roger, it's landed right in my rose garden.

SPELDING: I got General Powers. He's coming over. He said they've been watching this thing. They...they don't know what it is.

ELLEN: You mean it's nothing of ours?

SPELDING: They believe it...(*Swallows hard.*)...it's from outer space.

ELLEN: And John's down there! Daddy, get a gun or something.

SPELDING: Perhaps we'd better leave the house until the army gets here.

ELLEN: We can't leave John.

SPELDING: I can. (*Peers nearsightedly.*) Why, it's not much larger than a car. I'm sure it's some kind of meteor.

ELLEN: Meteors are blazing hot.

SPELDING: This is a cold one...

ELLEN: It's opening...the whole side's opening! (*Shouts.*) John! Come back! Quick...

MRS. SPELDING: Why, there's a man getting out of it! (*Sighs.*) I feel much better already. I'm sure if we ask him he'll move that thing for us. Roger, you ask him.

SPELDING: (*ominously*) If it's really a man?

ELLEN: John's shaking hands with him (*Calls.*) John darling, come on up here...

MRS. SPELDING: And bring your friend...

SPELDING: There's something wrong with the way that creature looks...if it is a man and not a...not a monster.

MRS. SPELDING: He looks perfectly nice to me.

*John and the visitor appear. The visitor is in his forties, a mild, pleasant-looking man with side-whiskers and dressed in the fashion of 1860. He pauses when he sees the three people, in silence for a moment. They stare back at him, equally interested.*

VISITOR: I seem to've made a mistake. I *am* sorry. I'd better go back and start over again.

SPELDING: My dear sir, you've only just arrived. Come in, come in. I don't need to tell you what a pleasure this is...Mister... Mister...

VISITOR: Kreton...This *is* the wrong costume, isn't it?

SPELDING: Wrong for what?

KRETON: For the country, and the time.

SPELDING: Well, it's a trifle old-fashioned.

MRS. SPELDING: But really awfully handsome.

KRETON: Thank you.

MRS. SPELDING: (*to husband*) Ask him about moving that thing off my rose bed.

*Spelding leads them all into living room.*

SPELDING: Come on in and sit down. You must be tired after your trip.

KRETON: Yes, I am a little (*Looks around delightedly.*) Oh, it's better than I'd hoped!

SPELDING: Better? What's better?

KRETON: The house...that's what you call it? Or is this an apartment?

SPELDING: This is a house in the State of Maryland, U.S.A.

KRETON: In the late twentieth century! To think this is really the twentieth century. I must sit down a moment and collect myself. The *real* thing! (*He sits down.*)

ELLEN: You...you're not an American, are you?

KRETON: What a nice thought! No, I'm not.

JOHN: You sound more English.

KRETON: Do I? Is my accent very bad?

JOHN: No, it's quite good.

SPELDING: Where *are* you from, Mr. Kreton?

KRETON: (*evasively*) Another place.

SPELDING: On this earth of course.

KRETON: No, not on this planet.

ELLEN: Are you from Mars?

KRETON: Oh dear no, not Mars. There's nobody on Mars...at least no one I know.

ELLEN: I'm sure you're teasing us and this is all some kind of publicity stunt.

KRETON: No, I really am from another place.

SPELDING: I don't suppose you'd consent to my interviewing you on television?

KRETON: I don't think your authorities will like that. They are terribly upset as it is.

SPELDING: How do you know?

KRETON: Well, I...pick up things. For instance, I know that in a few minutes a number of people from your Army will be here to question me and they...like you... are torn by doubt.

SPELDING: How extraordinary!

ELLEN: Why did you come here?

KRETON: Simply a visit to your small planet. I've been studying it for years. In fact, one might say, you people are my hobby. Especially, this period of your development.

JOHN: Are you the first person from your... your planet to travel in space like this?

KRETON: Oh my no! Everyone travels who wants to. It's just that no one wants to visit you. I can't think why. *I* always have. You'd be surprised what a thorough study I've made. (*Recites*.) The planet Earth is divided into five continents with a number of large islands. It is mostly water. There is one moon. Civilization is only just beginning....

SPELDING: Just beginning! My dear sir, we have had...

KRETON: (*blandly*) You are only in the initial stages, the most fascinating stages as far as I'm concerned....I do hope I don't sound patronizing.

ELLEN: Well, we are very proud.

KRETON: I know and that's one of your most endearing, primitive traits. Oh, I can't believe I'm here at last!

*General Powers, a vigorous product of the National Guard, and his Aide enter.*

POWERS: All right folks. The place is surrounded by troops. Where is the monster?

KRETON: I, my dear General, am the monster.

POWERS: What are you dressed up for, a fancy-dress party?

KRETON: I'd hoped to be in the costume of the period. As you see, I am about a hundred years too late.

POWERS: Roger, who is this joker?

SPELDING: This is Mr. Kreton...General Powers. Mr. Kreton arrived in that thing outside. He is from another planet.

POWERS: I don't believe it.

ELLEN: It's true. We saw him get out of the flying saucer.

POWERS: (*to Aide*) Captain, go down and look at that ship. But be careful. Don't touch anything. And don't let anybody else near it. (*Aide goes*.) So you're from another planet.

KRETON: Yes. My, that's a very smart uniform but I prefer the ones made of metal, the ones you used to wear, you know: with the feathers on top.

POWERS: That was five hundred years ago.... Are you *sure* you're not from the Earth?

KRETON: Yes.

POWERS: Well, I'm not. You've got some pretty tall explaining to do.

KRETON: Anything to oblige.

POWERS: All right, which planet?

KRETON: None that you have ever heard of.

POWERS: Where is it?

KRETON: You wouldn't know.

POWERS: This solar system?

KRETON: No.

POWERS: Another system?

KRETON: Yes.

POWERS: Look, Buster, I don't want to play games: I just want to know where you're from. The law requires it.

KRETON: It's possible that I could explain it to a mathematician but I'm afraid I couldn't explain it to you, not for another five hundred years and by then of course *you'd* be dead because you people do die, don't you?

POWERS: What?

KRETON: Poor fragile butterflies, such brief

little moments in the sun. . . . You see *we* don't die.

POWERS: You'll die all right if it turns out you're a spy or a hostile alien.

KRETON: I'm sure you wouldn't be so cruel.

*Aide returns; he looks disturbed.*

POWERS: What did you find?

AIDE: I'm not sure, General.

POWERS: (*heavily*) Then do your best to describe what the object is like.

AIDE: Well, it's elliptical, with a fourteen-foot diameter. And it's made of an unknown metal which shines and inside there isn't anything.

POWERS: Isn't anything?

AIDE: There's nothing inside the ship: No instruments, no food, nothing.

POWERS: (*to Kreton*) What did you do with your instrument board?

KRETON: With my what? Oh, I don't have one.

POWERS: How does the thing travel?

KRETON: I don't know.

POWERS: You don't know. Now look, Mister, you're in pretty serious trouble. I suggest you do a bit of co-operating. You claim you travelled here from outer space in a machine with no instruments. . . .

KRETON: Well, these cars are rather common in my world and I suppose, once upon a time, I must've known the theory on which they operate but I've long since forgotten. After all, General, we're not mechanics, you and I.

POWERS: Roger, do you mind if we use your study?

SPELDING: Not at all. Not at all, General.

POWERS: Mr. Kreton and I are going to have a chat. (*to Aide*) Put in a call to the Chief of Staff.

AIDE: Yes, General.

*Spelding rises, leads Kreton and Powers into* *next room, a handsomely furnished study with many books and a globe of the world.*

SPELDING: This way, gentlemen. (*Kreton sits down comfortably beside the globe which he twirls thoughtfully. At the door, Spelding speaks in a low voice to Powers.*) I hope I'll be the one to get the story first, Tom.

POWERS: There isn't any story. Complete censorship. I'm sorry but this house is under martial law. I've a hunch we're in trouble. (*He shuts the door. Spelding turns and rejoins his family.*)

ELLEN: I think he's wonderful, whoever he is.

MRS. SPELDING: I wonder how much damage he did to my rose garden. . . .

JOHN: It's sure hard to believe he's really from outer space. No instruments, no nothing . . . boy, they must be advanced scientifically.

MRS. SPELDING: Is he spending the night, dear?

SPELDING: What?

MRS. SPELDING: Is he spending the night?

SPELDING: Oh yes, yes, I suppose he will be.

MRS. SPELDING: Then I'd better go make up the bedroom. He seems perfectly nice to me. I like his whiskers. They're so very . . . comforting. Like Grandfather Spelding's. (*She goes.*)

SPELDING: (*bitterly*) I *know* this story will leak out before I can interview him. I just know it.

ELLEN: What does it mean, we're under martial law?

SPELDING: It means we have to do what General Powers tells us to do. (*He goes to the window as a soldier passes by.*) See?

JOHN: I wish I'd taken a closer look at that ship when I had the chance.

ELLEN: Perhaps he'll give us a ride in it.

JOHN: Travelling in space! Just like those stories. You know: intergalactic drive stuff.

SPELDING: *If* he's not an impostor.

ELLEN: I have a feeling he isn't.

JOHN: Well, I better call the family and tell them I'm all right. (*He crosses to telephone by the door which leads into hall.*)

AIDE: I'm sorry, sir, but you can't use the phone.

SPELDING: He certainly can. This is my house. . . .

AIDE: (*mechanically*) This house is a military reservation until the crisis is over: Order General Powers. I'm sorry.

JOHN: How am I to call home to say where I am?

AIDE: Only General Powers can help you. You're also forbidden to leave this house without permission.

SPELDING: You can't do this!

AIDE: I'm afraid, sir, we've done it.

ELLEN: Isn't it exciting!

*Cut to study.*

POWERS: Are you deliberately trying to confuse me?

KRETON: Not deliberately, no.

POWERS: We have gone over and over this for two hours now and all that you've told me is that you're from another planet in another solar system. . . .

KRETON: In another dimension. I think that's the word you use.

POWERS: In another dimension and you have come here as a tourist.

KRETON: Up to a point, yes. What did you expect?

POWERS: It is my job to guard the security of this country.

KRETON: I'm sure that must be very interesting work.

POWERS: For all I know, you are a spy, sent here by an alien race to study us, preparatory to invasion.

KRETON: Oh, none of my people would *dream* of invading you.

POWERS: How do I know that's true?

KRETON: You don't, so I suggest you believe me. I should also warn you: I can tell what's inside.

POWERS: What's inside?

KRETON: What's inside your mind.

POWERS: You're a mind reader?

KRETON: I don't really read it. I hear it.

POWERS: What am I thinking?

KRETON: That I am either a lunatic from the earth or a spy from another world.

POWERS: Correct. But then you could've guessed that. (*Frowns.*) What am I thinking now?

KRETON: You're making a picture. Three silver stars. You're pinning them on your shoulder, instead of the two stars you now wear.

POWERS: (*startled*) That's right. I was thinking of my promotion.

KRETON: If there's anything I can do to hurry it along, just let me know.

POWERS: You can. Tell me why you're here.

KRETON: Well, we don't travel much, my people. We used to but since we see everything through special monitors and recreators, there is no particular need to travel. However, *I* am a hobbyist. I love to gad about.

POWERS: (*taking notes*) Are you the first to visit us?

KRETON: Oh, no! We started visiting you long before there were people on the planet. However, we are seldom noticed on our trips. I'm sorry to say I slipped up, coming in the way I did . . . but then this visit was all rather impromptu. (*Laughs.*) I am a creature of impulse, I fear.

*Aide looks in.*

AIDE: Chief of Staff on the telephone, General.

POWERS: (*picks up phone*) Hello, yes, sir. Powers speaking. I'm talking to him now. No, sir. No, sir. No, we can't determine what method of power was used. He won't talk. Yes, sir. I'll hold him here. I've put the house under martial law...belongs to a friend of mine, Roger Spelding, the TV commentator. Roger Spelding, the TV... What? Oh, no, I'm sure he won't say anything. Who...oh, yes, sir. Yes, I realize the importance of it. Yes, I will. Goodbye. (*Hangs up*.) The President of the United States wants to know all about you.

KRETON: How nice of him! And I want to know all about him. But I do wish you'd let me rest a bit first. Your language is still not familiar to me. I had to learn them all, quite exhausting.

POWERS: You speak *all* our languages?

KRETON: Yes, all of them. But then it's easier than you might think since I can see what's inside.

POWERS: Speaking of what's inside, we're going to take your ship apart.

KRETON: Oh, I wish you wouldn't.

POWERS: Security demands it.

KRETON: In that case *my* security demands you leave it alone.

POWERS: You plan to stop us?

KRETON: I already have....Listen.

*Far-off shouting. Aide rushes into the study.*

AIDE: Something's happened to the ship, General. The door's shut and there's some kind of wall around it, an invisible wall. We can't get near it.

KRETON: (*to camera*) I hope there was no one inside.

POWERS: (*to Kreton*) How did you do that?

KRETON: I couldn't begin to explain. Now if you don't mind, I think we should go in and see our hosts.

*He rises, goes into living room. Powers and Aide look at each other.*

POWERS: Don't let him out of your sight.

*Cut to living room as Powers picks up phone. Kreton is with John and Ellen.*

KRETON: I don't mind curiosity but I really can't permit them to wreck my poor ship.

ELLEN: What do you plan to do, now you're here?

KRETON: Oh, keep busy. I have a project or two....(*Sighs.*) I can't believe you're real!

JOHN: Then we're all in the same boat.

KRETON: Boat? Oh, yes! Well, I should have come ages ago but I...I couldn't get away until yesterday.

JOHN: Yesterday? It only took you a *day* to get here?

KRETON: One of *my* days, not yours. But then you don't know about time yet.

JOHN: Oh, you mean relativity.

KRETON: No, it's much more involved than that. You won't know about time until... now let me see if I remember...no, I don't, but it's about two thousand years.

JOHN: What do we do between now and then?

KRETON: You simply go on the way you are, living your exciting primitive lives...you have no idea how much fun you're having now.

ELLEN: I hope you'll stay with us while you're here.

KRETON: That's very nice of you. Perhaps I will. Though I'm sure you'll get tired of having a visitor under foot all the time.

ELLEN: Certainly not. And Daddy will be deliriously happy. He can interview you by the hour.

JOHN: What's it like in outer space?

KRETON: Dull.

ELLEN: I should think it would be divine!

*Powers enters.*

KRETON: No, General, it won't work.

POWERS: What won't work?

KRETON: Trying to blow up my little force

field. You'll just plough up Mrs. Spelding's garden.

*Powers snarls and goes into study.*

ELLEN: Can you tell what we're *all* thinking?

KRETON: Yes. As a matter of fact, it makes me a bit giddy. Your minds are not at all like ours. You see, we control our thoughts while...well, it's extraordinary the things you think about!

ELLEN: Oh, how awful! You can tell *everything* we think?

KRETON: Everything! It's one of the reasons I'm here, to intoxicate myself with your primitive minds...with the wonderful rawness of your emotions! You have no idea how it excites me! You simply seethe with unlikely emotions.

ELLEN: I've never felt so sordid.

JOHN: From now on I'm going to think about agriculture.

SPELDING: (*entering*) You would.

ELLEN: Daddy!

KRETON: No, no. You must go right on thinking about Ellen. Such wonderfully *purple* thoughts!

SPELDING: Now see here, Powers, you're carrying this martial law thing too far....

POWERS: Unfortunately, until I have received word from Washington as to the final disposition of this problem, you must obey my orders: no telephone calls, no communication with the outside.

SPELDING: This is insupportable.

KRETON: Poor Mr. Spelding! If you like, I shall go. That would solve everything, wouldn't it?

POWERS: You're not going anywhere, Mr. Kreton, until I've had my instructions.

KRETON: I sincerely doubt if you could stop me. However, I put it up to Mr. Spelding. Shall I go?

SPELDING: Yes! (*Powers gestures a warning.*)

Do stay, I mean, we want you to get a good impression of us....

KRETON: And of course you still want to be the first journalist to interview me. Fair enough. All right, I'll stay on for a while.

POWERS: Thank you.

KRETON: Don't mention it.

SPELDING: General, may I ask our guest a few questions?

POWERS: Go right ahead, Roger. I hope you'll do better than I did.

SPELDING: Since you read our minds, you probably already know what our fears are.

KRETON: I do, yes.

SPELDING: We are afraid that you represent a hostile race.

KRETON: And I have assured General Powers that my people are not remotely hostile. Except for me, no one is interested in this planet's present stage.

SPELDING: Does this mean you might be interested in a *later* stage?

KRETON: I'm not permitted to discuss your future. Of course my friends think me perverse to be interested in a primitive society but there's no accounting for tastes, is there? You are my hobby. I love you. And that's all there is to it.

POWERS: So you're just here to look around...sort of going native.

KRETON: What a nice expression! That's it exactly. I am going native.

POWERS: (*grimly*) Well, it is my view that you have been sent here by another civilization for the express purpose of reconnoitring prior to invasion.

KRETON: That *would* be your view! The wonderfully primitive assumption that all strangers are hostile. You're almost too good to be true, General.

POWERS: You deny your people intend to make trouble for us?

KRETON: I deny it.

POWERS: Then are they interested in

establishing communication with us? trade? that kind of thing?

KRETON: We have always had communication with you. As for trade, well, we do not trade...that is something peculiar only to your social level. (*quickly*) Which I'm not criticizing! As you know, I approve of everything you do.

POWERS: I give up.

SPELDING: You have no interest then in... well, trying to dominate the earth.

KRETON: Oh, yes!

POWERS: I thought you said your people weren't interested in us.

KRETON: *They're* not, but *I* am.

POWERS: You!

KRETON: Me...I mean I. You see I've come here to take charge.

POWERS: Of the United States?

KRETON: No, of the whole world. I'm sure you'll be much happier and it will be great fun for me. You'll get used to it in no time.

POWERS: This is ridiculous. How can one man take over the world?

KRETON: (*gaily*) Wait and see!

POWERS: (*to Aide*) Grab him!

*Powers and aide rush Kreton but within a foot of him, they stop, stunned.*

KRETON: You can't touch me. That's part of the game. (*He yawns.*) Now, if you don't mind, I shall go up to my room for a little lie-down.

SPELDING: I'll show you the way.

KRETON: That's all right. I know the way. (*Touches his brow.*) Such savage thoughts! My head is vibrating like a drum. I feel quite giddy, all of you thinking away. (*He starts to the door; he pauses beside Mrs. Spelding.*) No, it's not a dream, dear lady. I shall be here in the morning when you wake up. And now, good night, dear, wicked children...(*He goes as we fade out.*)

## Act Two

*Fade in on Kreton's bedroom next morning. He lies fully clothed on bed with cat on his lap.*

KRETON: Poor cat! Of course I sympathize with you. Dogs *are* distasteful. What? Oh, I can well believe they do: yes, yes, how disgusting. They don't ever groom their fur! But you do *constantly*, such a fine coat. No, no, I'm not just saying that, I really mean it: exquisite texture. Of course, I wouldn't say it was *nicer* than skin but even so...What? Oh, no! They *chase* you! Dogs chase you for no reason at all except pure malice? You poor creature. Ah, but you *do* fight back! That's right! give it to them: slash, bite, scratch! Don't let them get away with a trick....No! Do dogs really do that? Well, I'm sure *you* don't. What...oh, well, yes I completely agree about mice. They *are* delicious! (Ugh!) Pounce, snap, and there is a heavenly dinner. No, I don't know any mice yet... they're not very amusing? But after all think how you must terrify them because you are so bold, so cunning, so beautifully predatory! (*knock at door*) Come in.

ELLEN: (*enters*) Good morning. I brought you your breakfast.

KRETON: How thoughtful! (*Examines bacon.*) Delicious, but I'm afraid my stomach is not like yours, if you'll pardon me. I don't eat. (*Removes pill from his pocket and swallows it.*) This is all I need for the day. (*Indicates cat.*) Unlike this creature, who would eat her own weight every hour, given a chance.

ELLEN: How do you know?

KRETON: We've had a talk.

ELLEN: You can *speak* to the cat?

KRETON: Not speak exactly but we communicate. I look inside the cat co-operates. Bright red thoughts, very exciting, though rather on one level.

ELLEN: Does kitty like us?

KRETON: No, I wouldn't say she did. But then she has very few thoughts not connected with food. Have you, my quadruped criminal? (*He strokes the cat, which jumps to the floor.*)

ELLEN: You know you've really upset everyone.

KRETON: I supposed that I would.

ELLEN: Can you really take over the world, just like that?

KRETON: Oh, yes.

ELLEN: What do you plan to do when you *have* taken over?

KRETON: Ah, that is my secret.

ELLEN: Well, I think you'll be a very nice President, *if* they let you of course.

KRETON: What a sweet girl you are! Marry him right away.

ELLEN: Marry John?

KRETON: Yes. I see it in your head *and* in his. He wants you very much.

ELLEN: Well, we plan to get married this summer, if father doesn't fuss too much.

KRETON: Do it before then. I shall arrange it all if you like.

ELLEN: How?

KRETON: I can convince your father.

ELLEN: That sounds awfully ominous. I think you'd better leave poor Daddy alone.

KRETON: Whatever you say. (*Sighs.*) Oh, I love it so! When I woke up this morning I had to pinch myself to prove I was really here.

ELLEN: We were all doing a bit of pinching too. Ever since dawn we've had nothing but visitors and phone calls and troops outside in the garden. No one has the faintest idea what to do about you.

KRETON: Well, I don't think they'll be confused much longer.

ELLEN: How do you plan to conquer the world?

KRETON: I confess I'm not sure. I suppose I must make some demonstration of strength, some colorful trick that will frighten everyone...though I much prefer taking charge quietly. That's why I've sent for the President.

ELLEN: The President? *Our* President?

KRETON: Yes, he'll be along any minute now.

ELLEN: But the President just doesn't go around visiting people.

KRETON: He'll visit me. (*Chuckles.*) It may come as a surprise to him, but he'll be in this house in a very few minutes. I think we'd better go downstairs now. (*to cat*) No, I will not give you a mouse. You must get your own. Be self-reliant. Beast!

*Dissolve to the study. Powers is reading book entitled:* The Atom and You. *Muffled explosions off-stage.*

AIDE: (*entering*) Sir, nothing seems to be working. Do we have the General's permission to try a fission bomb on the force field?

POWERS: No...no. We'd better give it up.

AIDE: The men are beginning to talk.

POWERS: (*thundering*) Well, keep them quiet! (*contritely*) I'm sorry, Captain. I'm on edge. Fortunately, the whole business will soon be in the hands of the World Council.

AIDE: What will the World Council do?

POWERS: It will be interesting to observe them

AIDE: You don't think this Kreton can really take over the world, do you?

POWERS: Of course not. Nobody can.

*Dissolve to living room. Mrs. Spelding and Spelding are talking.*

MRS. SPELDING: You still haven't asked Mr. Kreton about moving that thing, have you?

SPELDING: There are too many *important* things to ask him.

MRS. SPELDING: I hate to be a nag but you know the trouble I have had getting anything to grow in that part of the garden....

JOHN: (*enters*) Good morning.

MRS. SPELDING: Good morning, John.

JOHN: Any sign of your guest?

MRS. SPELDING: Ellen took his breakfast up to him a few minutes ago.

JOHN: They don't seem to be having much luck, do they? I sure hope you don't mind my staying here like this.

*Spelding glowers.*

MRS. SPELDING: Why, we love having you! I just hope your family aren't too anxious.

JOHN: One of the G.I.'s finally called them, said I was staying here for the weekend.

SPELDING: The rest of our *lives*, if something isn't done soon.

JOHN: Just how long do you think that'll be, Dad?

SPELDING: Who knows?

*Kreton and Ellen enter.*

KRETON: Ah, how wonderful to see you again! Let me catch my breath....Oh, your minds! It's not easy for me, you know. So many crude thoughts blazing away! Yes, Mrs. Spelding, I will move the ship off your roses.

MRS. SPELDING: That's awfully sweet of you.

KRETON: Mr. Spelding, if any interviews are to be granted you will be the first. I promise you.

SPELDING: That's very considerate, I'm sure.

KRETON: So you can stop thinking *those* particular thoughts. And now where is the President?

SPELDING: The President?

KRETON: Yes, I sent for him. He should be here. (*He goes to the terrace window.*) Ah, that must be he. (*A swarthy man in uniform with a sash across his chest is standing, bewildered, on the terrace. Kreton opens the glass doors.*) Come in, sir, come in, Your Excellency. Good of you to come on such short notice. (*Man enters.*)

MAN: (*in Spanish accent*) Where am I?

KRETON: You *are* the President, aren't you?

MAN: Of course I am the President. What am I doing here? I was dedicating a bridge and I find myself...

KRETON: (*aware of his mistake*) Oh, dear! *Where* was the bridge?

MAN: Where do you think, you idiot? In Paraguay!

KRETON: (*to others*) I seem to've made a mistake. Wrong President. (*Gestures and the man disappears.*) Seemed rather upset, didn't he?

JOHN: You can make people come and go just like that?

KRETON: Just like that.

*Powers looks into room from the study.*

POWERS: Good morning, Mr. Kreton. Could I see you for a moment?

KRETON: By all means.

*He crosses to the study.*

SPELDING: I believe I am going mad.

*Cut to study. The Aide stands at attention while Powers addresses Kreton.*

POWERS: ...and so we feel, the government of the United States feels, that this problem is too big for any one country, therefore we are turning the whole affair over to Paul Laurent, the Secretary-General of the World Council.

KRETON: Very sensible. I should've thought of that myself.

POWERS: Mr. Laurent is on his way here now. And I may add, Mr. Kreton, you've made me look singularly ridiculous.

KRETON: I'm awfully sorry. (*pause*) No, you can't kill me.

POWERS: You were reading my mind again.

KRETON: I can't really help it, you know. And such *black* thoughts today, but intense, very intense.

POWERS: I regard you as a menace.

KRETON: I know you do and I think it's awfully unkind. I do mean well.

POWERS: Then go back where you came from and leave us alone.

KRETON: I'm afraid I can't do that just yet....

*Phone rings, the Aide answers it.*

AIDE: He's outside? Sure, let him through. (*to Powers*) The Secretary-General of the World Council is here, sir.

POWERS: (*to Kreton*) I hope you'll listen to *him*.

KRETON: Oh, I shall, of course. I love listening.

*The door opens and Paul Laurent, middle-aged and serene, enters. Powers and his Aide stand to attention. Kreton goes forward to shake hands.*

LAURENT: Mr. Kreton?

KRETON: At your service, Mr. Laurent.

LAURENT: I welcome you to this planet in the name of the World Council.

KRETON: Thank you sir, thank you.

LAURENT: Could you leave us alone for a moment, General?

POWERS: Yes, sir.

*Powers and Aide go. Laurent smiles at Kreton.*

LAURENT: Shall we sit down?

KRETON: Yes, yes I love sitting down. I'm afraid my manners are not quite suitable, yet.

*They sit down.*

LAURENT: Now, Mr. Kreton, in violation of all the rules of diplomacy, may I come to the point?

KRETON: You may.

LAURENT: Why are you here?

KRETON: Curiosity. Pleasure.

LAURENT: You are a tourist, then, in this time and place?

KRETON: (*nods*) Yes. Very well put.

LAURENT: We have been informed that you have extraordinary powers.

KRETON: By your standards, yes, they must seem extraordinary.

LAURENT: We have also been informed that it is your intention to...to take charge of this world.

KRETON: That is correct.... What a remarkable mind you have! I have difficulty looking inside it.

LAURENT: (*laughs*) Practice. I've attended so many conferences.... May I say that your conquest of our world puts your status of tourist in a rather curious light?

KRETON: Oh, I said nothing about *conquest*.

LAURENT: Then how else do you intend to govern? The people won't allow you to direct their lives without a struggle.

KRETON: But I'm sure they will if I ask them to.

LAURENT: You believe you can do all this without, well, without violence?

KRETON: Of course I can. One or two demonstrations and I'm sure they'll do as I ask. (*Smiles.*) Watch this. (*Pause. Then shouting. Powers bursts into room.*)

POWERS: Now what've you done?

KRETON: Look out the window, Your Excellency. (*Laurent goes to to window. A rifle floats by, followed by an alarmed soldier.*) Nice isn't it? I confess I worked out a number of rather melodramatic tricks last night. Incidentally, all the rifles of all the soldiers in all the world are now floating in the air. (*Gestures.*) Now they have them back.

POWERS: (*to Laurent*) You see, sir, I didn't exaggerate in my report.

LAURENT: (*awed*) No, no, you certainly didn't.

KRETON: You were sceptical, weren't you?

LAURENT: Naturally. But now I...now I think it's possible.

POWERS: That this...this gentleman is going to run everything?

LAURENT: Yes, yes I do. And it might be wonderful.

KRETON: You *are* more clever than the others. You begin to see that I mean only good.

LAURENT: Yes, only good. General, do you realize what this means? We can have one government...

KRETON: With innumerable bureaus, and intrigue....

LAURENT: (*excited*) And the world could be incredibly prosperous, especially if he'd help us with his superior knowledge.

KRETON: (*delighted*) I will, I will. I'll teach you to look into one another's minds. You'll find it devastating but enlightening: all that self-interest, those *lurid* emotions...

LAURENT: No more countries. No more wars...

KRETON: (*startled*)What? Oh, but I like a lot of countries. Besides, at this stage of your development you're supposed to have lots of countries and lots of wars... innumerable wars....

LAURENT: But you can help us change all that.

KRETON: *Change* all that! My dear sir, I am your friend.

LAURENT: What do you mean?

KRETON: Why, your deepest pleasure is violence. How can you deny that? It is the whole point to you, the whole point to my hobby...and you are my hobby, all mine.

LAURENT: But our lives are devoted to *controlling* violence, and not creating it.

KRETON: Now, don't take me for an utter fool. After all, I can see into your minds. My dear fellow, don't you *know* what you are?

LAURENT: What are we?

KRETON: You are savages. I have returned to the dark ages of an insignificant planet simply because I want the glorious excitement of being among you and revelling in your savagery! There is murder in all your hearts and I love it! It intoxicates me!

LAURENT: (*slowly*) You hardly flatter us.

KRETON: I didn't mean to be rude but you did ask me why I am here and I've told you.

LAURENT: You have no wish then to...to help us poor savages.

KRETON: I couldn't even if I wanted to. You won't be civilized for at least two thousand years and you won't reach the level of my people for about a million years.

LAURENT: (*sadly*)Then you have come here only to...to observe?

KRETON: No, more than that. I mean to regulate your pastimes. But don't worry: I won't upset things too much. I've decided I don't want to be known to the people. You will go right on with your countries, your squabbles, the way you always have, while I will *secretly* regulate things through you.

LAURENT: The World Council does not govern. We only advise.

KRETON: Well, I shall advise you and you will advise the governments and we shall have a lovely time.

LAURENT: I don't know what to say. You obviously have the power to do as you please.

KRETON: I'm glad you realize that. Poor General Powers is now wondering if a

124

hydrogen bomb might destroy me. It won't, General.

POWERS: Too bad.

KRETON: Now, Your Excellency, I shall stay in this house until you have laid the groundwork for my first project.

LAURENT: And what is that to be?

KRETON: A war! I want one of your really splendid wars, with all the trimmings, all the noise and the fire . . .

LAURENT: A war! You're joking. Why at this moment we are working as hard as we know how *not* to have a war.

KRETON: But secretly you want one. After all, it's the one thing your little race does well. You'd hardly want me to deprive you of your simple pleasures, now would you?

LAURENT: I think you must be mad.

KRETON: Not mad, simply a philanthropist. Of course I myself shall get a great deal of pleasure out of a war (the vibrations must be incredible!) but I'm doing it mostly for you. So, if you don't mind, I want you to arrange a few incidents, so we can get one started spontaneously.

LAURENT: I refuse.

KRETON: In that event, I shall select someone else to head the World Council. Someone who *will* start a war. I suppose there exist a few people here who might like the idea.

LAURENT: How can you do such a horrible thing to us? Can't you see that we don't want to be savages?

KRETON: But you have no choice. Anyway, you're just pulling my leg! I'm sure you want a war as much as the rest of them do and that's what you're going to get: the biggest war you've ever had!

LAURENT: (*stunned*) Heaven help us!

KRETON: (*exuberant*) Heaven won't! Oh, what fun it will be! I can hardly wait! (*He strikes the globe of the world a happy blow as we fade out.*)

## Act Three

*Fade in on the the study, two weeks later. Kreton is sitting at desk on which a map is spread out. He has a pair of dividers, some models of jet aircraft. Occasionally he pretends to dive-bomb, imitating the sound of a bomb going off. Powers enters.*

POWERS: You wanted me, sir?

KRETON: Yes, I wanted those figures on radioactive fall-out.

POWERS: They're being made up now, sir. Anything else?

KRETON: Oh, my dear fellow, why do you dislike me so?

POWERS: I am your military aide, sir: I don't have to answer that question. It is outside the sphere of my duties.

KRETON: Aren't you at least happy about your promotion?

POWERS: Under the circumstances, no, sir.

KRETON: I find your attitude baffling.

POWERS: Is that all, sir?

KRETON: You have never once said what you thought of my war plans. Not once have I got a single word of encouragement from you, a single compliment . . . only black thoughts.

POWERS: Since you read my mind, sir, you know what I think.

KRETON: True, but I can't help but feel that deep down inside of you there is just a twinge of professional jealousy. You don't like the idea of an outsider playing your game better than you do. Now confess!

POWERS: I am acting as your aide only under duress.

KRETON: (*sadly*) Bitter, bitter . . . and to think I chose you especially as my aide. Think of all the other generals who would give anything to have your job.

POWERS: Fortunately, they know nothing about my job.

KRETON: Yes, I do think it wise not to advertise my presence, don't you?

POWERS: I can't see that it makes much difference, since you seem bent on destroying our world.

KRETON: I'm not going to destroy it. A few dozen cities, that's all, and not very nice cities either. Think of the fun you'll have building new ones when it's over.

POWERS: How many millions of people do you plan to kill?

KRETON: Well, quite a few, but they love this sort of thing. You can't convince me they don't. Oh, I know what Laurent says. But he's a misfit, out of step with his time. Fortunately, my new World Council is more reasonable.

POWERS: Paralysed is the word, sir.

KRETON: You don't think they like me either?

POWERS: You *know* they hate you, sir.

KRETON: But love and hate are so confused in your savage minds and the vibrations of the one are so very like those of the other that I can't always distinguish. You see, we neither love nor hate in my world. We simply have hobbies. (*He strokes the globe of the world tenderly.*) But now to work. Tonight's the big night: first, the sneak attack, then: boom! (*He claps his hands gleefully.*)

*Dissolve to the living room, to John and Ellen.*

ELLEN: I've never felt so helpless in my life.

JOHN: Here we all stand around doing nothing while he plans to blow up the world.

ELLEN: Suppose we went to the newspapers.

JOHN: He controls the press. When Laurent resigned they didn't even print his speech.

*A gloomy pause.*

ELLEN: What are you thinking about, John?

JOHN: Walnuts. (*They embrace.*)

ELLEN: Can't we do anything?

JOHN: No, I guess there's nothing.

ELLEN: (*vehemently*) Oh! I could kill him!

*Kreton and Powers enter.*

KRETON: Very good, Ellen, *very* good! I've never felt you so violent.

ELLEN: You heard what I said to John?

KRETON: Not in words, but you were absolutely bathed in malevolence.

POWERS: I'll get the papers you wanted, sir.

*Powers exits.*

KRETON: I don't think he likes me very much but your father does. Only this morning he offered to handle my public relations and I said I'd let him. Wasn't that nice of him?

JOHN: I think I'll go get some fresh air. (*He goes out through the terrace door.*)

KRETON: Oh, dear! (*Sighs.*) Only your father is really entering the spirit of the game. He's a much better sport than you, my dear.

ELLEN: (*exploding*) Sport! That's it! You think we're sport. You think we're animals to be played with: well, we're not. We're people and we don't want to be destroyed.

KRETON: (*patiently*) But *I* am not destroying you. You will be destroying one another of your own free will, as you have always done. I am simply a ...a kibitzer.

ELLEN: No, you are a vampire!

KRETON: A vampire? You mean I drink blood? Ugh!

ELLEN: No, you drink emotions, our emotions. You'll sacrifice us all for the sake of your ...your vibrations!

KRETON: Touché. Yet what harm am I really doing? It's true I'll enjoy the war more than anybody; but it will be *your*

126

destructiveness after all, not mine.

ELLEN: You could stop it.

KRETON: So could you.

ELLEN: I?

KRETON: Your race. They could stop altogether but they won't. And I can hardly intervene in their natural development. The most I can do is help out in small, practical ways.

ELLEN: We are not what you think. We're not so...so primitive.

KRETON: My dear girl, just take this one household: your mother dislikes your father but she is too tired to do anything about it so she knits and she gardens and she tries not to think about him. Your father, on the other hand, is bored with all of you. Don't look shocked: he doesn't like you any more than you like him....

ELLEN: Don't say that!

KRETON: I am only telling you the truth. Your father wants you to marry someone important; therefore he objects to John, while you, my girl...

ELLEN: (*with a fierce cry, Ellen grabs vase to throw*) You devil! (*Vase breaks in her hand.*)

KRETON: You see? That proves my point perfectly. (*gently*) Poor savage, I cannot help what you are. (*briskly*) Anyway, you will soon be distracted from your personal problems. Tonight is the night. If you're a good girl, I'll let you watch the bombing.

*Dissolve to study: Eleven forty-five. Powers and the Aide gloomily await the war.*

AIDE: General, isn't there anything we can do?

POWERS: It's out of our hands.

*Kreton, dressed as a Hussar with shako, enters.*

KRETON: Everything on schedule?

POWERS: Yes, sir. Planes left for their targets at twenty-two hundred.

KRETON: Good...good. I myself shall take off shortly after midnight to observe the attack first-hand.

POWERS: Yes, sir.

*Kreton goes into the living room where the family is gloomily assembled.*

KRETON: (*enters from study*) And now the magic hour approaches! I hope you're all as thrilled as I am.

SPELDING: You still won't tell us who's attacking whom?

KRETON: You'll know in exactly...fourteen minutes.

ELLEN: (*bitterly*) Are we going to be killed too?

KRETON: Certainly not! You're quite safe, at least in the early stages of the war.

ELLEN: Thank you.

MRS. SPELDING: I suppose this will mean rationing again.

SPELDING: Will...will we see anything from here?

KRETON: No, but there should be a good picture on the monitor in the study. Powers is tuning in right now.

JOHN: (*at window*) Hey look, up there! Coming this way!

*Ellen joins him.*

ELLEN: What is it?

JOHN: Why...it's *another* one! And it's going to land.

KRETON: (*surprised*) I'm sure you're mistaken. No one would dream of coming here.

*He has gone to the window, too.*

ELLEN: It's landing!

SPELDING: Is it a friend of yours, Mr. Kreton?

KRETON: (*slowly*) No, no, not a friend...

*Kreton retreats to the study; he inadvertently drops a lace handkerchief beside the sofa.*

JOHN: Here he comes.

ELLEN: (*suddenly bitter*) Now we have two of them.

MRS. SPELDING: My poor roses.

*The new Visitor enters in a gleam of light from his ship. He is wearing a most futuristic costume. Without a word, he walks past the awed family into the study. Kreton is cowering behind the globe. Powers and Aide stare, bewildered, as the Visitor gestures sternly and Kreton reluctantly removes shako and sword. They communicate by odd sounds.*

VISITOR: (*to Powers*) Please leave us alone.

*Cut to living room as Powers and the Aide enter from the study.*

POWERS: (*to Ellen*) Who on earth was that?

ELLEN: It's another one, another visitor.

POWERS: Now we're done for.

ELLEN: I'm going in there.

MRS. SPELDING: Ellen, don't you dare!

ELLEN: I'm going to talk to them. (*Starts to door.*)

JOHN: I'm coming, too.

ELLEN: (*grimly*) No, alone. I know what I want to say.

*Cut to interior of the study, to Kreton and the other Visitor as Ellen enters.*

ELLEN: I want you both to listen to me....

VISITOR: You don't need to speak. I know what you will say.

ELLEN: That you have no right here? That you mustn't...

VISITOR: I agree. Kreton has no right here. He is well aware that it is forbidden to interfere with the past.

ELLEN: The past?

VISITOR: (*nods*) You are the past, the dark ages: we are from the future. In fact, we are *your* descendants on another planet. We visit you from time to time but we never interfere because it would change *us* if we did. Fortunately, I have arrived in time.

ELLEN: There won't be a war?

VISITOR: There will be no war. And there will be no memory of any of this. When we leave here you will forget Kreton and me. Time will turn back to the moment before his arrival.

ELLEN: Why did you want to hurt us?

KRETON: (*heartbroken*) Oh, but I didn't! I only wanted to have...well, to have a little fun, to indulge my hobby...against the rules of course.

VISITOR: (*to Ellen*) Kreton is a rarity among us. Mentally and morally he is retarded. He is a child and he regards your period as his toy.

KRETON: A child, now really!

VISITOR: He escaped from his nursery and came back in time to you....

KRETON: And *every*thing went wrong, everything! I wanted to visit 1860...that's my *real* period but then something happened to the car and I ended up here, not that I don't find you nearly as interesting but...

VISITOR: We must go, Kreton.

KRETON: (*to Ellen*) You did like me just a bit, didn't you?

ELLEN: Yes, yes I did, until you let your hobby get out of hand. (*to Visitor*) What is the future like?

VISITOR: Very serene, very different...

KRETON: Don't believe him: it is dull, dull, dull beyond belief! One simply floats through eternity: no wars, no excitement...

VISITOR: It is forbidden to discuss these matters.

KRETON: I can't see what difference it makes since she's going to forget all about us anyway.

ELLEN: Oh, how I'd love to see the future....

VISITOR: It is against ...

KRETON: Against the rules: how tiresome you are. (*to Ellen*) But, alas, you can never pay us a call because you aren't born yet! I mean where we are you are not. Oh, Ellen, dear, think kindly of me, until you forget.

ELLEN: I will.

VISITOR: Come. Time has begun to turn back. Time is bending.

*He starts to door. Kreton turns conspiratorially to Ellen.*

KRETON: Don't be sad, my girl. I shall be back one bright day, but a bright day in 1860. I dote on the Civil War, so exciting ...

VISITOR: Kreton!

KRETON: Only next time I think it'll be more fun if the *South* wins!

*He hurries after the Visitor.*

*Cut to clock as the hands spin backwards. Dissolve to the living room, exactly the same as the first scene: Spelding, Mrs. Spelding, Ellen.*

SPELDING: There is nothing wrong with marrying a wealthy man. The horror of it has always eluded me. However, my only wish is that you marry someone hard-working, ambitious, a man who'll make his mark in the world. Not a boy who is content to sit on a farm all his life, growing peanuts....

ELLEN: English walnuts! And he won't just sit there.

SPELDING: Will you stop contradicting me?

ELLEN: But, Daddy, John grows walnuts....

*John enters.*

JOHN: Hello, everybody.

MRS. SPELDING: Good evening, John.

ELLEN: What kept you, darling? You missed Daddy's broadcast.

JOHN: I saw it before I left home. Wonderful broadcast, sir.

SPELDING: Thank you, John.

*John crosses to window.*

JOHN: That meteor you were talking about, well, for a while it looked almost like a space ship or something. You can just barely see it now.

*Ellen joins him at window. They watch, arms about one another.*

SPELDING: Space ship! Nonsense! Remarkable what some people will believe, *want* to believe. Besides, as I said in the broadcast: if there's any travelling to be done in space we'll do it first.

*He notices Kreton's handkerchief on sofa and picks it up. They all look at it, puzzled, as we cut to stock shot of the starry night against which two space ships vanish in the distance, one serene in its course, the other erratic, as we fade out.*

# Daphne du Maurier

# The Birds

They kept coming...
noiseless, silent, save for the beating wings.
The terrible, fluttering wings.

130

On December the third the wind changed overnight and it was winter. Until then the autumn had been mellow, soft. The earth was rich where the plough had turned it.

Nat Hocken, because of a wartime disability, had a pension and did not work full-time at the farm. He worked three days a week, and they gave him the lighter jobs. Although he was married, with three children, his was a solitary disposition; he liked best to work alone.

It pleased him when he was given a bank to build up, or a gate to mend, at the far end of the peninsula, where the sea surrounded the farmland on either side. Then, at mid-day, he would pause and eat the meat pie his wife had baked for him and, sitting on the cliff's edge, watch the birds.

In autumn great flocks of them came to the peninsula, restless, uneasy, spending themselves in motion; now wheeling, circling in the sky; now settling to feed on the rich, new-turned soil, but even when they fed, it was as though they did so without hunger, without desire.

Restlessness drove them to the skies again. Crying, whistling, calling, they skimmed the placid sea and left the shore.

Make haste, make speed, hurry and begone; yet where, and to what purpose? The restless urge of autumn, unsatisfying, sad, had put a spell upon them, and they must spill themselves of motion before winter came.

Perhaps, thought Nat, a message comes to the birds in autumn, like a warning. Winter is coming. Many of them will perish. And like people who, apprehensive of death before their time, drive themselves to work or folly, the birds do likewise; tomorrow we shall die.

Reprinted by permission of Mollie Waters, England.

The birds had been more restless than ever this fall of the year. Their agitation more remarked because the days were still.

As Mr. Trigg's tractor traced its path up and down the western hills, and Nat, hedging, saw it dip and turn, the whole machine and the man upon it were momentarily lost in the great cloud of wheeling, crying birds.

Nat remarked upon them to Mr. Trigg when the work was finished for the day.

"Yes," said the farmer, "there are more birds about than usual. I have a notion the weather will change. It will be a hard winter. That's why the birds are restless."

The farmer was right. That night the weather turned.

The bedroom in the cottage faced east. Nat woke just after two and heard the east wind, cold and dry. It sounded hollow in the chimney, and a loose slate rattled on the roof. Nat listened, and he could hear the sea roaring in the bay. He drew the blanket round him, leaned closer to the back of his wife, deep in sleep. Then he heard the tapping on the windowpane. It continued until, irritated by the sound, Nat got out of bed and went to the window. He opened it; and as he did so something brushed his hand, jabbing at his knuckles, grazing the skin. Then he saw the flutter of wings and the thing was gone again, over the roof, behind the cottage.

It was a bird. What kind of bird he could not tell. The wind must have driven it to shelter on the sill.

He shut the window and went back to bed but, feeling his knuckles wet, put his mouth to the scratch. The bird had drawn blood.

Frightened, he supposed, bewildered, seeking shelter, the bird had stabbed at him in the darkness. Once more he settled himself to sleep.

Presently the tapping came again – this time more forceful, more insistent. And now his wife woke at the sound and, turning in the bed, said to him, "See to the window, Nat; it's rattling."

"I've already been to it," he told her. "There's some bird there, trying to get in."

"Send it away," she said. "I can't sleep with that noise."

He went to the window for the second time, and now when he opened it there was not one bird on the sill but half a dozen; they flew straight into his face.

He shouted, striking out at them with his arms, scattering them; like the first one, they flew over the roof and disappeared.

He had let the window fall and latched it.

Suddenly a frightened cry came from the room across the passage where the children slept.

"It's Jill," said his wife, roused at the sound.

There came a second cry, this time from both children. Stumbling into their room, Nat felt the beating of wings about him in the darkness. The window was wide open. Through it came the birds, hitting first the ceiling and the walls, then swerving in mid-flight and turning to the children in their beds.

"It's all right. I'm here," shouted Nat, and the children flung themselves, screaming, upon him, while in the darkness the birds rose, and dived, and came for him again.

"What is it, Nat? What's happened?" his wife called. Swiftly he pushed the children through the door to the passage and shut it upon them, so that he was alone in their bedroom with the birds.

He seized a blanket from the nearest bed and, using it as a weapon, flung it right and left about him.

He felt the thud of bodies, heard the fluttering of wings; but the birds were not yet defeated, for again and again they returned to the assault, jabbing his hands, his head, their little stabbing beaks sharp as pointed forks.

The blanket became a weapon of defence. He wound it about his head, and then, in greater darkness, beat at the birds with his bare hands. He dared not stumble to the door and open it lest the birds follow him.

How long he fought with them in the darkness he could not tell; but at last the beating of the wings about him lessened, withdrew; and through the dense blanket he was aware of light.

He waited, listened; there was no sound except the fretful crying of one of the children from the bedroom beyond.

He took the blanket from his head and stared about him. The cold grey morning light exposed the room.

Dawn and the open window had called the living birds; the dead lay on the floor.

Sickened, Nat went to the window and stared out across his patch of garden to the fields.

It was bitter cold, and the ground had all the hard, black look of the frost that the east wind brings. The sea, fiercer now with turning tide, whitecapped and steep, broke harshly in the bay. Of the birds there was no sign.

Nat shut the window and door of the small bedroom and went back across the passage to his own room.

His wife sat up in bed, one child asleep beside her; the smaller one in her arms, his face bandaged.

"He's sleeping now," she whispered. "Something must have cut him; there was blood at the corners of his eyes. Jill said it was the birds. She said she woke up and the birds were in the room."

His wife looked up at Nat, searching his face for confirmation. She looked terrified, bewildered. He did not want her to know that he also was shaken, dazed almost, by the events of the past few hours.

"There are birds in there," he said. "Dead birds, nearly fifty of them."

He sat down on the bed beside his wife.

"It's the hard weather," he said. "It must be that; it's the hard weather. They aren't the birds, maybe, from around here. They've been driven down from up-country."

"But Nat," whispered his wife, "it's only this night that the weather turned. They can't be hungry yet. There's food for them out there in the fields."

"It's the weather," repeated Nat. "I tell you, it's the weather."

His face, too, was drawn and tired, like hers. They stared at one another for a while without speaking.

Nat went to the window and looked out. The sky was hard and leaden, and the brown hills that had gleamed in the sun the day before looked dark and bare. Black winter had descended in a single night.

The children were awake now. Jill was chattering, and young Johnny was crying once again. Nat heard his wife's voice, soothing, comforting them as he went downstairs.

Presently they came down. He had breakfast ready for them.

"Did you drive away the birds?" asked Jill.

"Yes, they've all gone now," Nat said. "It was the east wind brought them in."

"I hope they won't come again," said Jill.

"I'll walk with you to the bus," Nat said to her.

Jill seemed to have forgotten her experience of the night before. She danced ahead of him, chasing the leaves, her face rosy under her pixy hood.

All the while Nat searched the hedgerows for the birds, glanced over them to the fields beyond, looked to the small wood above the farm where the rooks and jackdaws gathered; he saw none. Soon the bus came ambling up the hill.

Nat saw Jill on to the bus, then turned and walked back toward the farm. It was not his day for work, but he wanted to satisfy himself that all was well. He went to the back door of the farmhouse; he heard Mrs. Trigg singing, the wireless making a background for her song.

"Are you there, missus?" Nat called.

She came to the door, beaming, broad, a good-tempered woman.

"Hullo, Mr. Hocken," she said. "Can you tell me where this cold is coming from? Is it Russia? I've never seen such a change. And it's going on, the wireless says. Something to do with the Arctic Circle."

"We didn't turn on the wireless this morning," said Nat. "Fact is, we had trouble in the night."

"Kiddies poorly?"

"No." He hardly knew how to explain. Now, in daylight, the battle of the birds would sound absurd.

He tried to tell Mrs. Trigg what had happened, but he could see from her eyes that she thought his story was the result of nightmare following a heavy meal.

"Sure they were real birds?" she said, smiling.

"Mrs. Triggs," he said, "there are fifty dead birds – robins, wrens, went for me; they tried to go for young Johnny's eyes."

Mrs. Trigg stared at him doubtfully. "Well, now," she answered. "I suppose the weather brought them; once in the bedroom they wouldn't know where they were. Foreign birds maybe, from that Arctic Circle."

"No," said Nat. "They were birds you see about here every day."

"Funny thing," said Mrs. Trigg. "No explaining, it really. You ought to write up and ask the *Guardian*. They'd have some answer for it. Well, I must be getting on."

Nat walked back along the lane to his cottage. He found his wife in the kitchen with young Johnny.

"See anyone?" she asked.

"Mrs. Trigg," he answered. "I don't think she believed me. Anyway, nothing wrong up there."

"You might take the birds away," she said. "I daren't go into the room to make the beds until you do. I'm scared."

"Nothing to scare you now," said Nat. "They're dead, aren't they?"

He went up with a sack and dropped the stiff bodies into it, one by one. Yes, there were fifty of them all told. Just the ordinary, common birds of the hedgerow; nothing as large even as a thrush. It must have been fright that made them act the way they did.

He took the sack out into the garden and was faced with a fresh problem. The ground was frozen solid, yet no snow had fallen; nothing had happened in the past hours but the coming of the east wind. It was unnatural, queer. He could see the whitecapped seas breaking in the bay. He decided to take the birds to the shore and bury them.

When he reached the beach below the headland, he could scarcely stand, the force of the east wind was so strong. It was low tide; he crunched his way over the shingle to the softer sand and then, his back to the wind, opened up his sack.

He ground a pit in the sand with his heel, meaning to drop the birds into it; but as he did so, the force of the wind lifted them as though in flight again, and they were blown away from him along the beach, tossed like feathers, spread and scattered.

The tide will take them when it turns, he said to himself.

He looked out to sea and watched the crested breakers, combing green. They rose stiffly, curled, and broke again; and because it was ebb tide, the roar was distant, more remote, lacking the sound and thunder of the flood.

Then he saw them. The gulls. Out there, riding the seas.

What he had thought at first were the whitecaps of the waves were gulls. Hundreds, thousands, tens of thousands.

They rose and fell in the troughs of the seas, heads to the wind, like a mighty fleet at anchor, waiting on the tide.

Nat turned; leaving the beach, he climbed the steep path home.

Someone should know of this. Someone should be told. Something was happening, because of the east wind and the weather, that he did not understand.

As he drew near the cottage, his wife came to meet him at the door. She called to him, excited. "Nat," she said, "it's on the wireless. They've just read out a special news bulletin. It's not only here, it's everywhere. In London, all over the country. Something has happened to the birds. Come and listen; they're repeating it."

Together they went into the kitchen to listen to the announcement.

"Statement from the Home Office, at eleven this morning. Reports from all over the country are coming in hourly about the vast quantity of birds flocking above towns, villages, and outlying districts, causing obstruction and damage and even attacking individuals. It is thought that the Arctic air stream at present covering the British Isles is causing birds to migrate south in immense numbers, and that intense hunger may drive these birds to attack human beings. Householders are warned to see to their windows, doors, and chimneys, and to take reasonable precautions for the safety of their children. A further statement will be issued later."

A kind of excitement seized Nat. He looked at his wife in triumph. "There you are," he said. "I've been telling myself all morning there's something wrong. And just now, down on the beach, I looked out to sea and there were gulls, thousands of them, riding on the sea, waiting."

"What are they waiting for, Nat?" she asked.

He stared at her. "I don't know," he said slowly.

He went over to the drawer where he kept his hammer and other tools.

"What are you going to do, Nat?"

"See to the windows and the chimneys, like they tell you to."

"You think they would break in with the windows shut? Those wrens and robins and such? Why, how could they?"

He did not answer. He was not thinking of the robins and the wrens. He was thinking of the gulls.

He went upstairs and worked there the rest of the morning, boarding the windows of the bedrooms, filling up the chimney bases.

"Dinner's ready." His wife called him from the kitchen.

"All right. Coming down."

When dinner was over and his wife was washing up, Nat switched on the one o'clock news. The same announcement was repeated, but the news bulletin enlarged upon it. "The flocks of birds have caused dislocation in all areas," said the announcer, "and in London the mass was so dense at ten o'clock this morning that it seemed like a vast black cloud. The birds settled on rooftops, on window ledges, and on chimneys. The species included blackbird, thrush, the common house sparrow, and as might be expected in the metropolis, a vast quantity of pigeons, starlings, and that frequenter of the London river, the black-headed gull. The sight was so unusual that traffic came to a standstill in many thoroughfares, work was abandoned in shops and offices, and the streets and pavements were crowded with people standing about to watch the birds."

The announcer's voice was smooth and suave; Nat had the impression that he treated the whole business as he would an elaborate joke. There would be others like him, hundreds of them, who did not know what it was to struggle in darkness with a flock of birds.

Nat switched off the wireless. He got up and started work on the kitchen windows. His wife watched him, young Johnny at her heels.

"What they ought to do," she said, "is to call the Army out and shoot the birds."

"Let them try," said Nat. "How'd they set about it?"

"I don't know. But something should be done. They ought to do something."

Nat thought to himself that "they" were no doubt considering the problem at that very moment, but whatever "they" decided to do in London and the big cities would not help them here, nearly three hundred miles away.

"How are we off for food?" he asked.

"It's shopping day tomorrow, you know that. I don't keep uncooked food about. Butcher doesn't call till the day after. But I can bring back something when I go in tomorrow."

Nat did not want to scare her. He looked in the larder for himself and in the cupboard where she kept her tins.

They could hold out for a couple of days.

He went on hammering the boards across the kitchen windows. Candles. They were low on candles. That must be another thing she meant to buy tomorrow. Well, they must go early to bed tonight. That was, if...

He got up and went out the back door and stood in the garden, looking down toward the sea.

There had been no sun all day, and now at barely three o'clock, a kind of darkness had already come; the sky was sullen, heavy, colorless like salt. He could hear the vicious sea drumming on the rocks.

He walked down the path halfway to the beach. And then he stopped. He could see the tide had turned. The gulls had risen. They were circling, hundreds of them, thousands of them, lifting their wings against the wind.

It was the gulls that made the darkening of the sky.

And they were silent. They just went on soaring and circling, rising, falling, trying their strength against the wind. Nat turned. He ran up the path back to the cottage.

"I'm going for Jill," he said to his wife.

"What's the matter?" she asked. "You've gone quite white."

"Keep Johnny inside," he said. "Keep the door shut. Light up now and draw the curtains."

"It's only gone three," she said.

"Never mind. Do what I tell you."

He looked inside the tool shed and took the hoe.

He started walking up the lane to the bus stop. Now and again he glanced over his shoulder, and he could see the gulls had risen higher now, their circles were broader, they were spreading out in huge formation across the sky.

He hurried on. Although he knew the bus would not come before four o'clock, he had to hurry.

He waited at the top of the hill. There was half an hour still to go.

The east wind came whipping across the fields from the higher ground. In the distance he could see the clay hills, white and clean against the heavy pallor of the sky.

Something black rose from behind them, like a smudge at first, then widening, becoming deeper. The smudge became a cloud; and the cloud divided again into five other clouds, spreading north, east, south, and west; and then they were not clouds at all but birds.

He watched them travel across the sky, within two or three hundred feet of him. He knew, from their speed, that they were bound inland; they had no business with the people here on the peninsula. They were

rooks, crows, jackdaws, magpies, jays, all birds that usually preyed upon the small species, but bound this afternoon on some other mission.

He went to the telephone call box, stepped inside, lifted the receiver. The exchange would pass the message on. "I'm speaking from the highway," he said, "by the bus stop. I want to report large formations of birds travelling up-country. The gulls are also forming in the bay."

"All right," answered the voice, laconic, weary.

"You'll be sure and pass this message on to the proper quarter?"

"Yes. Yes." Impatient now, fed up. The buzzing note resumed. She's another, thought Nat. She doesn't care.

The bus came lumbering up the hill. Jill climbed out.

"What's the hoe for, Dad?"

"I just brought it along," he said. "Come on now, let's get home. It's cold; no hanging about. See how fast you can run."

He could see the gulls now, still silent, circling the fields, coming in toward the land.

"Look, Dad; look over there. Look at all the gulls."

"Yes. Hurry now."

"Where are they flying? Where are they going?"

"Up-country, I dare say. Where it's warmer."

He seized her hand and dragged her after him along the lane.

"Don't go so fast. I can't keep up."

The gulls were copying the rooks and crows. They were spreading out, in formation, across the sky. They headed, in bands of thousands, to the four compass points.

"Dad, what is it? What are the gulls doing?"

They were not intent upon their flight, as the crows, as the jackdaws, had been. They

136 | still circled overhead. Nor did they fly so high. It was as though they waited upon some signal; as though some decision had yet to be given.

"I wish the gulls would go away." Jill was crying. "I don't like them. They're coming closer to the lane."

He started running, swinging Jill after him. As they went past the farm turning, he saw the farmer backing his car into the garage. Nat called to him.

"Can you give us a lift?" he said.

Mr. Trigg turned in the driver's seat and stared at them. Then a smile came to his cheerful, rubicund face. "It looks as though we're in for some fun," he said. "Have you seen the gulls? Jim and I are going to take a crack at them. Everyone's gone bird crazy, talking of nothing else. I hear you were troubled in the night. Want a gun?"

Nat shook his head.

The small car was packed, but there was room for Jill on the back seat.

"I don't want a gun," said Nat, "but I'd be obliged if you'd run Jill home. She's scared of the birds."

"O.K.," said the farmer. "I'll take her home. Why don't you stop behind and join in the shooting match? We'll make the feathers fly."

Jill climbed in and, turning the car, the driver sped up the lane. Nat followed after. Trigg must be crazy. What use was a gun against a sky of birds?

They were coming in now toward the farm, circling lower in the sky. The farm, then, was their target. Nat increased his pace toward his own cottage. He saw the farmer's car turn and come back along the lane. It drew up beside him with a jerk.

"The kid has run inside," said the farmer. "Your wife was watching for her. Well, what do you make of it? They're saying in town the Russians have done it. The Russians have poisoned the birds."

"How could they do that?" asked Nat.

"Don't ask me. You know how stories get around."

"Have you boarded your windows?" asked Nat.

"No. Lot of nonsense. I've had more to do today than to go round boarding up my windows."

"I'd board them now if I were you."

"Garn. You're windy. Like to come to our place to sleep?"

"No, thanks all the same."

"All right. See you in the morning. Give you a gull breakfast."

The farmer grinned and turned his car to the farm entrance. Nat hurried on. Past the little wood, past the old barn, and then across the stile to the remaining field. As he jumped the stile, he heard the whir of wings. A black-backed gull dived down at him from the sky. It missed, swerved in flight, and rose to dive again. In a moment it was joined by others – six, seven, a dozen.

Nat dropped his hoe. The hoe was useless. Covering his head with his arms, he ran toward the cottage.

They kept coming at him from the air – noiseless, silent, save for the beating wings. The terrible, fluttering wings. He could feel the blood on his hands, his wrists, upon his neck. If only he could keep them from his eyes. Nothing else mattered.

With each dive, with each attack, they became bolder. And they had no thought for themselves. When they dived low and missed, they crashed, bruised and broken on the ground.

As Nat ran he stumbled, kicking their spent bodies in front of him.

He found the door and hammered upon it with bleeding hands. "Let me in," he shouted. "It's Nat. Let me in."

Then he saw the gannet, poised for the dive, above him in the sky.

The gulls circled, retired, soared, one with another, against the wind.

Only the gannet remained. One single gannet, above him in the sky. Its wings folded suddenly to its body. It dropped like a stone.

Nat screamed; and the door opened.

He stumbled across the threshold, and his wife threw her weight against the door.

They heard the thud of the gannet as it fell.

His wife dressed his wounds. They were not deep. The backs of his hands had suffered most, and his wrists. Had he not worn a cap, the birds would have reached his head. As for the gannet – the gannet could have split his skull.

The children were crying, of course. They had seen the blood on their father's hands.

"It's all right now," he told them. "I'm not hurt."

His wife was ashen. "I saw them overhead," she whispered. "They began collecting, just as Jill ran in with Mr. Trigg. I shut the door fast, and it jammed. That's why I couldn't open it at once when you came."

"Thank God the birds waited for me," he said. "Jill would have fallen at once. They're flying inland, thousands of them. Rooks, crows, all the bigger birds. I saw them from the bus stop. They're making for the towns."

"But what can they do, Nat?"

"They'll attack. Go for everyone out in the streets. Then they'll try the windows, the chimneys."

"Why don't the authorities do something? Why don't they get the Army, get machine guns?"

"There's been no time. Nobody's prepared. We'll hear what they have to say on the six o'clock news."

"I can hear the birds," Jill said. "Listen, Dad."

Nat listened. Muffled sounds came from the windows, from the door. Wings brushing the surface, sliding, scraping, seeking a way of entry. The sound of many bodies pressed together, shuffling on the sills. Now and again came a thud, a crash, as some bird dived and fell.

Some of them will kill themselves that way, he thought, but not enough. Never enough.

"All right," he said aloud. "I've got boards over the windows, Jill. The birds can't get in."

He went and examined all the windows. He found wedges – pieces of old tin, strips of wood and metal – and fastened them at the sides of the windows to reinforce the boards.

His hammerings helped to deafen the sound of the birds, the shuffling, the tapping, and – more ominous – the splinter of breaking glass.

"Turn on the wireless," he said.

He went upstairs to the bedrooms and reinforced the windows there. Now he could hear the birds on the roof – the scraping of claws, a sliding, jostling sound.

He decided the whole family must sleep in the kitchen and keep up the fire. He was afraid of the bedroom chimneys. The boards he had placed at their bases might give way. In the kitchen they would be safe because of the fire.

He would have to make a joke of it. Pretend to the children they were playing camp. If the worst happened and the birds forced an entry by way of the bedroom chimneys, it would be hours, days perhaps, before they could break down the doors. The birds would be imprisoned in the bedrooms. They could do no harm there. Crowded together, they would stifle and die. He began to bring the mattresses downstairs.

At sight of them, his wife's eyes widened in apprehension.

"All right," he said cheerfully. 'We'll all sleep together in the kitchen tonight. More

138

cosy, here by the fire. Then we won't be worried by those silly old birds tapping at the windows."

He made the children help him rearrange the furniture, and he took the precaution of moving the dresser against the windows.

We're safe enough now, he thought. We're snug and tight. We can hold out. It's just the food that worries me. Food and coal for the fire. We've enough for two or three days, not more. By that time...

No use thinking ahead as far as that. And they'd be given directions on the wireless.

And now, in the midst of many problems, he realized that only dance music was coming over the air. He knew the reason. The usual programs had been abandoned; this only happened at exceptional times.

At six o'clock the records ceased. The time signal was given. There was a pause, and then the announcer spoke. His voice was solemn, grave. Quite different from midday.

"This is London," he said. "A national emergency was proclaimed at four o'clock this afternoon. Measures are being taken to safeguard the lives and property of the population, but it must be understood that these are not easy to effect immediately, owing to the unforeseen and unparalleled nature of the present crisis. Every householder must take precautions about his own building. Where several people live together, as in flats and hotels, they must unite to do the utmost that they can to prevent entry. It is absolutely imperative that every individual stay indoors tonight.

"The birds, in vast numbers, are attacking anyone on sight, and have already begun an assault upon buildings; but these, with due care, should be impenetrable.

"The population is asked to remain calm.

"Owing to the exceptional nature of the emergency, there will be no further transmission from any broadcasting station until 7:00 A.M. tomorrow."

They played "God Save the Queen." Nothing more happened.

Nat switched off the set. He looked at his wife. She stared back at him.

"We'll have supper early," suggested Nat. "Something for a treat — toasted cheese, eh? Something we all like."

He winked and nodded at his wife. He wanted the look of dread, of apprehension, to leave her face.

He helped with the supper, whistling, singing, making as much clatter as he could. It seemed to him that the shuffling and the tapping were not so intense as they had been at first, and presently he went up to the bedrooms and listened. He no longer heard the jostling for place upon the roof.

They've got reasoning powers, he thought. They know it's hard to break in here. They'll try elsewhere.

Supper passed without incident. Then, when they were clearing away, they heard a new sound, a familiar droning.

His wife looked up at him, her face alight.

"It's planes," she said. "They're sending out planes after the birds. That will get them. Isn't that gunfire? Can't you hear guns?"

It might be gunfire, out at sea. Nat could not tell. Big naval guns might have some effect upon the gulls out at sea, but the gulls were inland now. The guns couldn't shell the shore because of the population.

"It's good, isn't it," said his wife, "to hear the planes?"

Catching her enthusiasm, Jill jumped up and down with Johnny. "The planes will get the birds."

Just then they heard a crash about two miles distant. Followed by a second, then a third. The droning became more distant, passed away out to sea.

"What was that?" asked his wife.

"I don't know," answered Nat. He did not want to tell her that the sound they had heard was the crashing of aircraft.

It was, he had no doubt, a gamble on the part of the authorities to send out reconnaissance forces, but they might have known the gamble was suicidal. What could aircraft do against birds that flung themselves to death against propeller and fuselage but hurtle to the ground themselves?

"Where have the planes gone, Dad?" asked Jill.

"Back to base," he said. "Come on now, time to tuck down for bed."

There was no further drone of aircraft, and the naval guns had ceased. Waste of life and effort, Nat said to himself. We can't destroy enough of them that way. Cost too heavy. There's always gas. Maybe they'll try spraying with gas, mustard gas. We'll be warned first, of course, if they do. There's one thing, the best brains of the country will be on it tonight.

Upstairs in the bedrooms all was quiet. No more scraping and stabbing at the windows. A lull in battle. The wind hadn't dropped, though. Nat could still hear it roaring in the chimneys. And the sea breaking down on the shore.

Then he remembered the tide. The tide would be on the turn. Maybe the lull in battle was because of the tide. There was some law the birds obeyed, and it had to do with the east wind and the tide.

He glanced at his watch. Nearly eight o'clock. It must have gone high water an hour ago. That explained the lull. The birds attacked with the flood tide.

He reckoned the time limit in his head. They had six hours to go without attack. When the tide turned again, around 1:20 in the morning, the birds would come back.

He called softly to his wife and whispered to her that he would go out and see how they were faring at the farm, see if the telephone was still working there so that they might get news from the exchange.

"You're not to go," she said at once, "and leave me alone with the children. I can't stand it."

"All right," he said, "all right. I'll wait till morning. And we can get the wireless bulletin then, too, at seven. But when the tide ebbs again, I'll try for the farm; they may let us have bread and potatoes."

His mind was busy again, planning against emergency. They would not have milked, of course, this evening. The cows would be standing by the gate, waiting; the household would be inside, battened behind boards as they were here at the cottage.

That is, if they had had time to take precautions.

Softly, stealthily, he opened the back door and looked outside.

It was pitch-dark. The wind was blowing harder than ever, coming in steady gusts, icy, from the sea.

He kicked at the step. It was heaped with birds. These were the suicides, the divers, the ones with broken necks. Wherever he looked, he saw dead birds. The living had flown seaward with the turn of the tide. The gulls would be riding the seas now, as they had done in the forenoon.

In the far distance on the hill, something was burning. One of the aircraft that had crashed; the fire, fanned by the wind, had set light to a stack.

He looked at the bodies of the birds. He had a notion that if he stacked them, one upon the other, on the window sills, they would be added protection against the next attack.

Not much, perhaps, but something. The bodies would have to be clawed at, pecked, and dragged aside before the living birds gained purchase on the sills and attacked the panes.

He set to work in the darkness. It was queer. He hated touching the dead birds, but he went on with his work. He noticed grimly that every windowpane was shattered. Only the boards had kept the birds from breaking in.

He stuffed the cracked panes with the bleeding bodies of the birds and felt his stomach turn. When he had finished, he went back into the cottage and barricaded the kitchen door, making it doubly secure.

His wife had made him cocoa; he drank it thirstily. He was very tired. "All right," he said, smiling, "don't worry. We'll get through."

He lay down on his mattress and closed his eyes.

He dreamed uneasily because, through his dreams, ran the dread of something forgotten. Some piece of work that he should have done. It was connected, in some way, with the burning aircraft.

It was his wife, shaking his shoulder, who awoke him finally.

"They've begun," she sobbed. "They've started this last hour. I can't listen to it any longer alone. There's something smells bad too, something burning."

Then he remembered. He had forgotten to make up the fire.

The fire was smouldering, nearly out. He got up swiftly and lighted the lamp.

The hammering had started at the windows and the door, but it was not that he minded now. It was the smell of singed feathers.

The smell filled the kitchen. He knew what it was at once. The birds were coming down the chimney, squeezing their way down to the kitchen range.

He got sticks and paper and put them on the embers, then reached for the can of kerosene.

"Stand back," he shouted to his wife. He threw some of the kerosene on to the fire.

The flame roared up the pipe, and down into the fire fell the scorched, blackened bodies of the birds.

The children waked, crying. "What is it?" asked Jill. "What's happened?"

Nat had no time to answer her. He was raking the bodies from the chimney, clawing them out on to the floor.

The flames would drive away the living birds from the chimney top. The lower joint was the difficulty though. It was choked with the smouldering, helpless bodies of the birds caught by fire.

He scarcely heeded the attack on the windows and the door. Let them beat their wings, break their backs, lose their lives, in the desperate attempt to force an entry into his home. They would not break in.

"Stop crying," he called to the children. "There's nothing to be afraid of. Stop crying."

He went on raking out the burning, smouldering bodies as they fell into the fire.

This'll fetch them, he said to himself. The draft and the flames together. We're all right as long as the chimney doesn't catch.

Amid the tearing at the window boards came the sudden homely striking of the kitchen clock. Three o'clock.

A little more than four hours to go. He could not be sure of the exact time of high water. He reckoned the tide would not turn much before half-past seven.

He waited by the range. The flames were dying. But no more blackened bodies fell from the chimney. He thrust his poker up as far as it could go and found nothing.

The danger of the chimney's being choked up was over. It could not happen again, not if the fire was kept burning day and night.

I'll have to get more fuel from the farm tomorrow, he thought. I can do all that with the ebb tide. It can be worked; we can fetch what we need when the tide's turned. We've just got to adapt ourselves, that's all.

They drank tea and cocoa, ate slices of bread. Only half a loaf left, Nat noticed. Never mind, though; they'd get by.

If they could hang on like this until seven, when the first news bulletin came through, they would not have done too badly.

"Give us a smoke," he said to his wife. "It will clear away the smell of the scorched feathers."

"There's only two left in the packet," she said. "I was going to buy you some."

"I'll have one," he said.

He sat with one arm around his wife and one around Jill, with Johnny on his lap, the blankets heaped about them on the mattress.

"You can't help admiring the beggars," he said. "They've got persistency. You'd think they'd tire of the game, but not a bit of it."

Admiration was hard to sustain. The tapping went on and on; and a new, rasping note struck Nat's ear, as though a sharper beak than any hitherto had come to take over from its fellows.

He tried to remember the names of birds; he tried to think which species would go for this particular job.

It was not the tap of the woodpecker. That would be light and frequent. This was more serious; if it continued long, the wood would splinter as the glass had done.

Then he remembered the hawks. Could the hawks have taken over from the gulls? Were there buzzards now upon the sills, using talons as well as beaks? Hawks, buzzards, kestrels, falcons; he had forgotten the birds of prey. He had forgotten the gripping power of the birds of prey. Three hours to go; and while they waited, the sound of the splintering wood, the talons tearing at the wood.

Nat looked about him, seeing what furniture he could destroy to fortify the door.

The windows were safe because of the dresser. He was not certain of the door. He went upstairs; but when he reached the landing, he paused and listened.

There was a soft patter on the floor of the children's bedroom. The birds had broken through.

The other bedroom was still clear. He brought out the furniture to pile at the head of the stairs should the door of the children's bedroom go.

"Come down, Nat. What are you doing?" called his wife.

"I won't be long," he shouted. "I'm just making everything shipshape up here."

He did not want her to come. He did not want her to hear the pattering in the children's bedroom, the brushing of those wings against the door.

After he suggested breakfast, he found himself watching the clock, gazing at the hands that went so slowly around the dial. If his theory was not correct, if the attack did not cease with the turn of the tide, he knew they were beaten. They could not continue through the long day without air, without rest, without fuel.

A crackling in his ears drove away the sudden desperate desire for sleep.

"What is it? What now?" he said sharply.

"The wireless," said his wife. "I've been watching the clock. It's nearly seven."

The comfortable crackling of the wireless brought new life.

They waited. The kitchen clock struck seven.

The crackling continued. Nothing else. No chimes. No music.

"We heard wrong," he said. "They won't be broadcasting until eight o'clock."

They left the wireless switched on. Nat thought of the battery, wondered how much power was left in the battery. If it failed, they would not hear the instructions.

"It's getting light," whispered his wife. "I

can't see it but I can feel it. And listen! The birds aren't hammering so loud now."

She was right. The rasping, tearing sound grew fainter every moment. So did the shuffling, the jostling for place upon the step, upon the sills. The tide was on the turn.

By eight there was no sound at all. Only the wind. And the crackling of the wireless. The children, lulled at least by the stillness, fell asleep.

At half-past eight Nat switched the wireless off.

"We'll miss the news," said his wife.

"There isn't going to be any news," said Nat. "We've got to depend upon ourselves."

He went to the door and slowly pulled away the barricades. He drew the bolts and, kicking the broken bodies from the step outside the door, breathed the cold air.

He had six working hours before him, and he knew he must reserve his strength to the utmost, not waste it in any way.

Food and light and fuel; these were the most necessary things. If he could get them, they could endure another night.

He stepped into the garden; and as he did so, he saw the living birds. The gulls had gone to ride the sea, as they had done before. They sought sea food and the buoyancy of the tide before they returned to the attack.

Not so the land birds. They waited and watched.

Nat saw them on the hedgerows, on the soil, crowded in the trees, outside in the field – line upon line of birds, still, doing nothing. He went to the end of his small garden.

The birds did not move. They merely watched him.

I've got to get food, Nat said to himself. I've got to go to the farm to get food.

He went back to the cottage. He saw to the windows and the door.

"I'm going to the farm," he said.

His wife clung to him. She had seen the living birds from the open door.

"Take us with you," she begged. "We can't stay here alone. I'd rather die than stay here alone."

"Come on, then," he said. "Bring baskets and Johnny's pram. We can load up the pram."

They dressed against the biting wind. His wife put Johnny in the pram, and Nat took Jill's hand.

"The birds," Jill whimpered. "They're all out there in the fields."

"They won't hurt us," he said. "Not in the light."

They started walking across the field toward the stile, and the birds did not move. They waited, their heads turned to the wind.

When they reached the turning to the farm, Nat stopped and told his wife to wait in the shelter of the hedge with the two children. "But I want to see Mrs. Trigg," she protested. "There are lots of things we can borrow if they went to market yesterday, and..."

"Wait here," Nat interrupted. "I'll be back in a moment."

The cows were lowing, moving restlessly in the yard, and he could see a gap in the fence where the sheep had knocked their way through to roam unchecked in the front garden before the farmhouse.

No smoke came from the chimneys. Nat was filled with misgiving. He did not want his wife or the children to go down to the farm.

He went down alone, pushing his way through the herd of lowing cows, who turned this way and that, distressed, their udders full.

He saw the car standing by the gate. Not put away in the garage.

All the windows of the farmhouse were smashed. There were many dead gulls lying in the yard and around the house.

The living birds perched on the group of trees behind the farm and on the roof of the house. They were quite still. They watched him. Jim's body lay in the yard. What was left of it. His gun was beside him.

The door of the house was shut and bolted, but it was easy to push up a smashed window and climb through.

Trigg's body was close to the telephone. He must have been trying to get through to the exchange when the birds got him. The receiver was off the hook, and the instrument was torn from the wall.

No sign of Mrs. Trigg. She would be upstairs. Was it any use going up? Sickened, Nat knew what he would find there.

Thank God, he said to himself, there were no children.

He forced himself to climb the stairs, but halfway up he turned and descended again. He could see Mrs. Trigg's legs protruding from the open bedroom door. Beside her were the bodies of black-backed gulls and an umbrella, broken. It's no use doing anything, Nat thought. I've only got five hours; less than that. The Triggs would understand. I must load up with what I can find.

He tramped back to his wife and children.

"I'm going to fill up the car with stuff," he said. "We'll take it home and return for a fresh load."

"What about the Triggs?" asked his wife.

"They must have gone to friends," he said.

"Shall I come and help you then?"

"No, there's a mess down there. Cows and sheep all over the place. Wait; I'll get the car. You can sit in the car."

Her eyes watched his all the time he was talking. He believed she understood. Otherwise she certainly would have insisted on helping him find the bread and groceries.

They made three journeys altogether, to and from the farm, before he was satisfied they had everything they needed. It was surprising, once he started thinking, how many things were necessary. Almost the most important of all was planking for the windows. He had to go around searching for timber. He wanted to renew the boards on all the windows at the cottage.

On the final journey he drove the car to the bus stop and got out and went to the telephone box.

He waited a few minutes, jangling the hook. No good, though. The line was dead. He climbed on to a bank and looked over the countryside, but there was no sign of life at all, nothing in the fields but the waiting, watching birds.

Some of them slept; he could see their beaks tucked into their feathers.

You'd think they'd be feeding, he said to himself, not just standing that way.

Then he remembered. They were gorged with food. They had eaten their fill during the night. That was why they did not move this morning.

He lifted his face to the sky. It was colorless, grey. The bare trees looked bent and blackened by the east wind.

The cold did not affect the living birds, waiting out there in the fields.

This is the time they ought to get them, Nat said to himself. They're a sitting target now. They must be doing this all over the country. Why don't our aircraft take off now and spray them with mustard gas? What are all our chaps doing? They must know; they must see for themselves.

He went back to the car and got into the driver's seat.

"Go quickly past the second gate," whispered his wife. "The postman's lying there. I don't want Jill to see."

It was a quarter to one by the time they reached the cottage. Only an hour to go.

"Better have dinner," said Nat. "Hot up something for yourself and the children, some of that soup. I've no time to eat now. I've got to unload all this stuff from the car."

He got everything inside the cottage. It

could be sorted later. Give them all something to do during the long hours ahead.

First he must see to the windows and the door.

He went around the cottage methodically, testing every window and the door. He climbed on to the roof also, and fixed boards across every chimney except the kitchen's.

The cold was so intense he could hardly bear it, but the job had to be done. Now and again he looked up, searching the sky for aircraft. None came. As he worked, he cursed the inefficiency of the authorities.

He paused, his work on the bedroom chimney finished, and looked out to sea. Something was moving out there. Something grey and white among the breakers.

"Good old Navy," he said. "They never let us down. They're coming down channel; they're turning into the bay."

He waited, straining his eyes toward the sea. He was wrong, though. The Navy was not there. It was the gulls rising from the sea. And the massed flocks in the fields, with ruffled feathers, rose in formation from the ground and, wing to wing, soared upward to the sky.

The tide had turned again.

Nat climbed down the ladder and went inside the cottage. The family were at dinner. It was a little after two.

He bolted the door, put up the barricade, and lighted the lamp.

"It's nighttime," said young Johnny.

His wife had switched on the wireless once again. The crackling sound came, but nothing else.

"I've been all round the dial," she said, "foreign stations and all. I can't get anything but the crackling."

"Maybe they have the same trouble," he said. "Maybe it's the same right through Europe."

They ate in silence.

The tapping began at the windows, at the door, the rustling, the jostling, the pushing for position on the sills. The first thud of the suicide gulls upon the step.

When he had finished dinner, Nat planned, he would put the supplies away, stack them neatly, get everything shipshape. The boards were strong against the windows and across the chimneys. The cottage was filled with stores, with fuel, with all they needed for the next few days.

His wife could help him, and the children too. They'd tire themselves out between now and a quarter to nine, when the tide would ebb; then he'd tuck them down on their mattresses, see that they slept good and sound until three in the morning.

He had a new scheme for the windows, which was to fix barbed wire in front of the boards. He had brought a great roll of it from the farm. The nuisance was, he'd have to work at this in the dark, when the lull came between nine and three. Pity he had not thought of it before. Still, as long as the wife and the kids slept – that was the main thing.

The smaller birds were at the windows now. He recognized the light tap-tapping of their beaks and the soft brush of their wings.

The hawks ignored the windows. They concentrated their attack upon the door.

Nat listened to the tearing sound of splintering wood, and wondered how many million years of memory were stored in those little brains, behind the stabbing beaks, the piercing eyes, now giving them this instinct to destroy mankind with all the deft precision of machines.

"I'll smoke that last cigarette," he said to his wife. "Stupid of me. It was the one thing I forgot to bring back from the farm."

He reached for it, switched on the crackling wireless.

He threw the empty packet on to the fire and watched it burn.

# Yves Thériault

# Akua Nuten

"The city is small and
the bomb was a big one.
The reports indicate
there were no survivors."

Kakatso, the Montagnais Indian, felt the gentle flow of the air and noticed that the wind came from the south. Then he touched the moving water in the stream to determine the temperature in the highlands. Since everything pointed to nice June weather, with mild sunshine and light winds, he decided to go to the highest peak of the reserve, as he had been planning to do for the past week. There the Montagnais lands bordered those of the Waswanipis.

There was no urgent reason for the trip. Nothing really pulled him there except the fact that he hadn't been for a long time; and he liked steep mountains and frothy, roaring streams.

Three days before, he had explained his plan to his son, the thin Grand-Louis, who was well known to the white men of the

*Akua Nuten (The South Wind)* by Yves Thériault, translated by Howard Roiter, is reproduced with the permission of the publisher from *Stories from Quebec* by Philip Stratford (ed.). Copyright © 1974 by Van Nostrand Reinhold Ltd., Toronto.

North Shore. His son had guided many whites in the regions surrounding the Manicouagan and Bersimis rivers.

He had told him: "I plan to go way out, near the limits of the reserve."

This was clear enough, and Grand-Louis had simply nodded his head. Now he wouldn't worry, even if Kakatso disappeared for two months. He would know that his father was high in the hills, breathing the clean air and soaking up beautiful scenes to remember in future days.

Just past the main branch of the Manicouagan there is an enormous rock crowned by two pines and a fir tree which stand side by side like the fingers of a hand, the smallest on the left and the others reaching higher.

This point, which Kakatso could never forget, served as his signpost for every trail in the area; and other points would guide him north, west, or in any other direction. Kakatso, until his final breath, would easily find his way about there, guided only by the memory of a certain tree, the silhouette of the mountain outlined against the clear skies, the twisting of a river bed, or the slope of a hill.

In strange territory Kakatso would spend entire days precisely organizing his memories so that if he ever returned no trail there would be unknown to him.

Thus, knowing every winding path and every animal's accustomed lair, he could set out on his journey carrying only some salt, tea, and shells for his rifle. He could live by finding his subsistence in the earth itself and in nature's plenty.

Kakatso knew well what a man needed for total independence: a fish-hook wrapped in paper, a length of supple cord, a strong knife, waterproof boots and a well-oiled rifle. With these things a man could know the great joy of not having to depend on anyone but himself, of wandering as he pleased one day after another, proud and superior, the owner of eternal lands that stretched beyond the horizon.

(To despise the reserve and those who belonged there. Not to have any allegiance except a respect for the water, the sky, and the winds. To be a man, but a man according to the Indian image and not that of the whites. The Indian image of a real man was ageless and changeless, a true image of man in the bosom of a wild and immense nature.)

Kakatso had a wife and a house and grown-up children whom he rarely saw. He really knew little about them. One daughter was a nurse in a white man's city, another had married a turncoat Montagnais who lived in Baie-Comeau and worked in the factories. A son studied far away, in Montreal, and Kakatso would probably never see him again. A son who would repudiate everything, would forget the proud Montagnais language and change his name to be accepted by the whites in spite of his dark skin and slitty eyes.

The other son, Grand-Louis...but this one was an exception. He had inherited Montagnais instincts. He often came down to the coast, at Godbout or Sept-Îles, or sometimes at Natashquan, because he was ambitious and wanted to earn money. But this did not cause him to scorn or detest the forest. He found a good life there. For Kakatso, it was enough that his child, unlike so many others, did not turn into a phony white man.

As for Kakatso's wife, she was still at home, receiving Kakatso on his many returns without emotion or gratitude. She had a roof over her head, warmth, and food. With skilled fingers she made caribou skin jackets for the white man avid for the exotic. The small sideline liberated Kakatso from other obligations toward her. Soon after returning home, Kakatso always wanted to get away again. He was uncomfortable in

these white men's houses that were too high, too solid, and too neatly organized for his taste.

So Kakatso lived his life in direct contact with the forest, and he nurtured life itself from the forest's plenty. Ten months of the year he roamed the forest trails, ten months he earned his subsistence from hunting, trapping, fishing, and smoking the caribou meat that he placed in caches for later use. With the fur pelts he met his own needs and those of the house on the reserve near the forest, although these needs were minimal because his wife was a good earner.

He climbed, then, toward the northern limits of the Montagnais lands on this June day, which was to bring calamity of which he was completely unaware.

Kakatso had heard of the terrible bomb. For twenty years he had heard talk of it, and the very existence of these horrendous machines was not unknown to him. But how was he to know the complex fabric of events happening in the world just then? He never read the newspapers and never really listened to the radio when he happened to spend some hours in a warm house. How could he conceive of total annihilation threatening the whole world? How could he feel all the world's people trembling?

In the forest's vast peace, Kakatso, knowing nature's strength, could easily believe that nothing and nobody could prevail against the mountains, the rivers, and the forest itself stretching out all across the land. Nothing could prevail against the earth, the unchangeable soil that regenerated itself year after year.

He travelled for five days. On the fifth evening it took Kakatso longer to fall asleep. Something was wrong. A silent anguish he did not understand was disturbing him.

He had lit his evening fire on a bluff covered with soft moss, one hundred feet above the lake. He slept there, rolled in his blanket in a deeply dark country interrupted only by the rays of the new moon.

Sleep was slow and when it came it did not bring peace. A jumble of snarling creatures and swarming, roaring masses invaded Kakatso's sleep. He turned over time and again, groaning restlessly. Suddenly he awoke and was surprised to see that the moon had gone down and the night's blackness was lit only by stars. Here, on the bluff, there was a bleak reflection from the sky, but that long valley and the lake remained dark. Exhausted by his throbbing dreams, Kakatso got up, stretched his legs, and lit his pipe. On those rare occasions when his sleep was bad he had always managed to recover his tranquillity by smoking a bit, motionless in the night, listening to the forest sounds.

Suddenly the light came. For a single moment the southern and western horizons were illuminated by this immense bluish gleam that loomed up, lingered a moment, and then went out. The dark became even blacker and Kakatso muttered to himself. He wasn't afraid because fear had always been totally foreign to him. But what did this strange event mean? Was it the anger of some old mountain spirit?

All at once the gleam reappeared, this time even more westerly. Weaker this time and less evident. Then the shadows again enveloped the land.

Kakatso no longer tried to sleep that night. He squatted, smoking his pipe and trying to find some explanation for these bluish gleams with his simple ideas, his straightforward logic and vivid memory.

When dawn came the old Montagnais, the last of his people, the great Abenakis, carefully prepared his fire and boiled some water for his tea.

For some hours he didn't feel like moving. He no longer heard the inner voices calling him to the higher lands. He felt stuck there, incapable of going further until the tumult within him died down. What was there that he didn't know about his skies, he who had spent his whole life wandering in the woods and sleeping under the stars? The sky over his head was as familiar to him as the soil of the underbrush, the animal trails, and the games of the trout in their streams. But never before had he seen such gleams and they disturbed him.

At eight o'clock the sun was slowly climbing into the sky, and Kakatso was still there.

At ten he moved to the shore to look at the water in the lake. He saw a minnow run and concluded that the lake had many fish. He then attached his fire cord to the hook tied with partridge feathers he had found in the branches of a wild hawthorn bush. He cast the fly with a deliberate, almost solemn movement and it jumped on the smooth water. After Kakatso cast three more times a fat trout swallowed the hook and he pulled him in gently, quite slowly, letting him fight as much as he wanted. The midday meal was in hand. The Montagnais, still in no great hurry to continue his trip, began to prepare his fish.

He was finishing when the far-away buzz of a plane shook him out of his reveries. Down there, over the mountains around the end of the lake, a plane was moving through the sky. This was a familiar sight to Kakatso because all this far country was visited only by planes that landed on the lakes. In this way the Indian had come to know the white man. This was the most frequent place of contact between the two: a large body of quiet water where a plane would land, where the whites would ask for help and finding nothing better than an Indian to help them.

Even from a distance Kakatso recognized the type of plane. It was a single-engine, deluxe Bonanza, a type often used by the Americans who came to fish for their salmon in our rivers.

The plane circled the lake and flew over the bluff where Kakatso's fire was still burning. Then it landed gently, almost tenderly. The still waters were only lightly ruffled and quickly returned to their mirror smoothness. The plane slowed down, the motor coughed once or twice, then the craft made a complete turn and headed for the beach.

Kakatso, with one hand shading his eyes, watched the landing, motionless.

When the plane was finally still and the tips of its pontoons were pulled up on the sandy beach, two men, a young woman, and a twelve-year-old boy got out.

One of the men was massive. He towered a head over Kakatso although the Montagnais himself was rather tall.

"Are you an Indian?" the man asked suddenly.

Kakatso nodded slowly and blinked his eyes once.

"Good, I'm glad, you can save us," said the man.

"Save you?" said Kakatso. "Save you from what?"

"Never mind," said the woman, "that's our business."

Standing some distance away, she gestured to the big man who had first spoken to Kakatso.

"If you're trying to escape the police," said Kakatso, "I can't do anything for you."

"It has nothing to do with the police," said the other man who had not spoken previously.

He moved toward Kakatso and proffered a handshake. Now that he was close the Montagnais recognized a veteran bush pilot. His experience could be seen in his eyes, in the squint of his eyelids, and in the way he treated an Indian as an equal.

"I am Bob Ledoux," the man said. "I am a pilot. Do you know what nuclear war is?"

"Yes," answered Kakatso, "I know."

"All the cities in the south have been destroyed," said Ledoux. "We were able to escape."

"Is that a real one?" asked the boy, who had been closely scrutinizing Kakatso. "Eh, Mom, is it really one of those savages?"

"Yes," answered the woman, "certainly." And to Kakatso she said, "Please excuse him. He has never been on the North Shore."

Naturally Kakatso did not like to be considered a savage. But he didn't show anything and he swallowed his bitterness.

"So," said the pilot, "here we are without resources."

"I have money," said the man.

"This is Mr. Perron," said the pilot, "Mrs. Perron, and their son...."

"My name is Roger," said the boy. "I know how to swim."

The Montagnais was still undecided. He did not trust intruders. He preferred, in his simple soul, to choose his own objectives and decide his day's activities. And here were outsiders who had fallen from the sky, almost demanding his help...but what help?

"I can't do much for you," he said after a while.

"I have money," the man repeated.

Kakatso shrugged. Money? Why money? What would it buy up here?

Without flinching he had heard how all the southern cities had been destroyed. Now he understood the meaning of those sudden gleams that lit the horizon during the night. And because this event had been the work of whites, Kakatso completely lost interest in it.

So his problem remained these four people he considered spoilers.

"Without you," said the woman, "we are going to perish."

And because Kakatso looked at her in surprise, she added, in a somewhat different tone: "We have no supplies at all and we are almost out of fuel."

"That's true," said the pilot.

"So," continued the woman, "if you don't help us find food, we will die."

Kakatso, with a sweeping gesture, indicated the forest and the lake: "There is wild game there and fish in the waters...."

"I don't have a gun or fish-hooks," said the pilot. "And it's been a very long time since I came so far north."

He said this with a slightly abashed air and Kakatso saw clearly that the man's hands were too white; the skin had become too soft and smooth.

"I'll pay you whatever is necessary," said Mr. Perron.

"Can't you see," said the wife, "that money doesn't interest him?"

Kakatso stood there, looking at them with his shining, impassive eyes, his face unsmiling, and his arms dangling at his sides.

"Say something," cried the woman. "Will you agree to help us?"

"We got away as best we could," said the pilot. "We gathered the attack on Montreal was coming and we were already at the airport when the warning sirens went off. But I couldn't take on enough fuel. There were other planes leaving too. I can't even take off again from this lake. Do you know if there is a supply cache near here?"

Throughout the northern forests pilots left emergency fuel caches for use when necessary. But if Kakatso knew of several such places he wasn't letting on in front of the intruders.

"I don't know," he said.

There was silence.

The whites looked at the Indian and desperately sought words to persuade him. But Kakatso did not move and said nothing. He had always fled the society of whites and dealt with them only when it was unavoidable. Why should he treat those who surfaced here now any differently? They were without food; the forest nourishes those who know how to take their share. This knowledge was such an instinctive part of an Indian's being that he couldn't realize how some people could lack it. He was sure that these people wanted to impose their needs on him and enslave him. All his Montagnais pride revolted against this thought. And yet, he could help them. Less than one hour away there was one of those meat caches of a thousand pounds of smoked moose, enough to see them through a winter. And the fish in the lake could be caught without much effort. Weaving a simple net of fine branches would do it, or a trap of bulrushes.

But he didn't move a muscle.

Only a single fixed thought possessed Kakatso, and it fascinated him. Down there, in the south, the whites had been destroyed. Never again would they reign over these forests. In killing each other, they had rid the land of their kind. Would the Indians be free again? All the Indians, even those on the reserves? Free to retake the forests?

And these four whites: could they be the last survivors?

Brothers, thought Kakatso, all my brothers: it is up to me to protect your new freedom.

"The cities," he finally said, "they have really been destroyed?"

"Yes," said the pilot.

"Nothing is left any more," said the woman. "Nothing at all. We saw the explosion from the plane. It was terrible. And the wind pushed up for a quarter of an hour. I thought we were going to crash."

"Nothing left," said the boy, "nobody left. Boom! One bomb did it."

He was delighted to feel himself the hero

—a safe and sound hero—of such an adventure. He didn't seem able to imagine the destruction and death, only the spectacular explosion.

But the man called Perron had understood it well. He had been able to estimate the real power of the bomb.

"The whole city is destroyed," he said. "A little earlier, on the radio, we heard of the destruction of New York, then Toronto and Ottawa...."

"Many other cities too," added the pilot. "As far as I'm concerned, nothing is left of Canada, except perhaps the North Shore...."

"And it won't be for long," said Perron. "If we could get further up, further north. If we only had food and gasoline."

This time he took a roll of money out of his pocket and unfolded five bills, a sum Kakatso had never handled at one time. Perron offered them to the Indian.

"Here. The only thing we ask you for is a little food and gas if you can get some. Then we could leave."

"When such a bomb explodes," said Kakatso without taking the bills, "does it kill all the whites?"

"Yes," said the pilot. "In any case, nearly all."

"One fell on Ottawa?"

"Yes."

"Everybody is dead there?"

"Yes. The city is small and the bomb was a big one. The reports indicate there were no survivors."

Kakatso nodded his head two or three times approvingly. Then he turned away and took his rifle which had been leaning on a rock. Slowly, aiming at the whites, he began to retreat into the forest.

"Where are you going?" cried the woman.

"Here," said the man. "Here's all my money. Come back!"

Only the pilot remained silent. With his sharp eyes he watched Kakatso.

When the Indian reached the edge of the forest it was the boy's turn. He began to sob pitifully, and the woman also began to cry.

"Don't leave," she cried. "Please, help us...."

For all of my people who cried, thought Kakatso, all who begged, who wanted to defend their rights for the past two hundred years: I take revenge for them all.

But he didn't utter another word.

And when the two men wanted to run after him to stop him, he put his rifle to his shoulder. The bullet nicked the pilot's ear. Then the men understood that it would be futile to insist, and Kakatso disappeared into the forest which enclosed him. Bent low, he skimmed the ground, using every bush for cover, losing himself in the undergrowth, melting into the forest where he belonged.

Later, having circled the lake, he rested on a promontory hidden behind many spreading cedars. He saw that the pilot was trying to take off to find food elsewhere.

But the tanks were nearly empty and when the plane reached an altitude of a thousand feet the motor sputtered a bit, backfired, and stopped.

The plane went into a nosedive.

When it hit the trees it caught fire.

In the morning Kakatso continued his trip toward the highlands.

He felt his first nausea the next day and vomited blood two days later. He vomited once at first, then twice, then a third time, and finally one last time.

The wind kept on blowing from the south, warm and mild.

# David Crosby AND Stephen Stills

# Wooden Ships

If you smile at me, I will understand
'Cause that is something
Everybody everywhere does in the same language.

I can see by your coat, my friend,
You're from the other side.
There's just one thing I've got to know.
Can you tell me please, who won?

Say, can I have some of your purple berries?

Yes, I've been eating them for six or seven weeks now,
Haven't got sick once....

Prob'ly keep us both alive.

Wooden ships on the water very free and easy,
Easy you know the way it's supposed to be.
Silver people on the shoreline, let us be.
Talkin' 'bout very free and easy.

Horror grips us as we watch you die.
All we can do is echo your anguished cries,
Stare as all human feelings die.
We are leaving, you don't need us.

Go take a sister then by the hand.
Lead her away from this foreign land,
Far away where we might laugh again.
We are leaving, you don't need us.

And it's a fair wind,
Blowin' warm out of the south over my shoulder.
Guess I'll set a course and go.

# Gwendolyn MacEwen

# Flight One

Good afternoon ladies and gentlemen
This is your Captain speaking.

We are flying at an unknown altitude
And an incalculable speed.
The temperature outside is beyond words.

If you look out your windows you will see
Many ruined cities and enduring seas
But if you wish to sleep please close the blinds.

My navigator has been ill for many years
And we are on Automatic Pilot; regrettably
I cannot foresee our ultimate destination.

Have a pleasant trip.
You may smoke, you may drink, you may dance
You may die.
We may even land one day.

# Relationships

# Anonymous

# Love

There's the wonderful love of a beautiful maid,
　　And the love of a staunch true man,
And the love of a baby that's unafraid –
　　All have existed since time began.
But the most wonderful love, the Love of all loves,
　　Even greater than the love for Mother,
Is the infinite, tenderest, passionate love
　　Of one dead drunk for another.

# Al Purdy

# My '48 Pontiac

All winter long it wouldn't start
standing in the yard covered with snow
I'd go out at 10 below zero and coax
and say
       "Where's your pride?"
and kick it disgustedly
Finally snow covered everything
but television aerials and the world was
a place nobody came to
so white it couldn't be looked at
before nothing was something
But the old Pontiac lay there
affirming its identity
like some prehistoric vegetarian
stupidly unaware of snow
waiting for Tyrannosaurus Rex
to come along and bite off its fenders
"You no good American Pontiac you
(I'd say)
you're a disgrace to General Motors"
then go out and hitch up the dog team
When June hurried by it still wouldn't start
only stop
and the wreckers hauled it away

Now and then I go to visit my old friend
at Bud's Auto Wreckers
being sentimental about rubber and metal
I think it's glad to see me
and wags both tail lights
a true heart thumping eagerly
under the torn seat covers
I sit behind the wheel
on a parched August afternoon

and we drive thru a glitter of broken glass
among suicides and automotive murders
mangled chryslers and volkswagens
metal twisted into a look
of fierce helplessness
reversed violence in hunchback shapes
and containing it still
waiting to explode outward

We drive between dismantled buicks and
studebakers and one stuckup old cadillac
driven to Bud's by a doddering chauffeur
who used to play poker with Roman chariot drivers
and a silent crumpled grey plymouth
with bloodstains on the instrument panel
where a girl died
a '41 de soto with all the chrome gone
still excited from drag races
and quivering blondes whose bottoms it liked

My last visit was by moonlight and flashlight
to Bud's Auto Wreckers
where the old Pontiac waited
I turned the speedometer back to 5000 miles
changed the oil
polished the headlights to look at death
adjusted the rearview mirror to look at life
gave it back its ownership card
and went away
puzzled by things

From *The Poems of Al Purdy* by Al Purdy. Reprinted by
permission of The Canadian Publishers, McClelland
and Stewart Limited, Toronto.

# James Hurst

# The Scarlet Ibis

"Brother, Brother,
don't leave me!
Don't leave me!"

I t was in the clove of seasons, summer was dead but autumn had not yet been born, that the ibis lit in the bleeding tree. The flower garden was stained with rotting brown magnolia petals and ironweeds grew rank amid the purple phlox. The five o'clocks by the chimney still marked time, but the oriole nest in the elm was untenanted and rocked back and forth like an empty cradle. The last graveyard flowers were blooming, and their smell drifted across the cotton field and through every room of our house, speaking softly the names of our dead.

It's strange that all this is still so clear to me, now that that summer has long since

fled and time has had its way. A grindstone stands where the bleeding tree stood, just outside the kitchen door, and now if an oriole sings in the elm, its song seems to die up in the leaves, a silvery dust. The flower garden is prim, the house a gleaming white, and the pale fence across the yard stands straight and spruce. But sometimes (like right now), as I sit in the cool, green-draped parlor, the grindstone begins to turn, and time with all its changes is ground away – and I remember Doodle.

Doodle was just about the craziest brother a boy ever had. Of course, he wasn't a crazy crazy like old Miss Leedie, who was in love with President Wilson and wrote him a letter every day, but was nice crazy, like someone you meet in your dreams. He was born when I was six and was, from the outset, a disappointment. He seemed all head, with a tiny body which was red and shrivelled like an old man's. Everybody thought he was going to die – everybody except Aunt Nicey, who had delivered him. She said he would live because he was born in a caul and cauls were made from Jesus' nightgown. Daddy had Mr. Heath, the carpenter, build a little mahogany coffin for him. But he didn't die, and when he was three months old Mama and Daddy decided they might as well name him. They named him William Armstrong, which was like tying a big tail on a small kite. Such a name sounds good only on a tombstone.

I thought myself pretty smart at many things, like holding my breath, running, jumping, or climbing the vines in Old Woman Swamp, and I wanted more than anything else someone to race to Horsehead Landing, someone to box with, and someone to perch with in the top fork of the great pine behind the barn, where across the fields and swamps you could see the sea. I wanted a brother. But Mama, crying, told me that even if William Armstrong lived, he would never do these things with me. He might not, she sobbed, even be "all there." He might, as long as he lived, lie on the rubber sheet in the centre of the bed in the front bedroom where the white marquisette curtains billowed out in the afternoon sea breeze, rustling like palmetto fronds.

It was bad enough having an invalid brother, but having one who possibly was not all there was unbearable, so I began to make plans to kill him by smothering him with a pillow. However, one afternoon as I watched him, my head poked between the iron posts of the foot of the bed, he looked straight at me and grinned. I skipped through the rooms, down the echoing halls, shouting, "Mama, he smiled. He's all there! He's all there!" and he was.

When he was two, if you laid him on his stomach, he began to try to move himself, straining terribly. The doctor said that with his weak heart this strain would probably kill him, but it didn't. Trembling, he'd push himself up, turning first red, then a soft purple, and finally collapse back onto the bed like an old worn-out doll. I can still see Mama watching him, her hand pressed tight across her mouth, her eyes wide and unblinking. But he learned to crawl (it was his third winter), and we brought him out of the front bedroom, putting him on the rug before the fireplace. For the first time he became one of us.

As long as he lay all the time in bed, we called him William Armstrong, even though it was formal and sounded as if we were referring to one of our ancestors, but with his creeping around on the deerskin rug and beginning to talk, something had to be done about his name. It was I who renamed him. When he crawled, he crawled backward, as if he were in reverse and couldn't change gears. If you called him, he'd turn around as

if he were going in the other direction, then he'd back right up to you to be picked up. Crawling backward made him look like a doodlebug, so I began to call him Doodle, and in time even Mama and Daddy thought it was a better name than William Armstrong. Only Aunt Nicey disagreed. She said caul babies should be treated with special respect since they might turn out to be saints. Renaming my brother was perhaps the kindest thing I ever did for him, because nobody expects much from someone called Doodle.

Although Doodle learned to crawl, he showed no signs of walking, but he wasn't idle. He talked so much that we all quit listening to what he said. It was about this time that Daddy built him a gocart and I had to pull him around. At first I just paraded him up and down the piazza, but then he started crying to be taken out into the yard and it ended up by my having to lug him wherever I went. If I so much as picked up my cap, he'd start crying to go with me and Mama would call from wherever she was, "Take Doodle with you."

He was a burden in many ways. The doctor had said that he mustn't get too excited, too hot, too cold, or too tired and that he must always be treated gently. A long list of don'ts went with him, all of which I ignored once we got out of the house. To discourage his coming with me, I'd run with him across the ends of the cotton rows and careen him around corners on two wheels. Sometimes I accidentally turned him over, but he never told Mama. His skin was very sensitive, and he had to wear a big straw hat whenever he went out. When the going got rough and he had to cling to the sides of the gocart, the hat slipped all the way down over his ears. He was a sight. Finally, I could see I was licked. Doodle was my brother and he was going to cling to me forever, no matter what I did, so I dragged him across the burning cotton field to share with him the only beauty I knew, Old Woman Swamp. I pulled the gocart through the saw-tooth fern, down into the green dimness where the palmetto fronds whispered by the stream. I lifted him out and set him down in the soft rubber grass beside a tall pine. His eyes were round with wonder as he gazed about him, and his little hands began to stroke the rubber grass. Then he began to cry.

"For heaven's sake, what's the matter?" I asked, annoyed.

"It's so pretty," he said. "So pretty, pretty, pretty."

After that day Doodle and I often went down into Old Woman Swamp. I would gather wildflowers, wild violets, honeysuckle, yellow jasmine, snakeflowers, and water lilies, and with wire grass we'd weave them into necklaces and crowns. We'd bedeck ourselves with our handiwork and loll about thus beautified, beyond the touch of the everyday world. Then when the slanted rays of the sun burned orange in the tops of the pines, we'd drop our jewels into the stream and watch them float away toward the sea.

There is within me (and with sadness I have watched it in others) a knot of cruelty borne by the stream of love, much as our blood sometimes bears the seed of our destruction, and at times I was mean to Doodle. One day I took him up to the barn loft and showed him his casket, telling him how we all had believed he would die. It was covered with a film of Paris green sprinkled to kill the rats, and screech owls had built a nest inside it.

Doodle studied the mahogany box for a long time, then said, "It's not mine."

"It is," I said. "And before I'll help you down from the loft, you're going to have to touch it."

"I won't touch it," he said sullenly.

"Then I'll leave you here by yourself," I threatened, and made as if I were going down.

Doodle was frightened of being left. "Don't leave me, Brother," he cried, and he leaned toward the coffin. His hand, trembling, reached out, and when he touched the casket he screamed. A screech owl flapped out of the box into our faces, scaring us and covering us with Paris green. Doodle was paralysed, so I put him on my shoulder and carried him down the ladder, and even when we were outside in the bright sunshine, he clung to me, crying, "Don't leave me. Don't leave me."

When Doodle was five years old, I was embarrassed at having a brother of that age who couldn't walk, so I set out to teach him. We were down in Old Woman Swamp and it was spring and the sick-sweet smell of bay flowers hung everywhere like a mournful song. "I'm going to teach you to walk, Doodle," I said.

He was sitting comfortably on the soft grass, leaning back against the pine. "Why?" he asked.

I hadn't expected such an answer. "So I won't have to haul you around all the time."

"I can't walk, Brother," he said.

"Who says so?" I demanded.

"Mama, the doctor – everybody."

"Oh, you can walk," I said, and I took him by the arms and stood him up. He collapsed onto the grass like a half-empty flour sack. It was as if he had no bones in his little legs.

"Don't hurt me, Brother," he warned.

"Shut up. I'm not going to hurt you. I'm going to teach you to walk." I heaved him up again, and again he collapsed.

This time he did not lift his face up out of the rubber grass. "I just can't do it. Let's make honeysuckle wreaths."

"Oh yes you can, Doodle," I said. "All you

got to do is try. Now come on," and I hauled him up once more.

It seemed so hopeless from the beginning that it's a miracle I didn't give up. But all of us must have something or someone to be proud of, and Doodle had become mine. I did not know then that pride is a wonderful, terrible thing, a seed that bears two vines, life and death. Every day that summer we went to the pine beside the stream of Old Woman Swamp, and I put him on his feet at least a hundred times each afternoon. Occasionally I too became discouraged because it didn't seem as if he was trying, and I would say, "Doodle, don't you *want* to learn to walk?"

He'd nod his head, and I'd say, "Well, if you don't keep trying, you'll never learn." Then I'd paint for him a picture of us as old men, white-haired, him with a long white beard and me still pulling him around in the gocart. This never failed to make him try again.

Finally one day, after many weeks of practising, he stood alone for a few seconds. When he fell, I grabbed him in my arms and hugged him, our laughter pealing through the swamp like a ringing bell. Now we knew it could be done. Hope no longer hid in the dark palmetto thicket but perched like a cardinal in the lacy toothbrush tree, brilliantly visible. "Yes, yes," I cried, and he cried it too, and the grass beneath us was soft and the smell of the swamp was sweet.

With success so imminent, we decided not to tell anyone until he could actually walk. Each day, barring rain, we sneaked into Old Woman Swamp, and by cotton-picking time Doodle was ready to show what he could do. He still wasn't able to walk far, but we could wait no longer. Keeping a nice secret is very hard to do, like holding your breath. We chose to reveal all on October eighth, Doodle's sixth birthday, and for

weeks ahead we mooned around the house, promising everybody a most spectacular surprise. Aunt Nicey said that, after so much talk, if we produced anything less tremendous than the Resurrection, she was going to be disappointed.

At breakfast on our chosen day, when Mama, Daddy, and Aunt Nicey were in the dining room, I brought Doodle to the door in the gocart just as usual and had them turn their backs, making them cross their hearts and hope to die if they peeked. I helped Doodle up, and when he was standing alone I let them look. There wasn't a sound as Doodle walked slowly across the room and sat down at his place at the table. Then Mama began to cry and ran over to him, hugging him and kissing him. Daddy hugged him too, so I went to Aunt Nicey, who was thanks praying in the doorway, and began to waltz her around. We danced together quite well until she came down on my big toe with her brogans, hurting me so badly I thought I was crippled for life.

Doodle told them it was I who had taught him to walk, so everyone wanted to hug me, and I began to cry.

"What are you crying for?" asked Daddy, but I couldn't answer. They did not know that I did it for myself; that pride, whose slave I was, spoke to me louder than all their voices, and that Doodle walked only because I was ashamed of having a crippled brother.

Within a few months Doodle had learned to walk well and his gocart was put up in the barn loft (it's still there) beside his little mahogany coffin. Now, when we roamed off together, resting often, we never turned back until our destination had been reached, and to help pass the time, we took up lying. From the beginning Doodle was a terrible liar and he got me in the habit. Had anyone stopped to listen to us, we would have been sent off to Dix Hill.

My lies were scary, involved, and usually pointless, but Doodle's were twice as crazy. People in his stories all had wings and flew wherever they wanted to go. His favorite lie was about a boy named Peter who had a pet peacock with a ten-foot tail. Peter wore a golden robe that glittered so brightly that when he walked through the sunflowers they turned away from the sun to face him. When Peter was ready to go to sleep, the peacock spread his magnificent tail, enfolding the boy gently like a closing go-to-sleep flower, burying him in the gloriously iridescent, rustling vortex. Yes, I must admit it. Doodle could beat me lying.

Doodle and I spent lots of time thinking about our future. We decided that when we were grown we'd live in Old Woman Swamp and pick dog-tongue for a living. Beside the stream, he planned, we'd build us a house of whispering leaves and the swamp birds would be our chickens. All day long (when we weren't gathering dog-tongue) we'd swing through the cypresses on the rope vines, and if it rained we'd huddle beneath an umbrella tree and play stickfrog. Mama and Daddy could come and live with us if they wanted to. He even came up with the idea that he could marry Mama and I could marry Daddy. Of course, I was old enough to know this wouldn't work out, but the picture he painted was so beautiful and serene that all I could do was whisper "Yes, Yes."

Once I had succeeded in teaching Doodle to walk, I began to believe in my own infallibility and I prepared a terrific development program for him, unknown to Mama and Daddy, of course. I would teach him to run, to swim, to climb trees, and to fight. He, too, now believed in my infallibility, so we set the deadline for these accomplishments less than a year away, when, it had been decided, Doodle could start to school.

That winter we didn't make much progress, for I was in school and Doodle suffered from one bad cold after another. But when spring came, rich and warm, we raised our sights again. Success lay at the end of summer like a pot of gold, and our campaign got off to a good start. On hot days, Doodle and I went down to Horsehead Landing and I gave him swimming lessons or showed him how to row a boat. Sometimes we descended into the cool greenness of Old Woman Swamp and climbed the rope vines or boxed scientifically beneath the pine where he had learned to walk. Promise hung about us like the leaves, and wherever we looked, ferns unfurled and birds broke into song.

That summer, the summer of 1918, was blighted. In May and June there was no rain and the crops withered, curled up, then died under the thirsty sun. One morning in July a hurricane came out of the east, tipping over the oaks in the yard and splitting the limbs of the elm trees. That afternoon it roared back out of the west, blew the fallen oaks around, snapping their roots and tearing them out of the earth like a hawk at the entrails of a chicken. Cotton bolls were wrenched from the stalks and lay like green walnuts in the valleys between the rows, while the cornfield leaned over uniformly so that the tassels touched the ground. Doodle and I followed Daddy out into the cotton field, where he stood, shoulders sagging, surveying the ruin. When his chin sank down onto his chest, we were frightened, and Doodle slipped his hand into mine. Suddenly Daddy straightened his shoulders, raised a giant, knuckly fist, and with a voice that seemed to rumble out of the earth itself began cursing heaven, hell, the weather, and the Republican Party. Doodle and I, prodding each other and giggling, went back to the house, knowing that everything would be all right.

And during that summer, strange names were heard through the house: Château

Thierry, Amiens, Soissons, and in her blessing at the supper table, Mama once said, "And bless the Pearsons, whose boy Joe was lost at Belleau Wood."

So we came to that clove of seasons. School was only a few weeks away, and Doodle was far behind schedule. He could barely clear the ground when climbing up the rope vines and his swimming was certainly not passable. We decided to double our efforts, to make that last drive and reach our pot of gold. I made him swim until he turned blue and row until he couldn't lift an oar. Wherever we went, I purposely walked fast, and although he kept up, his face turned red and his eyes became glazed. Once, he could go no further, so he collapsed on the ground and began to cry.

"Aw, come on, Doodle," I urged. "You can do it. Do you want to be different from everybody else when you start school?"

"Does it make any difference?"

"It certainly does," I said. "Now, come on," and I helped him up.

As we slipped through dog days, Doodle began to look feverish, and Mama felt his forehead, asking him if he felt ill. At night he didn't sleep well, and sometimes he had nightmares, crying out until I touched him and said, "Wake up, Doodle. Wake up."

It was Saturday noon, just a few days before school was to start. I should have already admitted defeat, but my pride wouldn't let me. The excitement of our program had now been gone for weeks, but still we kept on with a tired doggedness. It was too late to turn back, for we had both wandered too far into a net of expectations and had left no crumbs behind.

Daddy, Mama, Doodle, and I were seated at the dining-room table having lunch. It was a hot day, with all the windows and doors open in case a breeze should come. In the kitchen Aunt Nicey was humming softly.

After a long silence, Daddy spoke. "It's so calm, I wouldn't be surprised if we had a storm this afternoon."

"I haven't heard a rain frog," said Mama, who believed in signs, as she served the bread around the table.

"I did," declared Doodle. "Down in the swamp."

"He didn't," I said contrarily.

"You did, eh?" said Daddy, ignoring my denial.

"I certainly did," Doodle reiterated, scowling at me over the top of his iced-tea glass, and we were quiet again.

Suddenly, from out in the yard, came a strange, croaking noise. Doodle stopped eating, with a piece of bread poised ready for his mouth, his eyes popped round like two blue buttons. "What's that?" he whispered.

I jumped up, knocking over my chair, and had reached the door when Mama called, "Pick up the chair, sit down again, and say excuse me."

By the time I had done this, Doodle had excused himself and had slipped out into the yard. He was looking up into the bleeding tree. "It's a great big red bird!" he called.

The bird croaked loudly again, and Mama and Daddy came out into the yard. We shaded our eyes with our hands against the hazy glare of the sun and peered up through the still leaves. On the topmost branch a bird the size of a chicken, with scarlet feathers and long legs, was perched precariously. Its wings hung down loosely, and as we watched, a feather dropped away and floated slowly down through the green leaves.

"It's not even frightened of us," Mama said.

"It looks tired," Daddy added. "Or maybe sick."

Doodle's hands were clasped at his

throat, and I had never seen him stand still so long. "What is it?" he asked.

Daddy shook his head. "I don't know, maybe it's . . ."

At that moment the bird began to flutter, but the wings were unco-ordinated, and amid much flapping and a spray of flying feathers, it tumbled down, bumping through the limbs of the bleeding tree and landing at our feet with a thud. Its long, graceful neck jerked twice into an S, then straightened out, and the bird was still. A white veil came over the eyes and the long white beak unhinged. Its legs were crossed and its clawlike feet were delicately curved at rest. Even death did not mar its grace, for it lay on the earth like a broken vase of red flowers, and we stood around it, awed by its exotic beauty.

"It's dead," Mama said.

"What is it?" Doodle repeated.

"Go bring me the bird book," said Daddy.

I ran into the house and brought back the bird book. As we watched, Daddy thumbed through its pages. "It's a scarlet ibis," he said, pointing to a picture. "It lives in the tropics – South America to Florida. A storm must have brought it here."

Sadly, we all looked back at the bird. A scarlet ibis! How many miles it had travelled to die like this, in *our* yard, beneath the bleeding tree.

"Let's finish lunch," Mama said, nudging us back toward the dining room.

"I'm not hungry," said Doodle, and he knelt down beside the ibis.

"We've got peach cobbler for dessert," Mama tempted from the doorway.

Doodle remained kneeling. "I'm going to bury him."

"Don't you dare touch him," Mama warned. "There's no telling what disease he might have had."

"All right," said Doodle. "I won't."

Daddy, Mama, and I went back to the dining-room table, but we watched Doodle through the open door. He took out a piece of string from his pocket and, without touching the ibis, looped one end around its neck. Slowly, while singing softly "Shall We Gather at the River," he carried the bird around to the front yard and dug a hole in the flower garden, next to the petunia bed. Now we were watching him through the front window, but he didn't know it. His awkwardness at digging the hole with a shovel whose handle was twice as long as he was made us laugh, and we covered our mouths with our hands so he wouldn't hear.

When Doodle came into the dining room, he found us seriously eating our cobbler. He was pale and lingered just inside the screen door. "Did you get the scarlet ibis buried?" asked Daddy.

Doodle didn't speak but nodded his head.

"Go wash your hands, and then you can have some peach cobbler," said Mama.

"I'm not hungry," he said.

"Dead birds is bad luck," said Aunt Nicey, poking her head from the kitchen door. "Specially *red* dead birds!"

As soon as I had finished eating, Doodle and I hurried off to Horsehead Landing. Time was short, and Doodle still had a long way to go if he was going to keep up with the other boys when he started school. The sun, gilded with the yellow cast of autumn, still burned fiercely, but the dark green woods through which we passed were shady and cool. When we reached the landing, Doodle said he was too tired to swim, so we got into a skiff and floated down the creek with the tide. Far off in the marsh a rail was scolding, and over on the beach locusts were singing in the myrtle trees. Doodle did not speak and kept his head turned away, letting one hand trail limply in the water.

After we had drifted a long way, I put the oars in place and made Doodle row back against the tide. Black clouds began to gather in the southwest, and he kept watching them, trying to pull the oars a little faster. When we reached Horsehead Landing, lightning was playing across half the sky and thunder roared out, hiding even the sound of the sea. The sun disappeared and darkness descended, almost like night. Flocks of marsh crows flew by, heading inland to their roosting trees, and two egrets, squawking, arose from the oyster-rock shallows and careened away.

Doodle was both tired and frightened, and when he stepped from the skiff he collapsed onto the mud, sending an armada of fiddler crabs rustling off into the marsh grass. I helped him up, and as he wiped the mud off his trousers, he smiled at me ashamedly. He had failed and we both knew it, so we started back home, racing the storm. We never spoke (What are the words that can solder cracked pride?), but I knew he was watching me, watching for a sign of mercy. The lightning was near now, and from fear he walked so close behind me he kept stepping on my heels. The faster I walked, the faster he walked, so I began to run. The rain was coming, roaring through the pines, and then, like a bursting Roman candle, a gum tree ahead of us was shattered by a bolt of lightning. When the deafening peal of thunder had died, and in the moment before the rain arrived, I heard Doodle, who had fallen behind, cry out, "Brother, Brother, don't leave me! Don't leave me!"

The knowledge that Doodle's and my plans had come to naught was bitter, and that streak of cruelty within me awakened. I ran as fast as I could, leaving him far behind with a wall of rain dividing us. The drops stung my face like nettles, and the wind flared the wet glistening leaves of the bordering trees. Soon I could hear his voice no more.

I hadn't run too far before I became tired, and the flood of childish spite evanesced as well. I stopped and waited for Doodle. The sound of rain was everywhere, but the wind had died and it fell straight down in parallel paths like ropes hanging from the sky. As I waited, I peered through the downpour, but no one came. Finally I went back and found him huddled beneath a red nightshade bush beside the road. He was sitting on the ground, his face buried in his arms, which were resting on his drawn-up knees. "Let's go, Doodle," I said.

He didn't answer, so I placed my hand on his forehead and lifted his head. Limply, he fell backwards onto the earth. He had been bleeding from the mouth, and his neck and the front of his shirt was stained a brilliant red.

"Doodle! Doodle!" I cried, shaking him, but there was no answer but the ropy rain. He lay very awkwardly, with his head thrown far back, making his vermilion neck appear unusually long and slim. His little legs, bent sharply at the knees, had never before seemed so fragile, so thin.

I began to weep, and the tear-blurred vision in red before me looked very familiar. "Doodle!" I screamed above the pounding storm and threw my body to the earth above his. For a long long time, it seemed forever, I lay there crying, sheltering my fallen scarlet ibis from the heresy of rain.

## William Blake

# A Poison Tree

I was angry with my friend:
I told my wrath, my wrath did end.
I was angry with my foe:
I told it not, my wrath did grow.

And I water'd it in fears,
Night and morning with my tears;
And I sunned it with smiles,
And with soft deceitful wiles.

And it grew both day and night,
Till it bore an apple bright;
And my foe beheld it shine,
And he knew that it was mine,

And into my garden stole
When the night had veil'd the pole:
In the morning glad I see
My foe outstretch'd beneath the tree.

## Morley Callaghan

# Two Fishermen

The line was out full length.

The only reporter on the town paper, the *Examiner*, was Michael Foster, a tall, long-legged, eager young fellow, who wanted to go to the city some day and work on an important newspaper.

The morning he went into Bagley's Hotel, he wasn't at all sure of himself. He went over to the desk and whispered to the proprietor, Ted Bagley, "Did he come here, Mr. Bagley?"

Bagley said slowly, "Two men came here from this morning's train. They're registered." He put his spatulate forefinger on the open book and said, "Two men. One of them's a drummer. This one here, T. Woodley. I know because he was through this way last year and just a minute ago he walked across the road to Molson's hardware store. The other one...here's his name, K. Smith."

"Who's K. Smith?" Michael asked.

"I don't know. A mild, harmless-looking little guy."

"Did he look like the hangman, Mr. Bagley?"

"I couldn't say that, seeing as I never saw one. He was awfully polite and asked where he could get a boat so he could go fishing on the lake this evening, so I said likely down at Smollet's place by the powerhouse."

"Well, thanks. I guess if he was the hangman, he'd go over to the jail first," Michael said.

He went along the street, past the Baptist church to the old jail with the high brick fence around it. Two tall maple trees, with branches drooping low over the sidewalk, shaded one of the walls from the morning sunlight. Last night, behind those walls, three carpenters, working by lamplight, had nailed the timbers for the scaffold. In the morning, young Thomas Delaney, who had grown up in the town, was being hanged: he had killed old Mathew Rhinehart whom he had caught molesting his wife when she had been berry-picking in the hills behind the town. There had been a struggle and Thomas Delaney had taken a bad beating before he had killed Rhinehart. Last night a crowd had gathered on the sidewalk by the lamppost, and while moths and smaller insects swarmed around the high blue carbon light, the crowd had thrown sticks and bottles and small stones at the out-of-town workmen in the jail yard. Billy Hilton, the town constable, had stood under the light with his head down, pretending not to notice anything. Thomas Delaney was only three years older than Michael Foster.

Michael went straight to the jail office, where Henry Steadman, the sheriff, a squat, heavy man, was sitting on the desk idly wetting his long moustaches with his tongue. "Hello, Michael, what do you want?" he asked.

"Hello, Mr. Steadman, the *Examiner* would like to know if the hangman arrived yet."

"Why ask me?"

"I thought he'd come here to test the gallows. Won't he?"

"My, you're a smart young fellow, Michael, thinking of that."

"Is he in there now, Mr. Steadman?"

"Don't ask me. I'm saying nothing. Say, Michael, do you think there's going to be trouble? You ought to know. Does anybody seem sore at me? I can't do nothing. You can see that."

"I don't think anybody blames you, Mr. Steadman. Look here, can't I see the hangman? Is his name K. Smith?"

"What does it matter to you, Michael? Be a sport, go on away and don't bother us any more."

"All right, Mr. Steadman," Michael said very competently, "just leave it to me."

Early that evening, when the sun was setting, Michael Foster walked south of the town on the dusty road leading to the powerhouse and Smollet's fishing pier. He knew that if Mr. K. Smith wanted to get a boat he would go down to the pier. Fine powdered road dust whitened Michael's shoes. Ahead of him he saw the powerplant, square and low, and the smooth lake water. Behind him the sun was hanging over the blue hills beyond the town and shining brilliantly on square patches of farm land. The air around the powerhouse smelt of steam.

Out on the jutting, tumble-down pier of rock and logs, Michael saw a little fellow without a hat, sitting down with his knees hunched up to his chin, a very small man with little grey baby curls on the back of his neck, who stared steadily far out over the water. In his hand he was holding a stick with a heavy fishing line twined around it and a gleaming copper spoon bait, the hooks brightened with bits of feathers such as they used in the neighborhood when trolling for lake trout. Apprehensively Michael walked out over the rocks toward the stranger and called, "Were you thinking of going fishing, mister?" Standing up, the man smiled. He had a large head, tapering down to a small chin, a birdlike neck, and a very wistful smile. Puckering his mouth up, he said shyly to Michael, "Did you intend to go fishing?"

"That's what I came down here for. I was going to get a boat back at the boathouse there. How would you like if we went together?"

"I'd like it first rate," the shy little man said eagerly. "We could take turns rowing. Does that appeal to you?"

"Fine. Fine. You wait here and I'll go back to Smollet's place and ask for a rowboat and I'll row around here and get you."

"Thanks. Thanks very much," the mild little man said as he began to untie his line. He seemed very enthusiastic.

When Michael brought the boat around to the end of the old pier and invited the stranger to make himself comfortable so he could handle the line, the stranger protested comically that he ought to be allowed to row.

Pulling strong at the oars, Michael was soon out in the deep water and the little man was letting his line out slowly. In one furtive glance, he had noticed that the man's hair, grey at the temples, was inclined to curl to his ears. The line was out full length. It was twisted around the little man's forefinger, which he let drag in the water. And then Michael looked full at him and smiled because he thought he seemed so meek and quizzical. "He's a nice little guy," Michael assured himself and he said, "I work on the town paper, the *Examiner*."

"Is it a good paper? Do you like the work?"

"Yes, but it's nothing like a first-class city paper and I don't expect to be working on it long. I want to get a reporter's job on a city paper. My name's Michael Foster."

"Mine's Smith. Just call me Smitty."

"I was wondering if you'd been over to the jail yet."

Up to this time the little man had been smiling with the charming ease of a small boy who finds himself free, but now he became furtive and disappointed. Hesitating, he said, "Yes, I was over there first thing this morning."

"Oh, I just knew you'd go there," Michael said. They were a bit afraid of each other. By this time they were far out on the water, which had a mill-pond smoothness. The town seemed to get smaller, with white houses in rows and streets forming geometric patterns, just as the blue hills behind the town seemed to get larger at sundown.

Finally Michael said, "Do you know this Thomas Delaney that's dying in the morning?" He knew his voice was slow and resentful.

"No. I don't know anything about him. I never read about them.

"Aren't there any fish at all in this old lake? I'd like to catch some fish," he said rapidly. "I told my wife I'd bring her home some fish." Glancing at Michael, he was appealing, without speaking, that they should do nothing to spoil an evening's fishing.

The little man began to talk eagerly about fishing as he pulled out a small flask from his hip pocket. "Scotch," he said, chuckling with delight. "Here, take a swig." Michael drank from the flask and passed it back. Tilting his head back and saying, "Here's to you, Michael," the little man took a long pull at the flask. "The only time I take a drink," he said still chuckling, "is when I go on a fishing trip by myself. I usually go by myself," he added apologetically as if he wanted the young fellow to see how much he appreciated his company.

They had gone far out on the water but they had caught nothing. It began to get dark. "No fish tonight, I guess, Smitty," Michael said.

"It's a crying shame," Smitty said. "I looked forward to coming up here when I found out the place was on the lake. I wanted to get some fishing in. I promised my wife I'd bring her back some fish. She'd often like to go fishing with me, but of course, she can't because she can't travel around from place to place like I do. Whenever I get a call to go some place, I always look at the map to see if it's by a lake or on a river, then I take my lines and hooks along."

"If you took another job, you and your wife could probably go fishing together," Michael suggested.

"I don't know about that. We sometimes

go fishing together anyway." He looked away, waiting for Michael to be repelled and insist that he ought to give up the job. And he wasn't ashamed as he looked down at the water, but he knew that Michael thought he ought to be ashamed. "Somebody's got to do my job. There's got to be a hangman," he said.

"I just meant that if it was such disagreeable work, Smitty."

The little man did not answer for a long time. Michael rowed steadily with sweeping, tireless strokes. Huddled at the end of the boat, Smitty suddenly looked up with a kind of melancholy hopelessness and said mildly, "The job hasn't been so disagreeable."

"Good God, man, you don't mean you like it?"

"Oh, no," he said, to be obliging, as if he knew what Michael expected him to say. "I mean you get used to it, that's all." But he looked down again at the water, knowing he ought to be ashamed of himself.

"Have you got any children?"

"I sure have. Five. The oldest boy is fourteen. It's funny, but they're all a lot bigger and taller than I am. Isn't that funny?"

They started a conversation about fishing rivers that ran into the lake farther north. They felt friendly again. The little man, who had an extraordinary gift for storytelling, made many quaint faces, puckered up his lips, screwed up his eyes, and moved around restlessly as if he wanted to get up in the boat and stride around for the sake of more expression. Again he brought out the whiskey flask and Michael stopped rowing. Grinning, they toasted each other and said together, "Happy days." The boat remained motionless on the placid water. Far out, the sun's last rays gleamed on the waterline. And then it got dark and they could only see the town lights. It was time to turn around and pull for the shore. The little man tried to take

the oars from Michael, who shook his head resolutely and insisted that he would prefer to have his friend catch a fish on the way back to the shore.

"It's too late now, and we may have scared all the fish away," Smitty laughed happily. "But we're having a grand time, aren't we?"

When they reached the old pier by the powerhouse, it was full night and they hadn't caught a single fish. As the boat bumped against the rocks Michael said, "You can get out here. I'll take the boat around to Smollet's."

"Won't you be coming my way?"

"Not just now. I'll probably talk with Smollet a while."

The little man got out of the boat and stood on the pier looking down at Michael. "I was thinking dawn would be the best time to catch some fish," he said. "At about five o'clock. I'll have an hour and a half to spare anyway. How would you like that?" He was speaking with so much eagerness that Michael found himself saying, "I could try. But if I'm not here at dawn, you go on without me."

"All right. I'll walk back to the hotel now."

"Good night, Smitty."

"Good night, Michael. We had a fine neighborly time, didn't we?"

As Michael rowed the boat around to the boathouse, he hoped that Smitty wouldn't realize he didn't want to be seen walking back to town with him. And later, when he was going slowly along the dusty road in the dark and hearing all the crickets chirping in the ditches, he couldn't figure out why he felt so ashamed of himself.

At seven o'clock next morning Thomas Delaney was hanged in the town jail yard. There was hardly a breeze on that leaden grey morning and there were no small whitecaps out over the lake. It would have been a fine morning for fishing. Michael went down to the jail, for he thought it his duty as a newspaperman to have all the facts, but he was afraid he might get sick. He hardly spoke to all the men and women who were crowded under the maple trees by the jail wall. Everybody he knew was staring at the wall and muttering angrily. Two of Thomas Delaney's brothers, big, strapping fellows with bearded faces, were there on the sidewalk. Three automobiles were at the front of the jail.

Michael, the town newspaperman, was admitted into the courtyard by old Willie Mathews, one of the guards, who said that two newspapermen from the city were at the gallows on the other side of the building. "I guess you can go around there, too, if you want to," Mathews said, as he sat down slowly on the step. Whitefaced, and afraid, Michael sat down on the step with Mathews and they waited and said nothing.

At last the old fellow said, "Those people outside there are pretty sore, ain't they?"

"They're pretty sullen, all right. I saw two of Delaney's brothers there."

"I wish they'd go," Mathews said. "I don't want to see anything. I didn't even look at Delaney. I don't want to hear anything. I'm sick." He put his head back against the wall and closed his eyes.

The old fellow and Michael sat close together till a small procession came around the corner from the other side of the yard. First came Mr. Steadman, the sheriff, with his head down as though he were crying, then Dr. Parker, the physician, then two hard-looking young newspapermen from the city, walking with their hats on the backs of their heads, and behind them came the little hangman, erect, stepping out with military precision and carrying himself with a strange cocky dignity. He was dressed in a long black cutaway coat with grey striped trousers, a gates-ajar collar, and a narrow red tie, as if he alone felt the formal importance of the occasion. He walked with brusque precision till he saw Michael, who was standing up, staring at him with his mouth open.

The little hangman grinned and as soon as the procession reached the doorstep, he shook hands with Michael. They were all looking at Michael. As though his work were over now, the hangman said eagerly to Michael, "I thought I'd see you here. You didn't get down to the pier at dawn?"

"No. I couldn't make it."

"That was tough, Michael. I looked for you," he said. "But never mind. I've got something for you." As they all went into the jail, Dr. Parker glanced angrily at Michael, then turned his back on him. In the office, where the doctor prepared to sign a certificate, Smitty was bending down over his fishing basket which was in the corner. Then he pulled out two good-sized salmon-bellied trout, folded in a newspaper, and said, "I was saving these for you, Michael. I got four in an hour's fishing." Then he said, "I'll talk about that later, if you'll wait. We'll be busy here, and I've got to change my clothes."

Michael went out to the street with Dr. Parker and the two city newspapermen. Under his arm he was carrying the fish, folded in the newspaper. Outside, at the jail door, Michael thought that the doctor and the two newspapermen were standing a little apart from him. Then the small crowd, with their clothes all dust-soiled from the road, surged forward, and the doctor said to them, "You might as well go home, boys. It's all over."

"Where's old Steadman?" somebody demanded.

"We'll wait for the hangman," somebody else shouted.

The doctor walked away by himself. For

a while Michael stood beside the two city newspapermen, and tried to look as nonchalant as they were looking, but he lost confidence in them when he smelled whiskey. They only talked to each other. Then they mingled with the crowd, and Michael stood alone. At last he could stand there no longer looking at all those people he knew so well, so he, too, moved out and joined the crowd.

When the sheriff came out with the hangman and two of the guards, they got halfway down to one of the automobiles before someone threw an old boot. Steadman ducked into one of the cars, as the boot hit him on the shoulder, and the two guards followed him. The hangman, dismayed, stood alone on the sidewalk. Those in the car must have thought at first that the hangman was with them for the car suddenly shot forward, leaving him alone on the sidewalk. The crowd threw small rocks and sticks, hooting at him as the automobile backed up slowly toward him. One small stone hit him on the head. Blood trickled from the side of his head as he looked around helplessly at all the angry people. He had the same expression on his face, Michael thought, as he had had last night when he had seemed ashamed and had looked down steadily at the water. Only now, he looked around wildly, looking for someone to help him as the crowd kept pelting him. Farther and farther Michael backed into the crowd and all the time he felt dreadfully ashamed as though he were betraying Smitty, who last night had had such a good neighborly time with him. "It's different now, it's different," he kept thinking, as he

held the fish in the newspaper tight under his arm. Smitty started to run toward the automobile, but James Mortimer, a big fisherman, shot out his foot and tripped him and sent him sprawling on his face.

Mortimer, the big fisherman, looking for something to throw, said to Michael, "Sock him, sock him."

Michael shook his head and felt sick.

"What's the matter with you, Michael?"

"Nothing. I got nothing against him."

The big fisherman started pounding his fists up and down in the air. "He just doesn't mean anything to me at all," Michael said quickly. The fisherman, bending down, kicked a small rock loose from the road bed and heaved it at the hangman. Then he said, "What are you holding there, Michael, what's under your arm? Fish. Pitch them at him. Here, give them to me." Still in a fury, he snatched the fish, and threw them one at a time at the little man just as he was getting up from the road. The fish fell in the thick dust in front of him, sending up a little cloud. Smitty seemed to stare at the fish with his mouth hanging open, then he didn't even look at the crowd. That expression on Smitty's face as he saw the fish on the road made Michael hot with shame and he tried to get out of the crowd.

Smitty had his hands over his head, to shield his face as the crowd pelted him, yelling "Sock the little rat. Throw the runt in the lake." The sheriff pulled him into the automobile. The car shot forward in a cloud of dust.

# Carly Simon

# You're So Vain

You walked into the party like you
    were walking onto a yacht
Your hat strategically dipped below
    one eye
Your scarf it was apricot
You had one eye in the mirror as you
    watched yourself gavotte
And all the girls dreamed that they'd
    be your partner
They'd be your partner, and . . .
You're so vain, you probably think
    this song is about you
You're so vain, I'll bet you think
    this song is about you
Don't you? Don't you?

You had me several years ago when I
    was still quite naïve
Well you said that we made such a
    pretty pair
And that you would never leave
But you gave away the things you
    loved and one of them was me
I had some dreams, they were clouds
    in my coffee
Clouds in my coffee, and . . .

You're so vain, you probably think
    this song is about you
You're so vain, I'll bet you think
    this song is about you
Don't you? Don't you?

Well I hear you went up to Saratoga
    and your horse naturally won
Then you flew your Lear jet up to
    Nova Scotia
To see the total eclipse of the sun
Well you're where you should be
    all the time and when you're not
    you're with
Some underworld spy or the wife of
    a close friend
Wife of a close friend, and . . .
You're so vain, you probably think
    this song is about you
You're so vain, I'll bet you think
    this song is about you
Don't you? Don't you?

# Glen Kirkland

# Hitchhiker

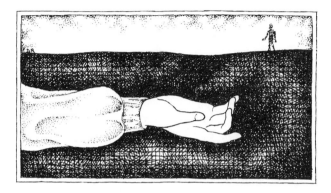

I have watched you
hitchhike
through trips of
self-destruction

becoming what is
becoming

With you
I am pensive
and remote
like a lone driver
on a northern
highway

How can I
tell you that
I do not want
you

becoming
lost in
me

Reprinted by permission of the author.

Gordon Lightfoot

# If You Could Read My Mind

If you could read my mind, love,
What a tale my thoughts could tell,
Just like an old-time movie
About a ghost from a wishing-well,
In a castle dark or a fortress strong,
With chains upon my feet.
You know that ghost is me.
And I will never be set free
As long as I'm a ghost that you can't see.

If I could read your mind, love,
What a tale your thoughts could tell,
Just like a paperback novel,
The kind the drugstores sell.
When you reach the part where the heartaches come,
The hero would be me,
But heroes often fall,
And you won't read that book again
Because the ending's just too hard to take.

I'd walk away like a movie star
Who gets burned in a three-way script.
Enter number two:
A movie queen to play the scene
Of bringing all the good things out in me.
But for now, love, let's be real.
I never thought I could act this way
And I've got to say that I just don't get it.
I don't know where we went wrong,
But the feeling's gone
And I just can't get it back.

If you could read my mind, love,
What a tale my thoughts could tell,
Just like an old-time movie
About a ghost from a wishing-well,
In a castle dark or a fortress strong,
With chains upon my feet.
But stories always end,
And if you read between the lines,
You'll know that I'm just trying to understand
The feelings that you lack.
I never thought I could feel this way
And I've got to say
That I just don't get it.
I don't know where we went wrong,
But the feeling's gone
And I just can't get it back.

# Charles M. Schulz

Louis MacKay

# The Ill-Tempered Lover

I wish my tongue were a quiver the size of a huge cask
Packed and crammed with long black venomous rankling
    darts.
I'd fling you more full of them, and joy in the task,
Than ever Sebastian was, or Caesar, with thirty-three swords
    in his heart.

I'd make a porcupine out of you, or a pin-cushion, say;
The shafts should stand so thick you'd look like a headless
    hen
Hung up by the heels, with the long bare red neck
    stretching, curving, and dripping away
From the soiled floppy ball of ruffled feathers standing on
    end.

You should bristle like those cylindrical brushes they use to
    scrub out bottles,
Not even to reach the kindly earth with the soles of your
    prickled feet.
And I would stand by and watch you wriggle and writhe,
    gurgling through the barbs in your throttle
Like a woolly caterpillar pinned on its back – man, that
    would be sweet!

Reprinted by permission of the author.

# Elizabeth Barrett Browning

# How
# Do I
# Love Thee?

How do I love thee? Let me count the ways.
I love thee to the depth and breadth and height
My soul can reach, when feeling out of sight
For the ends of Being and ideal Grace.
I love thee to the level of every day's
Most quiet need, by sun and candlelight.
I love thee freely, as men strive for Right;
I love thee purely, as they turn from Praise.
I love thee with the passion put to use
In my old griefs, and with my childhood's faith;
I love thee with a love I seemed to lose
With my lost saints, – I love thee with the breath,
Smiles, tears, of all my life! – and, if God choose,
I shall but love thee better after death.

Sidney Katz

# A Sociologist Foresees the Eclipse of Romantic Love in Marriage

"Romantic love
will
practically disappear."

The year is 1990.

Boy meets girl at a party in a Toronto apartment. He's strongly attracted to her and his interest steadily mounts. He sees a serious relationship looming, so he asks her, "What's your code number? I want to look you up."

The boy is referring to the computer-compiled profile of the young lady that is stored in a central depot, available for instant retrieval. In 1990 everyone has such a document; compiled by specialists, it records family background, health history, religious and political beliefs, philosophical convictions, leisure-time interests, and personality traits.

But the girl at the party declines to disclose her code number, leading the boy to conclude either that she isn't interested in him or that she has something to hide.

"That's the way courtship will be conducted within twenty years," says Dr. Leo Davids, thirty-three, a former orthodox rabbi and now a sociologist at York University. "Young people won't be wasting their time courting partners who are grossly incompatible."

Davids' appearance bespeaks orthodoxy. He dresses conservatively, his face is adorned with a neat black beard, and a yarmulke is perched on his head. But there's nothing traditional about his forecasts of what courtship, love, and marriage will be like in the year 1990.

"My predictions are not guesswork," explained the York sociologist in an interview. "They're scientific estimates based on trends already underway or coming very soon. Given a number of known facts, you can figure out the rest.

"Fatherhood, for example, is going to be vastly changed two decades from now."

Reprinted with permission – the *Toronto Star*.

180

Picture the office of the human relations director in an industrial plant. A young husband is explaining that he's just become a father – therefore he'll only be working part-time for the next eight or ten years. The director is not surprised. Legal provision exists that frees fathers to spend at least twenty leisure hours a week with their younger children.

"It's becoming increasingly appreciated that working fathers are responsible for more child neglect than working mothers," observed Davids. "Remedial action will be taken in the future."

Indeed, labor unions in British Columbia and New York State have already bargained for an extended paternity leave when a new child is born.

If Davids' forecasts prove to be accurate, the 1990's will be a bleak period for the writers of traditional-style songs, poems, movies, and novels.

He stated flatly, "Romantic love will practically disappear."

At present, he explained, it's perfectly acceptable to meet a stranger and form a sudden emotional attachment to that person – without logic or contemplation – and proceed to marriage. The accepted myth is that we search until we find the one-and-only perfect mate. The advent of that person is accompanied by emotional thunder and lightning.

"Young people today are rejecting this romantic myth," said Davids. "They are drawn, generally, to what they call 'beautiful people.' They don't fall in love at first sight. Rather, a gradual process of mutual discovery sometimes results in love.

"A boy meets a girl but before he commits himself deeply, he makes sure that her values and personal philosophy are akin to his. In other words, the beautiful creature is being asked to state her views.

"In the future, the only people retaining a belief in romantic love will be found among the uneducated and the poor."

If a couple should decide on marriage, there will be several forms of marriage available – all recognized by law and entered into by civil contract.

A popular type of union will be the three- to five-year, childless, trial marriage. At the end of the term, the contract comes up for discussion. The couple can decide to continue as before, opt out, or renew it on different terms.

"If the couple separates, no divorce or legal red tape is necessary," explained Davids. "The trial marriage would be a normal, perhaps minor, part of the average person's marital career."

For those who want to conduct a series of short, casual sexual affairs, no publicly registered marriage will be necessary. There will be a large number of people, in Davids' view, who will not enter any sort of marriage on any sort of terms.

Another option will be the "permanently childless" marriage. The couple have agreed in advance that there will be no offspring. If one partner changes his or her mind, then the contract can be ended or redrawn on mutually acceptable terms.

Davids predicts that perhaps seventy percent of all couples in 1990 will choose the permanently childless marriage.

He also foresees the advent of legal multiple marriages: "The extent to which polyandry (several husbands) or polygamy (several wives) is practised will depend on local conditions."

For example, many women over the age of fifty-five may be ready for polygamy. Women outlive their husbands and so there's a surplus of women in this age group who might happily settle for a half or a third of a husband.

Or, conversely, polyandry may be practised in certain regions where there are only a few women available for a large number of men. This situation prevails in several rugged outposts. Multiple marriages, explains Davids, have proven to be workable in various cultures. But he warns, "The people involved all have to be compatible with each other."

The York University sociologist predicts that the most radical changes will occur in our approaches to parenthood.

For one thing, the long-popular "parenthood is fun" myth will be abandoned. Young people will no longer accept the traditional belief that being a parent is a natural, instinctive role for everyone – something to be entered into very much in the same spirit that you embark on a new hobby, like boating or antique collecting.

"The younger generation see parenthood as a very serious business – a responsibility to be assumed only by those who are qualified and properly trained."

To upgrade the quality of parenthood, society in the future will impose a series of obstacles in the path of would-be parents.

Adults wanting to reproduce will be required to tender an application to a local "Parenthood Board" that consists of physicians, psychologists, geneticists, and social workers.

"The applicants," explained Davids, "would be subject to the same intensive investigating and interviewing that is now applied to couples who seek to adopt a child.

"We'll want to know about the husband-wife relationship, the physical and mental health of the couple, their motivation in seeking a child, and their ability to handle stress."

Once accepted, the would-be parents would be required to take an intensive parent-training course. The curriculum would embrace several topics, including human reproduction, infant care, life values, and the impact of mass media and the urban environment on children.

"And the mid-term and final oral and written exams will not be cinch tests," explained Davids. "If the student fails – too bad. Remember we also flunk out candidates for law and medicine. We can't afford to expose helpless children to adults with no talent for parenthood. Battered babies, mental illness, delinquency are the all-too-common aftermath of substandard parental care."

Davids foresees a striking change in the age at which marriage and child-bearing will take place in the future.

At present, most women get married in their early twenties and have children two or three years later. Typically, the husband is three or four years older than his wife.

"Women in the future will have their family when they're in their middle or late thirties," said Davids. "They will have used the extra years to travel, pursue interests – in general to enjoy themselves. During this period they will probably have been a partner in trial, companionate marriage."

The age difference between husbands and wives will also disappear. Traditionally, Davids explains, men have married younger women because of the patriarchal sentiment that the male is the "senior" in the home.

"But that will be a thing of the past," said Davids. Husband and wife will truly be equals in marriage – sharing alike, in all decisions. Women's Liberation is not a passing fad.

"It's the beginning of the end. Male dominance is doomed."

Charles Webb

# There Goes the Bride

*The following story is the conclusion of Charles Webb's novel* The Graduate. *At this point, Benjamin Braddock, a recent college graduate, has decided to marry Elaine Robinson, who loves him also. However, her parents disapprove of such a move and push their daughter into a hasty marriage with Carl Smith.*

J ust before dawn Benjamin landed at the San Francisco airport and hurried off the plane and into a phone booth. There was only one Carl Smith in the directory. He called but there was no answer. Then he tore the page out of the phone book and had a taxi take him to the address. The front door of the apartment building was unlocked. Benjamin pushed it open and hurried up the three flights of stairs and down a darkened hall to the door of Carl Smith's apartment. Just as he was about to knock he noticed a white envelope thumbtacked to the wood of the door next to the doorknob. He tore it off and ran back down the hall with it to a window. On the front of the envelope the name *Bob* was written. Benjamin ripped it open, pulled out a sheet of paper from inside, and read it quickly by the grey light coming in through the dirty glass of the window.

Bob,

Prepare yourself for a real jolt, old boy. Believe it or not I am getting hitched. Elaine Robinson, the girl I brought up to your party last month, has accepted my proposal and in fact insists that we tie the knot this very weekend. I cannot believe my luck and am, needless to say, in quite a daze at the moment so I know you will forgive me for cancelling out on our plans.

It was all arranged in a midnight visit from her and her father. There are many strange and bizarre circumstances surrounding the whole thing which I don't have time to go into now. Elaine is down in Santa Barbara staying with my folks and I am on my way down. We will be married in the First Presbyterian Church on Allen Street in S.B. at eleven o'clock Saturday morning. If perchance you find this note soon enough, be sure and hop it down there as I think I can promise you a pretty good show. Janie is frantically trying to dig up bridesmaids and Mother is telegramming invitations to everyone in sight. Dad is too stunned to do anything.

I will be back early in the week, bride in tow, and will see you then if not before, Hallelujah!

Carl

His airplane touched down in a small airport in the outskirts of Santa Barbara just at eleven o'clock. Benjamin was the first out of its door and down the ramp. Several minutes later his taxi pulled to a stop in front of the First Presbyterian Church on Allen Street. He jumped out and handed the driver a bill through the window.

The church was in a residential section of large houses and neat green lawns and was itself an extremely large building with a broad expanse of stained-glass windows across the front and wide concrete stairs leading up to a series of doors, all of which were closed. Benjamin squeezed between the bumpers of two limousines parked in front of the church and hurried up the stairs. He grabbed the handles of two doors and pulled. They were locked. He rushed to the next pair of handles and pulled again. They were also locked. He began banging with his fist on one of the doors, then turned around and ran down the steps. He ran to the side of the church. A stairway led up the wall of the church to a door. Benjamin hurried back along the wall, then ran two steps at a time up to the top of the stairs. He tried the door. It opened. Thick organ music poured out from inside the building. He ran down a hall to a door and pushed it open, then hurried through it and stopped.

Beneath him were the guests. They were standing. Nearly all of them were turned part way around and looking back toward the rear of the church under the balcony where he was standing. Most of the women were wearing white gloves. One was holding a handkerchief up to her eye. A man with a red face near the front of the church was turned around and was smiling broadly toward the back. Carl Smith and another boy were standing at the front of the church. Both were wearing black tuxedos with white carnations in their lapels. Benjamin saw Mrs. Robinson. She was standing in the first pew in the church and wearing a small hat on her head. He stared at her a moment, then a girl wearing a bright green dress came walking slowly under him and down the aisle of the church toward the altar. Another girl appeared, also wearing a bright green dress, then another and another. Then suddenly Elaine appeared. Benjamin rushed closer to the railing and leaned over to stare down at a piece of white lace on the top of her head. He began clenching and unclenching his hands in front of him. She was walking with her arm in her father's arm and wearing a white wedding dress whose long train followed her slowly over the thick red carpet and toward the front of the church. Benjamin began shaking his head, still staring at her and clenching and unclenching his hands. The guests turned slowly as she passed them. The girls in green dresses formed two rows at either side of the altar. Then Benjamin slammed his hands down on the railing of the balcony and yelled.

"Elaine!!!"

The organ music stopped.

He slammed his hands down again. "Elaine!!! Elaine!!! Elaine!!!"

From the altar the minister looked up quickly. The girls in green all looked up toward the back of the church. Mrs. Robinson stepped part way into the aisle, stared up at him, then took another step toward him and began shaking her head. The man with the red face near the front of the church looked up and stopped smiling.

Benjamin slammed his hands down on the wooden railing. "Elaine!!!"

Elaine had turned around and was staring up at him. Behind her Carl Smith was looking up at him with his head tilted slightly to the side. Mr. Robinson made a move toward the back of the church. Then he turned around quickly and took Elaine's hand. He pulled her up toward the front of the church and to the minister. He said something to the minister, the minister bent slightly forward, he said it again, gesturing at Carl Smith, then the minister nodded. Mr. Robinson took Carl Smith's arm and brought him over beside Elaine in front of the minister. The minister opened a small book he was holding.

"No!!!"

Benjamin turned in a circle. Then he lifted one of his legs up and put it over the railing. A woman screamed. Several guests immediately beneath him began pushing and shoving each other to get out of the way. Elaine turned around and took several steps down the aisle toward the back of the church and stared up at him, holding her hands up over part of her face. Then her father grabbed her arm and pulled her back up to the minister again.

Benjamin removed his leg from over the railing. He ran across the balcony to the door and through the door and down through a wooden hallway leading to the front part of the church. At the end of the hallway were two doors. He threw one of them open and a man wearing black clergyman's clothes looked up at him over a desk and began rising from his chair. Benjamin turned around and pushed open the other door. It opened onto a flight of wooden stairs. He ran down. There were two more doors. He grabbed the doorknob of one and pushed it open.

Mr. Robinson was waiting for him. He was standing crouched in front of Benjamin with his arms spread out beside him. Behind Mr. Robinson Elaine was standing staring at him with her hands still up beside her face. Benjamin jumped one way to get around him but Mr. Robinson moved in front of him. He jumped the other. Mr. Robinson dove in toward him and grabbed him around the waist. Benjamin twisted away but before he could reach Elaine he felt Mr. Robinson grabbing at his neck and then grabbing at the collar of his shirt and pulling him backward and ripping the shirt down his back. He spun around and slammed his fist into Mr. Robinson's face. Mr. Robinson reeled backward and crumpled into a corner.

Benjamin hurried forward. Elaine stepped toward him and he grabbed her hand. "Come on," he said. "Don't faint."

He pulled her part way back toward the door but then suddenly the man in black clergyman's clothes from upstairs stepped in through it and closed it behind him.

"Get out of my way," Benjamin said.

The man didn't move. Benjamin bent his knees slightly and was about to move toward the door when he felt an arm closing around his neck. He thrashed away. Carl Smith was standing behind him breathing heavily. His carnation had fallen off. Benjamin looked quickly back and forth from Carl Smith to the man still standing in front of the door; then he grabbed a large bronze cross from off an altar beside him and raised it up beside his ear. He rushed at Carl Smith. Carl Smith stumbled backward, then turned and fled back down to the other guests. Benjamin gripped Elaine's hand as tightly as he could and pulled her toward the door.

"Move!!!" he said. He drew the cross farther back behind his head. The man in clergyman's clothes hurried away from the door. Benjamin dropped the cross and pulled Elaine through the door and across the hallway and out another door onto a sidewalk in back of the church.

"Run!" he said. He pulled her after him. "Run, Elaine! Run!"

She tripped and fell. "Benjamin, this dress!" she said.

"Come on!" he said. He pulled her up.

They ran for several blocks. Crossing one street a car had to slam on its brakes and turn up onto the curb to avoid hitting them. Finally Benjamin saw a bus stopped half a block ahead of them loading passengers.

"There!" he said, pointing at it as he ran.

The doors of the bus closed just as they reached it. Benjamin banged against them with his free hand and they were opened. He pushed Elaine up ahead of him and carried the train of her dress in after her.

"Where does this bus go?" he said to the driver, trying to catch his breath.

The driver was staring at Elaine and didn't answer.

"Where does this bus go?!"

"Morgan Street," he said.

"All right then," Benjamin said. He pulled a handful of change out of one of his pockets and dropped it in the coin box. Then he let go of Elaine's dress and took her hand again to lead her toward the back of the bus. The driver got up out of his seat to watch them. Most of the passengers stood part way up in their seats and stared at Benjamin's torn shirt hanging down around his knees and then turned their heads to stare down at the train of Elaine's dress as it dragged slowly past over the ends of cigarettes and gum wrappers in the aisle. There was a little girl sitting by herself on the seat at the rear.

"Excuse me," Benjamin said. He helped Elaine in next to the window and sat down beside her.

Most of the passengers were standing, turned around in their seats. One old man was bending his head around someone and out into the aisle to look back at them. The driver was still standing in the front next to the coin box staring at them.

"Get this bus moving!" Benjamin said.

The driver stood where he was.

"Get it moving!" Benjamin said, beginning to rise up again from the seat. "Get this bus moving!"

The driver waited a moment, then turned around and climbed back up into his seat. He pulled a handle and the doors of the bus closed. Benjamin sat back down.

Elaine was still trying to catch her breath. She turned her face to look at him. For several moments she sat looking at him, then she reached over and took his hand.

"Benjamin?" she said.

"What?"

The bus began to move.

# Michael Novak

# The Courage to Have Children

## What strengthens the family strengthens society.

Recently a friend told me the following anecdote. At lunch in a restaurant one day he had mentioned that he and his wife intended to have a second child soon. His companion stood and reached out his hand. "Congratulations!" he said. "You are making a political statement."

Choosing to have a family used to be routine. But so many, so varied, and so aggressive are the antifamily sentiments in society that today it is an act of intelligence and courage. To love family life, to see in family life the most potent moral, intellectual, and political cell in the body politic, is to be marked today as a heretic.

The great corporations and universities, the political professions, the foundations, the publishing empires, and the film industry diminish the moral and economic importance of the family. They demand travel and frequent change of residence. Teasing the heart with glittering entertainment and gratifying the demands of ambition, they dissolve attachments and loyalties.

To insist, in the face of such forces, that marriage and family still express our highest moral ideals is to awaken hostility and opposition. For many, marriage has been a bitter disappointment. They long to be free of it and of the guilt they feel. They celebrate its demise, since each sign of weakness in the institution exonerates them of personal failure.

Urban industrial life is not designed to assist families. Expressways divide neighborhoods and parishes. Small family stores are boarded up. Social engineers plan for sewers, power lines, access roads, but not for the cultural ecology which allows families to flower and prosper. The workplace is not designed with family needs in mind; neither are working hours.

Yet, clearly, the family is the critical centre of social force. It is a seedbed of economic skills, money habits, attitudes toward work and the arts of financial independence. It is a stronger agency of educational success than the school and a stronger teacher of the religious imagination than the church. Political and social planning in a wise social order begins with the axiom: *What strengthens the family strengthens society*.

Even when poverty and disorientation strike, as over the generations they so often do, it is family strength that most defends individuals against alienation, lassitude, or despair. The world around the family is fundamentally unjust, but one unforgettable law has been learned painfully through all the oppressions, disasters, and injustices of the last thousand years: *If things go well with the family, life is worth living; when the family falters, life falls apart*.

Yet marriage is pictured these days as a form of imprisonment, oppression, boredom, and chafing hindrance. Not all these accusations are wrong; but the superstition surrounding them is. Marriage *is* an assault upon the lonely, atomic ego. Marriage *is* a threat to the solitary individual. Marriage *does* impose gruelling, humbling, baffling, and frustrating responsibilities. Yet if one supposes that precisely such things are the preconditions for all true liberation, marriage is not the enemy of moral development in adults. Quite the opposite.

In our society, of course, there is no need to become an adult. One may remain – one is exhorted daily to remain – a child forever. In such a life, the central aim is self-fulfilment. Marriage is merely an alliance, entailing as minimal an abridgment of inner privacy as one partner may allow. Children are not a welcome responsibility, for to have children

is, plainly, to cease being a child oneself. One tries instead to live as angels once were believed to live – soaring, free, unencumbered.

People say marriage is boring when they mean that it terrifies them: too many and too deep are its searing revelations, its angers, its rages, its hates, and its loves. They say of marriage that it is deadening, when what they mean is that it drives us beyond adolescent fantasies and romantic dreams. They say of children that they are brats, when what they mean is that the importance of parents with respect to the future of their children is now known with greater clarity and exactitude than ever before.

Marriage, like every other serious use of one's freedom, is an enormous risk, and one's likelihood of failure is high. No tame project, marriage. The raising of children, now that so few die in childbirth or infancy, and now that fate takes so little responsibility out of the hands of affluent and well-educated parents, brings each of us breathtaking vistas of our inadequacy. Fear of freedom – more exactly, fear of taking the consequences – adds enormously to the tide of evasion.

Being married and having children has impressed on my mind certain lessons, and most of what I am forced to learn about myself is not pleasant. The quantity of sheer impenetrable selfishness in the human breast (in *my* breast) is a never-failing source of wonderment. I do not want to be disturbed, challenged, troubled. Huge regions of myself belong only to me. Getting used to thinking of life as bicentred, even multi-centred, is a struggle of which I had no suspicion when I lived alone. Seeing myself through the unblinking eyes of an intelligent, honest spouse is humiliating. Trying to act fairly to children, each of whom is temperamentally different from myself and from each other, each of whom is at a different stage of perception and aspiration, is baffling.

Nothing is more poignant and private than one's sense of failing as a father. When my own sense of identity was that of a son, I expected great perfection from my father. Now that I am a father, I know the taste of uncertainty. To be a father rather than a son is to learn the inevitability of failure.

It would be a lie, however, to write only of the difficulties of marriage and family, and not of the beauty. Quiet pleasures and perceptions flow: the movement of new life within a woman's belly; the total dependence of life upon the generosity and wisdom of its parents; the sense that these poor muscles, nerves, and cells of one's own flesh have re-created a message to the future, carried in relays generation after generation, carried since the dim beginnings. Parents *do* forge a link in the humble chain of human beings, encircling heirs to ancestors. To hold a new child in one's hands, only ounces heavy, and to feel its helplessness, is to know responsibilities sweet and awesome, to walk within a circle of magic as primitive as humans knew in caves.

But it is not the private pleasures of family life that most need emphasis today. Those who love family life do not begrudge the price paid for adulthood. What needs elucidation is the political significance of the family. A people whose marriages and families are weak can have no solid institutions.

To marry, to have children, is to make a political statement hostile to what passes as "liberation" today. It is a statement of flesh, intelligence, and courage. It draws its strength from nature, from tradition, and from the future. For apart from millions of decisions by couples to bring forth children they will nourish, teach, and launch against the void, the human race *has* no future – no wisdom, no advance, no community, no grace. Only the emptiness of solitary space, the dance of death. It is the destiny of flesh and blood to be familial.

Gail Fox

# Lines in Contentment

*(for Milton)*

My son, whose small age
barely confirms my motherhood,
sings into my sleep
with hungry insistence
and catches me always
on the verge of forgetting
who I now am and must be:
loving, honest, possessed of my senses.
I pick him up and
he grows in my hands,
grows into each successive morning,
singing me into a semblance of identity.
He grows, and in his excessive joy,
takes me along.

Reprinted by permission of the author.

## Don Owen

# Nobody Waved Goodbye

"Your life is so mixed up, Peter, you wouldn't know what to do with it. You're a bad investment."

*Characters*

FATHER    PETER    CUSTOMER    BARBER

*Medium shot: Int. Car showroom where* FATHER *works. Day.*

PETER *stands with his arms crossed, waiting impatiently to talk to his* FATHER. FATHER *is off-stage. His voice is heard talking to a customer.*

FATHER: . . .on our popular options and accessories, so we have the change-over to the Fordomatic, automatic, the whitewall tires and the transistorized push-button radios . . .

*Long shot*: FATHER *and* CUSTOMER, *as they stand talking by a new car.*

FATHER: And I might mention here also that this little trunk – it looks little – but there's 23.7 cubic feet in it.

*Close shot*: PETER. *He is very tense.*

FATHER: It's a lot for a compact car I would say!

CUSTOMER: Yeah. Yeah, that's very nice. Yes, I stayed a little longer than I intended to.

*Medium shot, reverse angle*: FATHER *and* CUSTOMER, *with* PETER *standing in background.*

CUSTOMER: Nice to have met you. I'll call you . . .right away . . .tomorrow.

FATHER: (*enthusiastically*) Fine. We are looking forward to it.

CUSTOMER: I'm pretty sold on it. 'Bye.

FATHER: (*shakes hands with customer*) Ah-ha. Thank you, sir.

CUSTOMER: Goodbye.

FATHER: Thank you for dropping in.

PETER: Hey, Dad. (*Walks over to his father.*) Have you got a minute, Dad?

FATHER: (*somewhat annoyed*) It's a fine way to come down here to see me, for a minute.

PETER: Well it's something special.

FATHER: Well, when it's something special, at least you can put something on to come down here to see me. (*He looks at* PETER *disparagingly.*) Some clothes that...

PETER: (*interrupting him − quietly*) I'm sorry. But, really it was a last-minute thing and I had to see you. It's something special. Just a second.

FATHER: Well, I have to get a haircut.... (*firmly*) And I don't like this!

*Cut to: Int. Barber shop. Day.*

*Medium shot*: BARBER. *Camera zooms back as the* BARBER *puts cape on* PETER'S FATHER, *who sits in the chair. Continues zoom in full shot of* BARBER *and* FATHER *(backs toward camera) and* PETER *who stands facing his father.*

PETER: (*apologetically*) Dad, I'm sorry about dropping in, in the middle of a business day.

FATHER: (*more gently*) I'd like you to have some decent clothes, coming down to my place. It's stupid....

PETER: Yeah, I'm sorry about that too. But you know I got up, and I'm just going down to work this afternoon....

*Medium shot*: PETER, FATHER, *and* BARBER. PETER *stands next to the mirror, and we see, in the mirror, his* FATHER *having his hair cut, as* PETER *talks.*

PETER: Well, you know things haven't been going too well with us lately. The business with the car...and then...and now Sullivan, the probation officer.

FATHER: Yes.

PETER: (*sincerely*)...and (*sighs*) I'm sorry about that too! I know it's not great having a son who gets into trouble and has to go and see the probation officer every week and...but I don't know, you know....It isn't that I set out to do something to hurt you or anything....It's just that...that...

FATHER: (*flatly*) You did hurt me, that's all.

PETER: (*expressing himself with some difficulty*) Well...well, it's a funny time you know when you are as old as I am. And things aren't as clear as they are when you are older...you know I...I just am not sure where I'm going and what I'm going to do. Well, since it's probably just a stage, you know...it's probably just a matter of...I'm not finding a direction. I thought it would be a good idea if I...sort of... went away for a year. I just want to try something else. I want to see places and... I've been going to school for thirteen years, and I thought it would be a good idea to take a breather now. Then when I come back, if I want to start again, I can always do it. I can always get the three papers that I missed...and go to school...and go to university if I want to. But just to sort of work and be on my own for a year. Away from the city. And all I need is something...just something to start on. (*hopefully*) Can you loan me some money? Can you loan me three hundred bucks to start with?

FATHER: (*quietly*) Three hundred dollars?

PETER: I know it sounds crazy, but it's just a start....It's like a fund, you know. Three hundred bucks.

FATHER: How long are you going to be away?

PETER: A year.

FATHER: (*straightforwardly*) Look, Peter, I'm a businessman. Three hundred dollars is three hundred dollars. Now don't give me that jazz that I've got all kinds of money....

PETER: (*uncomprehendingly*) Yeah, you're a businessman, but I'm your son. It's not a business proposition. It's a loan....It's a favor....It's a gift from father to son... can't you do that?

FATHER: I wonder how many sons just go to their fathers all the time and say: "Dad I want three hundred bucks." I wish I'd been able to do it.

PETER: Well, but...you didn't have you for a father, did you?

*Medium shot*: FATHER. BARBER's *hands are seen cutting his hair. Sound of* BARBER's *scissors.*

PETER: (*bitingly*) How long does it take to earn three hundred bucks anyway? You sell one car and you make three hundred dollars commission.

FATHER: (*tellingly*) You know how much work it is to sell one car.

PETER: You were sweet-talking that guy in there pretty good. He'll probably come back tomorrow and buy the car and with that money...you can give it to me.

FATHER: (*simply*) No.

*Medium shot*: PETER, FATHER, *and* BARBER. PETER *is angry.*

PETER: (*frustrated*) You know you're a bloody poor excuse for a father. I'm telling you that much. Who needs you anyway? You talk about money and that you're.... (*vindictively*) You're just a money-grabbing old bastard, that's what you are.

*Medium close shot*: FATHER.

FATHER: (*furious*) Now listen! Don't you dare start talking to me like that! I've been listening to you for a long time now. You're not worth three hundred dollars. Your life is so mixed up, Peter, you wouldn't know what to do with it. You're a bad investment....(*He reaches over and grabs* PETER. *Then, threateningly:*) And until such time as you get your life unscrambled, don't you come anywhere near me. You get the hell out of here! Get out! Now! (*He flings* PETER *past camera toward the door.*)

*Camera zooms back to medium shot of* FATHER *and* BARBER. *In the mirror, we see* PETER *leaving the shop.*

# Morley Callaghan

# A
# Sick Call

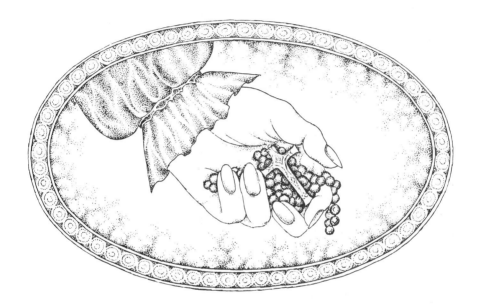

*"Pray for me, father."*

Sometimes Father Macdowell mumbled out loud and took a deep wheezy breath as he walked up and down the room and read his office. He was a huge old priest, white-headed except for a shiny baby-pink bald spot on the top of his head, and he was a bit deaf in one ear. His florid face had many fine red interlacing vein lines. For hours he had been hear-

ing confessions and he was tired, for he always had to hear more confessions than any other priest at the cathedral; young girls who were in trouble, and wild but at times repentant young men, always wanted to tell their confessions to Father Macdowell, because nothing seemed to shock or excite him, or make him really angry, and he was even tender with those who thought they were most guilty.

While he was mumbling and reading and trying to keep his glasses on his nose, the house girl knocked on the door and said,

"There's a young lady here to see, father. I think it's about a sick call."

"Did she ask for me especially?" he said in a deep but slightly cracked voice.

"Indeed she did, father. She wanted Father Macdowell and nobody else."

So he went out to the waiting room, where a girl about thirty years of age, with fine brown eyes, fine cheek-bones, and rather square shoulders, was sitting daubing her eyes with a handkerchief. She was wearing a dark coat with a grey wolf collar. "Good evening, father," she said. "My sister is sick. I wanted you to come and see her. We think she's dying."

"Be easy, child; what's the matter with her? Speak louder. I can hardly hear you."

"My sister's had pneumonia. The doctor's coming back to see her in an hour. I wanted you to anoint her, father."

"I see, I see. But she's not lost yet. I'll not give her extreme unction now. That may not be necessary. I'll go with you and hear her confession."

"Father, I ought to let you know, maybe. Her husband won't want to let you see her. He's not a Catholic, and my sister hasn't been to church in a long time."

"Oh, don't mind that. He'll let me see her," Father Macdowell said, and he left the room to put on his hat and coat.

When he returned, the girl explained that her name was Jane Stanhope, and her sister lived only a few blocks away. "We'll walk and you tell me about your sister," he said. He put his black hat square on the top of his head, and pieces of white hair stuck out awkwardly at the sides. They went to the avenue together.

The night was mild and clear. Miss Stanhope began to walk slowly, because Father Macdowell's rolling gait didn't get him along the street very quickly. He walked as if his feet hurt him, though he wore a pair of large, soft, specially constructed shapeless shoes. "Now, my child, you go ahead and tell me about your sister," he said, breathing with difficulty, yet giving the impression that nothing could have happened to the sister which would make him feel indignant.

There wasn't much to say, Miss Stanhope replied. Her sister had married John Williams two years ago, and he was a good, hard-working fellow, only he was very bigoted and hated all church people. "My family wouldn't have anything to do with Elsa after she married him, though I kept going to see her," she said. She was talking in a loud voice to Father Macdowell so that he could hear her.

"Is she happy with her husband?"

"She's been very happy, father. I must say that."

"Where is he now?"

"He was sitting beside her bed. I ran out because I thought he was going to cry. He said if I brought a priest near the place he'd break the priest's head."

"My goodness. Never mind, though. Does your sister want to see me?"

"She asked me to go and get a priest, but she doesn't want John to know she did it."

Turning into a side street, they stopped at the first apartment house, and the old priest followed Miss Stanhope up the stairs. His breath came with great difficulty. "Oh dear, I'm not getting any younger, not one day younger. It's a caution how a man's legs go back on him," he said. As Miss Stanhope rapped on the door, she looked pleadingly at the old priest, trying to ask him not to be offended at anything that might happen, but he was smiling and looking huge in the narrow hallway. He wiped his head with his handkerchief.

The door was opened by a young man in a white shirt with no collar, with a head of thick, black, wavy hair. At first he looked dazed, then his eyes got bright with excitement when he saw the priest, as though he were glad to see someone he could destroy with pent-up energy. "What do you mean, Jane?" he said. "I told you not to bring a priest around here. My wife doesn't want to see a priest."

"What's that you're saying, young man?"

"No one wants you here."

"Speak up. Don't be afraid. I'm a bit hard of hearing," Father Macdowell smiled rosily. John Williams was confused by the unexpected deafness in the priest, but he stood there, blocking the door with sullen resolution as if waiting for the priest to try to launch a curse at him.

"Speak to him, father," Miss Stanhope said, but the priest didn't seem to hear her; he was still smiling as he pushed past the young man, saying, "I'll go in and sit down, if you don't mind, son. I'm here on God's errand, but I don't mind saying I'm all out of breath from climbing those stairs."

John was dreadfully uneasy to see he had been brushed aside, and he followed the priest into the apartment and said loudly, "I don't want you here."

Father Macdowell said, "Eh, eh?" Then he smiled sadly. "Don't be angry with me, son," he said. "I'm too old to try and be fierce and threatening." Looking around, he said, "Where's your wife?" and he started to walk along the hall, looking for the bedroom.

John followed him and took hold of his arm. "There's no sense in your wasting your time talking to my wife, do you hear?" he said angrily.

Miss Stanhope called out suddenly, "Don't be rude, John."

"It's he that's being rude. You mind your business," John said.

"For the love of God let me sit down a moment with her, anyway. I'm tired," the priest said.

"What do you want to say to her? Say it to me, why don't you?"

Then they both heard someone moan softly in the adjoining room, as if the sick woman had heard them. Father Macdowell, forgetting that the young man had hold of his arm, said, "I'll go in and see her for a moment, if you don't mind," and he began to open the door.

"You're not going to be alone with her, that's all," John said, following him into the bedroom.

Lying on the bed was a white-faced, fair girl, whose skin was so delicate that her cheekbones stood out sharply. She was feverish, but her eyes rolled toward the door, and she watched them coming in. Father Macdowell took off his coat, and as he mumbled to himself he looked around the room, at the mauve-silk bed-light and the light wallpaper with the tiny birds in flight. It looked like a little girl's room. "Good evening, father," Mrs. Williams whispered. She looked scared. She didn't glance at her husband. The notion of dying had made her afraid. She loved her husband and wanted to die loving him, but she was afraid, and she looked up at the priest.

"You're going to get well, child," Father Macdowell said, smiling and patting her hand gently.

John, who was standing stiffly by the door, suddenly moved around the big priest, and he bent down over the bed and took his wife's hand and began to caress her forehead.

"Now, if you don't mind, my son, I'll hear your wife's confession," the priest said.

"No, you won't," John said abruptly. "Her people didn't want her and they left us together, and they're not going to separate us now. She's satisfied with me." He kept looking down at her face as if he could not bear to turn away.

Father Macdowell nodded his head up and down and sighed. "Poor boy," he said. "God bless you." Then he looked at Mrs. Williams, who had closed her eyes, and he saw a faint tear on her cheek. "Be sensible, my boy," he said. "You'll have to let me hear your wife's confession. Leave us alone a while."

"I'm going to stay right here," John said, and he sat down on the end of the bed. He was working himself up and staring savagely at the priest. All of a sudden he noticed the tears on his wife's cheeks, and he muttered as though bewildered, "What's the matter, Elsa? What's the matter, darling? Are we bothering you? Just open your eyes and we'll get out of the room and leave you alone till the doctor comes." Then he turned and said to the priest, "I'm not going to leave you here with her, can't you see that? Why don't you go?"

"I could revile you, my son. I could threaten you; but I ask you, for the peace of your wife's soul, leave us alone." Father Macdowell spoke with patient tenderness. He looked very big and solid and immovable as he stood by the bed. "I liked your face as soon as I saw you," he said to John. "You're a good fellow."

John still held his wife's wrist, but he rubbed one hand through his thick hair and said angrily, "You don't get the point, sir. My wife and I were always left alone, and we merely want to be left alone now. Nothing is going to separate us. She's been content with me. I'm sorry, sir; you'll have to speak to her with me here, or you'll have to go."

"No; you'll have to go for a while," the priest said patiently.

Then Mrs. Williams moved her head on the pillow and said jerkily, "Pray for me, father."

So the old priest knelt down by the bed, and with a sweet unruffled expression on his florid face he began to pray. At times his breath came with a whistling noise as though a rumbling were inside him, and at other times he sighed and was full of sorrow. He was praying that young Mrs. Williams might get better, and while he prayed he knew that her husband was more afraid of losing her to the Church than losing her to death.

All the time Father Macdowell was on his knees, with his heavy prayer book in his two hands, John kept staring at him. John couldn't understand the old priest's patience and tolerance. He wanted to quarrel with him, but he kept on watching the light from overhead shining on the one baby-pink bald spot on the smooth, white head, and at last he burst out, "You don't understand, sir! We've been very happy together. Neither you nor her people came near her when she was in good health, so why should you bother her now? I don't want anything to separate us now; neither does she. She came with me. You see you'd be separating us, don't you?" He was trying to talk like a reasonable man who had no prejudices.

Father Macdowell got up clumsily. His knees hurt him, for the floor was hard. He said to Mrs. Williams in quite a loud voice, "Did you really intend to give up everything for this young fellow?" and he bent down close to her so he could hear.

"Yes, father," she whispered.

"In Heaven's name, child, you couldn't have known what you were doing."

"We loved each other, father. We've been very happy."

"All right. Supposing you were. What now? What about all eternity, child?"

"Oh, father, I'm very sick and I'm afraid." She looked up to try to show him how scared she was, and how much she wanted him to give her peace.

He sighed and seemed distressed, and at

last he said to John, "Were you married in the Church?"

"No, we weren't. Look here, we're talking pretty loud and it upsets her."

"Ah, it's a crime that I'm hard of hearing, I know. Never mind, I'll go." Picking up his coat, he put it over his arm; then he sighed as if he were very tired, and he said, "I wonder if you'd just fetch me a glass of water. I'd thank you for it."

John hesitated, glancing at the tired old priest, who looked so pink and white and almost cherubic in his utter lack of guile.

"What's the matter?" Father Macdowell said.

John was ashamed of himself for appearing so sullen, so he said hastily, "Nothing's the matter. Just a moment. I won't be a moment." He hurried out of the room.

The old priest looked down at the floor and shook his head; and then, sighing and feeling uneasy, he bent over Mrs. Williams, with his good ear down to her, and he said, "I'll just ask you a few questions in a hurry, my child. You answer them quickly and I'll give you absolution." He made the sign of the cross over her and asked if she repented for having strayed from the Church, and if she had often been angry, and whether she had always been faithful, and if she had ever lied or stolen – all so casually and quickly as if it hadn't occurred to him that such a young woman could have serious sins. In the same breath he muttered, "Say a good act of contrition to yourself and that will be all, my dear." He had hardly taken a minute.

When John returned to the room with the glass of water in his hand, he saw the old priest making the sign of the cross. Father Macdowell went on praying without even looking up at John. When he had finished, he turned and said, "Oh, there you are. Thanks for the water. I needed it. Well, my boy, I'm sorry if I worried you."

John hardly said anything. He looked at his wife, who had closed her eyes, and he sat down on the end of the bed. He was too disappointed to speak.

Father Macdowell, who was expecting trouble, said "Don't be harsh, lad."

"I'm not harsh," he said mildly, looking up at the priest. "But you weren't quite fair. And it's as though she turned away from me at the last moment. I didn't think she needed you."

"God bless you, bless the both of you. She'll get better," Father Macdowell said. But he felt ill at ease as he put on his coat, and he couldn't look directly at John.

Going along the hall, he spoke to Miss Stanhope, who wanted to apologize for her brother-in-law's attitude. "I'm sorry if it was unpleasant for you, father," she said.

"It wasn't unpleasant," he said. "I was glad to meet John. He's a fine fellow. It's a great pity he isn't a Catholic. I don't know as I played fair with him."

As he went down the stairs, puffing and sighing, he pondered the question of whether he had played fair with the young man. But by the time he reached the street he was rejoicing amiably to think he had so successfully ministered to one who had strayed from the faith and had called out to him at the last moment. Walking along with the rolling motion as if his feet hurt him, he muttered, "Of course they were happy as they were . . . in a worldly way. I wonder if I did come between them?"

He shuffled along, feeling very tired, but he couldn't help thinking, "What beauty there was to his staunch love for her!" Then he added quickly, "But it was just a pagan beauty, of course."

As he began to wonder about the nature of this beauty, for some reason he felt inexpressibly sad.

W.D. Valgardson

# A
# Business
# Relationship

Carl had found her
ten years before
in the personal column
of the Winnipeg *Free Press.* . . .

Olga woke just before dawn. Even so, Carl was already up, huddled before the stove, his winter jacket pulled close around his shoulders. Although he was intent on splicing a broken cable, as soon as Olga entered, he looked up.

Ever since he had become sick, he had been unable to keep warm. His feet were constantly cold. Around the house, he wore two pairs of heavy wool socks inside his slippers. Lately, the growing pain had made him so restless that he was unable to sleep more than two or three hours at a time.

"I never heard you get up," she said. For the past week he had been sleeping on the chesterfield. Neither of them liked the arrangement, but, more and more, the chores had become Olga's responsibility and they both knew that if she was going to do them herself, she needed to get her sleep.

"It's all right. I had some work to do."

"I'll make some fresh coffee," she offered, bustling forward and taking the pot from the stove. "That's bitter from standing all night. Would you like some cinnamon toast?"

He shook his head. He no longer ate or drank much except coffee.

Olga busied herself with her breakfast. She was a large, rawboned woman with a pink, hearty face and big hands and feet. She had a high forehead and a round chin which, like her cheeks, was always red. Carl had found her ten years before in the personal column of the Winnipeg *Free Press*, where she was crammed into sixteen words – *Lady, 32, good character, cook, housekeeper, religious, wants to meet man of similar age. Object matrimony.*

Writing was difficult for Carl but he managed two short letters about himself. Then, the preliminaries over, he boarded the

"A Business Relationship" by W.D. Valgardson is reprinted from *God Is Not a Fish Inspector* by permission of Oberon Press.

Saturday-morning bus to Winnipeg. They met over a cup of tea in her landlady's shabby parlor. The air had been sour with stale grease and her landlady hid behind the door. Although they could not see her, her asthmatic breathing had rasped back and forth across their nervous conversation. Because Carl kept milk cows, he was only able to stay until shortly before departure time for the afternoon bus. The visit was unsatisfactory for both of them but it had to do. Before he left, they had reached an agreement. They both prided themselves on being practical and they both knew what to expect out of their relationship. They were not a couple of romantic teenagers. He was to provide her with a husband and home while she was to be a housekeeper and helpmate.

After the door closed behind him, the landlady, her back as round as a stone with age, her eyes that greedily consumed the scraps of other people's lives, came scampering in, her hands washing themselves with excitement.

"Are you taking him? He's not much to look at." She skittered to one side, then the other, in a dance of anticipation. Olga had carefully kept Carl's letters in her purse so that they would not be read while she was out.

"Yes," she answered abruptly. "I'll be leaving at the end of the month."

There were no children or relatives to explain to so they were married exactly two weeks later. She wore her good striped green dress and a large hat decorated with paper carnations. He wore his black suit, which smelled of mothballs and dust. The minister's wife and the janitor were their witnesses.

She brought her belongings with her in a suitcase and a cardboard box that had originally held twenty-four cans of Campbell's soup. While they waited for the evening bus, they ate bacon and eggs in the depot coffee-shop. At Eddyville, the bus stopped in front of the drugstore. From there it was a mile to Carl's house. She was unused to the country and as they started off down the road she had become more and more afraid.

Although he had not been a large man even then, during the last few months he seemed to be constantly shrinking. Every morning, more bone showed. His loss of flesh was like a constant erosion around the roots of trees. His black hair had stiffened to the texture of dry grass. His eyes had begun to cloud, as though a thin layer of calcium was settling over them, and his nose and mouth had grown more prominent.

While she ate, Carl worked the strands of wire together, joining the pieces so tightly that they would be inseparable. He could never stand to be idle and lately, as he had had to give up more and more of the heavy work, he had taken to repairing small pieces of equipment.

The kitchen was just big enough for the two of them but it was bright and cheerful. When she had come, Carl was living in the kitchen and bedroom. She had opened the living and dining room and had cleaned and arranged until she was satisfied. He had made no objection. She had painted the kitchen cupboards white and the walls light yellow. Around the edges of the cupboard, she had stencilled red poppies.

The house was a storey and a half with four concrete pillars holding up the porch roof. The pillars made the house feel permanent, as though it had been tightly screwed into the soil. To the south of the porch were the graves of Carl's parents. Set side by side, they were old graves, levelled, covered with grass, joined by a single headstone. Behind the headstone were purple and white lilacs. At first, she had been nervous about graves being so close but, after a while, she was glad they were there. Her own mother had disap-peared during the Nazi occupation of Poland. She and her father had fled to Can-ada, living first in Halifax, then Toronto and Winnipeg. On a trip to Toronto to buy cloth for his tailor's shop, her father had died of a heart attack. She could not afford to have his body returned so he had been buried without anyone at his funeral. After that, she lived on what she earned from making alterations for a men's store.

Now, against all habit, she lingered over her breakfast, taking a second cup of coffee that she did not want. There was a sudden squeal from below, which she immediately identified as coming from the sump-pump. In ten years, she had come to know the house and land so well that it was as though she had never lived anywhere else. Since she had married, she had never returned to Win-nipeg, not even to visit.

The yellow house sitting on the curve, a spruce tree set at each side of the entrance to the driveway, the wild grass cropped to a lawn by their dozen sheep and seven cows, made up her entire life. Once or twice a month, they went together to Eddyville for bingo on a Wednesday. Saturdays, if they needed groceries, she walked into town to the Co-op. Sundays, they went to church.

Crowded between a dirt road and the lake, their half-mile of land was only a thou-sand feet at its widest point but it was big enough for them. Behind the house, there was a narrow path that angled down to the dock where a green skiff was moored.

"It may not be much," he had said when they first stood on the road together in the growing dusk, studying the fading house and barn and listening to the cattle moving softly along the fence, "but it's *ours*." She never forgot that.

She knew nothing of the country but she learned as quickly as she could. From the moment she put her ad in the paper, she was determined to see that whoever agreed to have her would never have reason to regret his decision. Olga had added a dozen each of chickens and ducks and a brace of geese. Besides taking care of the house, she helped with the chores. She planted a vegetable garden, gradually expanding it each year until it provided them with vegetables and fruit from one year's end to the next. The year before last, they had a few dollars to spare and Carl had brought her marigolds and snapdragons to add to her border of wildflowers.

"You should let me take you to the hospital," she said quietly.

His eyes rested on her, then he went back to splicing the cable, his thin hands moving with practised familiarity.

"We've got two thousand dollars. Do you know what a day in the hospital costs? Fifty dollars, maybe seventy-five dollars. And then there's the doctor and the medicine." He said it evenly, without rancor or bitterness but with a puzzled tone as if unable to understand how lying in bed could cost so much.

She knew there was no use trying to explain. Like most people who had to work hard for everything, he was careful with his money. She did not blame him. For ten dollars' worth of fish, he had often gone out at dawn and stood all morning in a lurching, choppy sea, pulling nets from the bitter water. When he came back, he returned to farm chores that lasted into the evening.

"Everything is in your name. The two thousand dollars is in the metal foot-locker." They had been over it all before but she listened without reminding him. "The title to the farm is in the top drawer and the money to pay the taxes." He paused, thinking ahead. "The worst will be when the cows are calving. You won't get much rest. Maybe," he added, momentarily unsure of himself, "you'll not want to stay by yourself. There are a lot of heavy chores."

"I should feed the cows," she answered but she did not move.

"You can't do all the work and look after me at the same time."

She, like him, was a realist. She knew her own limits. "Yes," she agreed, "I can't do both."

"The black cow always has trouble with its calf. The vet from Eddyville will cost a few dollars but you'll need him."

"What about the boat and nets?"

As he considered the question, he sat with his mouth pursed. "Sell them. You won't use them and every season they sit, they lose value."

She knew he was right but she wished she could have kept the boat. Sometimes, in nice weather, she had gone with him to his nets and they had eaten lunch together. Rocking gently on a vast silver plain, they seemed, at those times, to be the only two people on earth.

"I'll put up a sign in the Co-op store and the skating rink."

He nodded with approval.

She knew he was worried about money and she wanted him not to worry so she said, "If I need more, I can get a job cleaning the school or the bank. It isn't hard work and it only takes a couple of hours a day."

"Good." He nodded his head in approval. "They are not the best jobs but you have to be practical."

They both liked to be practical but sometimes it was difficult. During Olga's first week on the farm, a woman had come to the door with chickens for a dollar fifty each. She had thought they were a wonderful bargain and bought four. She had roasted one for their supper but when she tried to cut it, the knife slid off the breast. Carl had managed to hack off a piece but no amount of chewing would soften it. They had eaten leftover cabbage rolls for supper. The next day, she had stewed the chicken for eight hours.

From time to time, Carl had come to ask if the chicken was cooked. His asking made her feel terrible but then she realized he was teasing and they had started to laugh. Ever since then, it had been their own private joke. Whenever she cooked chicken, he would ask if she was sure that it was ready and prod it gently with a fork before carving it.

"Maybe you'll prefer to go back to the city," he said. "It'll be lonely."

She thought about the sad, grey room that had made her desperate enough to advertise in the paper, desperate enough to expose herself to the ridicule of the world, and wished she had some way to explain what it meant to have her own pots and pans, her own kitchen, her own husband. Having always had a place of his own, he could not, she knew, ever really understand what it had been like to have to live in other people's rooms.

After a while she replied, "I'd rather be here. There are the animals and the garden. Eddyville is close enough for me to walk. If the roads are muddy, I can take the tractor."

They fell silent again, then more to himself than her, he said, "Jimmy, the Englishman, you know, the one I've told you about. He lived beside where I pull up my boat for the winter. He got sick and before it was finished, everything was gone. His wife had to live on welfare."

He had finished the cable. He pulled it tight, inspecting it to see that there were no loose strands. Satisfied, he coiled it and carefully put it in a box at his feet. She liked the fact that he was tidy and picked up after himself.

"The garden was good this year," he remarked. "You've learned to make a good garden. No one would ever know you hadn't come from the country."

She flushed with pride.

He lifted himself up from the seat of his chair with one hand and craned to look out the window. He was not a carpenter but when she had mentioned that she would like to be able to look out as she worked at the counter, he had put in a window right away.

"It's really nice to have that window," she said. "The light is good for working."

He ducked his head, the way he did when he was embarrassed. "You need to feed the cows. They can't wait any longer."

She got up and put her mug in the sink.

"I'm going," he informed her, "to the marsh for some hay." He pulled on his rubber boots then, as if it was an afterthought, and added, "I'll see if I can shoot a mallard for tomorrow's supper. If I'm a little bit late, don't worry."

"I won't," she lied. "Are you going right away?"

He took the shotgun out of the cupboard and stuffed a handful of shells into his pocket.

"Yes. It's already late." He hesitated at the door and she thought he was going to say something more but then he quickly went out. The tractor started with a roar. When she looked, he was turning out of the yard. She watched until he jolted out of sight behind a thicket of leafless poplars.

She went outside and saw that both pitchforks were leaning against the fence. The sky was clear and the air brisk. The blue dome of the sky went on forever. She thought that this was wrong, that it should have been grey and cloudy with a cold drizzle. The sun was too bright to look at directly so she stood watching it from an angle, wishing she could reach up and hold it in place with her bare hands, but then she heard the cows shuffling impatiently in the barn and, since there was no one else to do the work, she went to pitch them hay from the loft.

# The
# Road
# Ahead

# David McFadden

# The Stoker

*for Barry*

From *Intense Pleasure* by David McFadden. Reprinted
by permission of The Canadian Publishers, McClelland
and Stewart Limited, Toronto.

They try to teach you things so fast in school
& if you can't learn that fast they fail you
but when you get out in the world
you don't have to be that fast,
you find things go slower.

I'm slow. That's my problem.
I can do anything but it takes me longer, that's all.

Used to be I could only eat certain things, no bread & so on
but now I can eat anything. The way I see it
it was all nerves. Whenever I got nervous my stomach
would act up, or whenever I got scared.

I got as far as Grade 6 & now they say I'm too old, at 18,
to be in Grade 6. I have to get three years'
work experience before taking Adult Training.
They told me I'd never be able to work on an assembly line.
    They said
I didn't have the co-ordination. Can't move my hands fast enough.

I heard about this course at Mohawk College
where they teach you to move your arms faster
but when I phoned up to ask if I could take it
they said they were all filled up. They said
*Don't call us, we'll call you.*

I make $28 a week in the parking lot
& also I make $12 a week in my other job at the poolroom
filling the stoker. My mother's down in the dumps a lot lately.
She worries we don't have enough money.
She thinks I spend my money foolishly.
But with two jobs I make $40 a week,
that's not good but it's not bad.

To be a garbage man you have to have Grade 10.
Why should that be? That's just not right.
I may not have perfect co-ordination but you don't have to be able
to recite Shakespeare to throw garbage on to a truck.

I saw this advertisement for a radio announcer,
a free course. So I phoned them.
They said *Do you have a thousand dollars?*
I said I thought it was free. They said *Yes it's free*

*but you need a thousand dollars for books & equipment.*
*Besides that you need Grade 10.*

I said I only had Grade 6 & they said I'd be eligible
for the technician's course.
All I needed was $50.
My mother just said *Forget it!*

I want to get my chauffeur's licence
but no one in the family will teach me to drive.
They say I'm a risk.
I'll have to take lessons from a driving school but I can't afford it.
Anyway my mother says I'll be heartbroken
when I get my licence & find I can't afford a car.

I'm a good worker.
All the people I've worked for
say I'm reliable & competent.
Maybe I'm no good at reading and writing
but I'm good at arithmetic. And I've learned
to make change beautifully
since starting at the parking lot.

I want to have my own store some day.
I wanted to have my own grocery store
but I guess that idea went up in smoke.
*There are already too many grocery stores in town.*
*Too much competition,* everyone told me.

I really wanted to work in a grocery store.
I wanted to be a stock boy. But no,
you need Grade 10 & they said I'd run into trouble trying
to figure out what merchandise to put on what shelf.

Maybe I'll get my own bookstore.
My brother Clyde has a friend who has a bookstore in Toronto.
He gets these books – hardcovered – worth 4 or 5 dollars
that no one wants, they would just throw them in the fire.
He gets them & sells them for 50 cents. All profit!

But I want to be a salesman most of all. I can really talk.
They told me at Parkview Vocational I'd make a good salesman
so when I get my three years' work experience over & done with
I'll be taking an adult training course in salesmanship.

Frank W. Lanham, Marie M. Stewart, and Kenneth Zimmer

# The Employment Interview

"Why
have you selected
this kind
of work?"

Of all oral communication, none is more important to the business person than the employment interview; for his career may depend on its success. The employment interview is also one of the best examples of total communication, because it is in the interview that the job applicant is able to show that he possesses the communication skills required in a business job.

## PREPARING FOR THE INTERVIEW

An employment interviewer judges a job applicant on how well he knows his own qualifications, how well he knows the job, and how effectively he is able to relate the two. Careful planning and preparation for the interview are required. Study the follow-

From *Business English and Communication*, 2nd Edition/Canadian by Frank W. Lanham, Marie M. Stewart, and Kenneth Zimmer. Copyright 1977. Reproduced with permission.

ing suggestions thoroughly, for the way you apply them will be a big factor in determining your standing among the other applicants.

**Know your qualifications** Before the interview, be sure you have collected and reviewed the needed information about your personal qualifications. If you wrote a letter of application, refresh your memory about what you said. If you prepared a qualifications summary, memorize the facts you included. Have a transcript of school credits at hand and review the subjects you have taken. Have available, too, a list of class activities in which you have participated, clubs and organizations you belong to, honors you have won, and your hobbies and favorite sports. Know your school average and your attendance record. How embarrassing to be asked about your personal qualifications and not be able to remember exactly!

On his desk, the interviewer may have

written information such as your application letter or form, your qualifications summary, school records, statements from previous employers, and letters of reference. In all probability, he will ask you about these records in order to expand or clarify them. And the interviewer will note how accurately your knowledge of your qualifications tallies with the written records he has before him. Prepare yourself, therefore, by collecting and reviewing all data on your qualifications. And have the information at the tip of your tongue so that you can answer questions readily and accurately.

**Know the job**  Many employers advertise for experienced applicants to fill a position because they believe an experienced person is more likely to know the job – what is expected and how to perform. But the requirement of experience is not the handicap it may at first seem to an inexperienced applicant. The latter may be able to compensate for his lack of experience by learning all he can about the specific job for which he is applying. He is then prepared to show the interviewer that he makes up for lack of experience by a realistic understanding of what the job involves.

To learn about a job, you can talk with employees in that field. Before you leave school, you might invite a recent graduate who is now working in the company of your choice to speak to the class. If you have an opportunity to do so, take a field trip through the offices or plant. Read about the products manufactured or about the services or goods sold. Through friends, you may even be able to learn something about the people who own or operate the company and about the particular person who will interview you. The more you know about the job, the company, and the people you will meet, the better equipped you will be to relate your abilities to the specific job.

**Relate your qualifications to the job**  Well-intentioned, well-qualified applicants have been known to enter a personnel office with a general statement such as, "I want to apply for a job." This shows a lack of wisdom and an immaturity not wanted in business. The person might as well say that he has not considered what job he wishes to apply for, what qualifications are needed, or how his qualifications are related to the needs of the job. This applicant usually does not get past the receptionist. To avoid such a disappointment, you must prepare for the employment interview by considering how your abilities fit you for the specific job for which you are applying.

## CONDUCTING YOURSELF DURING THE INTERVIEW

Having prepared carefully for the interview, try to radiate self-confidence and poise as you enter the employment office. At the interview, however, you will also be judged on decorum; that is, on the propriety of your dress and conduct as well as on what you say.

**Your appearance**  Meticulous care in grooming and in the selection of clothing is of major importance to you as an applicant. The clothing you wear to the interview should be neat, clean, comfortable, and, of course, appropriate. As the interviewer talks with you, he will notice such details as nails, teeth, make-up, and hair. A full eight hours of sleep the night before will contribute to your fresh, alert appearance. On the other hand, any detail of appearance and dress that attracts unfavorable attention will count against you. The trained interviewer knows that there is a direct relation between personal habits and work habits – slovenly appearance, slovenly work; neat appearance, neat work. Make your appearance speak favorably for you at the interview.

**Your manner and manners** Good manners are often taken for granted; but any lapse or omission is noticed immediately. Practise the following five tips on common courtesy and etiquette.

1. *Be on time or a few minutes early.* Not only is it rude to be tardy for an appointment, but lack of punctuality may make the interviewer wonder whether you as an employee would be late often. The interviewer might also conclude that you do not really want the job since you are late. Rushing to arrive on time will leave you breathless, however; so start early enough to allow for unforeseen delays.

2. *Meet the unexpected with poise, tact, and humor.* If the interviewer is not ready to see you, take a seat and occupy yourself while you're waiting. Imagine the childish impression a person makes who says, "But Mr. White told me that he would see me at ten o'clock."

3. *Follow the lead of the interviewer.* Remember, you are his guest. Shake hands if he offers to do so, and grasp his hand firmly. A limp handshake indicates weakness. Wait for an invitation before seating yourself. It is the host's privilege to seat you where and when he wishes. You are being a good guest if you follow the interviewer's lead.

4. *Exhibit tact and graciousness in your conversation.* Listen carefully. Don't interrupt, even if the interviewer is long-winded and you think of something you wish to tell him right away. Follow his conversation leads and show him that you understand the implications of what he says. Don't bore him with long, overly detailed answers; but do give him more than a meek "Yes" or "No" in answer to his questions. Of course you would not contradict him or imply that you think he is wrong; this is rude under any circumstances.

5. *Show appreciation for the interviewer's time and interest.* At the close of the interview, remember to thank the interviewer, just as you would thank your host when leaving his home. Don't let the excitement and tension of the interview make you forget this courtesy. Failing to show appreciation spoils an otherwise effective interview.

**Your speech and conversation** Speech principles you have studied will aid you in demonstrating your oral communication. Have you worked to improve your voice? How are your enunciation, vocabulary, and pronunciation? Do you still say "yeah" when you mean "yes"? If you have worked hard and applied all you have learned, you can forget how your voice and speech sound; they will do you credit. You can concentrate on what you say.

Did you know that what you say reflects your attitudes and tells what kind of person you are? During the interview, for example, if you betray that you are overly interested in salary, your lunch hour, vacation, sick leave, or short working hours, you may reveal that you are more interested in loafing than in working. And interviewers have a responsibility to employ people who want to work!

**Typical interview questions** Understanding the intent of the interviewer's questions will help you answer more intelligently. Here are some typical interview questions, with the reasons behind them and suggestions as to what you might say in reply.

1. *Why have you selected this kind of work?* The interviewer wishes to know how interested you are in the work and what your goals are. An answer like "Oh, I just need a job" shows lack of purpose. Isn't the following a better answer? "I've wanted to be a secretary ever since I started school. That was my reason for studying stenography. I believe I'll like this type of job, too." This

person knows what she wants from a job; she has interest; and she has a purpose.

2. *If you had your choice of job and company, what would you most like to be doing and where?* Watch your answer to this question! The interviewer is trying to gauge just how satisfied you will be working in this job and in this company. The best answer, if you can truthfully say so, is: "Mr. Shaw, the job I want is the one for which I am now applying. The company? Yours. Before too long, I hope to have proved myself and to have been promoted to greater responsibility."

3. *What are your hobbies?* The interviewer is not interested in swapping information about his stamp collection. He wants to find out whether you have broad interests, for a person who has few outside interests is likely to become listless about himself and about his job. Be ready to list briefly your major interests in hobbies and sports.

4. *In what extra-curricular activities have you participated?* To what clubs do you belong? What offices have you held? What honors have you received? These and similar questions are asked to determine the scope of your interest in people – whether you are able to work with people and whether you have leadership qualities. These are the characteristics of a well-rounded, well-adjusted individual. In preparing for the interview, review your extra-curricular activities so that you can give the facts without hesitation.

5. *Would you be willing to work overtime?* Employers like to see a willingness, even an eagerness, to perform well in a job. Overtime may be required seldom; but if it is, employers want to have people who will accept this responsibility. You would be entering a job with the wrong attitude if you were not willing to work overtime when necessary.

# Jim Unger

# Herman

"The man we're looking for
will be dynamic and aggressive."

# Morgan D. Parmenter

# Your First Job

Remember,
when starting
your first job,
that you are
a beginner who
has a great deal
to learn.

The first day, week, perhaps month, at any new job – particularly your first full-time one – can be exciting, but it may also be confusing and a little frightening. In common with most beginners you may suffer for a while from "new-job jitters." This affliction may, in fact, develop some days before you start your first job. The symptoms are acute concern as to whether you will do well, what the boss will think of you, and how things will work out.

There is nothing abnormal in feeling anxious about your first full-time job. After all, it represents your entry into the earn-a-living work-world. First impressions do count and the impression you make during early days on your first job may very well have quite a bit to do with your future progress. Becoming overly concerned, however, tends to defeat your chances of getting off to a good start. It may be a good idea, therefore,

to think calmly and well ahead of time about that first job situation – what you should expect, what you should know. You should also think about do's and don'ts of behavior which will, if kept in mind, make for a happier, more rewarding initiation period.

One of the first things to realize is that you have, as a result of an interview or other contact, been hired; you have been invited as it were to join the staff; to become a member of a work team. Employers are usually pretty able judges of applicants. Being hired means, then, that an employer believes you have certain knowledge and skills which will prove helpful to him. The fact that your employer-to-be does believe this should, in itself, tend to bolster your confidence in yourself.

The next thing, and here much can be done in advance of the job-starting date, is to consider carefully where you are inclined to be weak in matters related to doing well whatever may be required of you in a first-job setting. At first blush such consideration may seem impossible until you know very definitely the nature of the work to be done in your first job. We are thinking here, however, not so much about details as they relate to a specific job with a specific employer, but about matters which apply generally in the case of most first-job situations – matters such as understanding requirements and conditions which apply to the job world generally, knowing how to work with and get along well with others, having desirable attitudes toward work, being personally efficient, and so on. Such preliminary consideration may help you to develop a self-improvement list of things to do something about now and also a special "Watch It!" list of do's and don'ts to keep in mind as you settle in at your first job.

It may prove helpful when you are preparing these lists to consider a number of factors which others have found important in affecting, for better or worse, their chances for maximum success on a first job. Where certain of these factors seem especially significant in your case, include them on your lists. Awareness of the following matters and determination to take them into account now and later on the job should help you very definitely to cut down on first-job jitters and should help you to perform in such a way as to ensure first-job success.

1. *Remember, when starting your first job, that you are a beginner who has a great deal to learn.* Do not let the fact that you were, perhaps, very able at school, or that you know or are related to someone of considerable importance in the organization, go to your head. Keep quiet about such matters. Your attitude, as a novice, should be one of humility.

2. *Welcome information, suggestions, and advice from fellow workers.* Most of those at work in the same office, factory, or other organization are inclined to be friendly and willing to help the newcomer to settle in. Be careful, however, about imposing and taking too much of someone's time to assist you with things you can discover for yourself. Be cautious, too, about following suggestions or taking the advice of the occasional worker who may have some gripe about the company and who may try to steer you in the wrong direction.

3. *Try to find out, as soon as possible, as much as you can about the establishment where you are employed.* Become familiar with the layout of the building, with what you are supposed to do in your job, with rules and regulations as these relate to hours of work, car parking, coffee breaks, locker allotment, vacation periods, sick leave, and salary or wage payment dates. Determine, too, approved and disapproved customs with regard to smoking, dress, and so on. Get to know the persons closely associated with you and find out about lines of authority. Newcomers do have difficulty sometimes in becoming properly aware of important matters such as those set forth above. Many modern industrial organizations, realizing that this is the case and realizing, too, that the worker who settles in quickly and happily is usually a more productive employee, have set up what are called orientation programs aimed at assisting the newcomer along the lines outlined above. Some of these organizations provide for each new employee a handbook of information. Then, too, at some plants the first two or three days are given over entirely, before the newcomer starts work, to showing him around and making him familiar with the organization and what is to be done. At still others a long-time, able employee is appointed as "sponsor" to a newcomer for the first two or three months. In the case of quite a few organizations, however, very little is done in organized fashion along orientation lines. Brief instruction is provided on how to handle tasks related to the immediate job and then the beginner is left pretty much on his own. The newcomer is expected, nevertheless, to be productively and constantly busy. Under such circumstances it will be necessary to take the initiative in checking with others and asking questions. If your first job is with the latter type of organization, do not be afraid to reveal ignorance. It is much better to do this and to find out than to proceed, make serious mistakes, and perhaps be considered lacking in good

214

judgment because of failure to investigate before going ahead.

**4.** *No matter what your beginning job may be, give to it your full attention and very best effort.* The chances are that your first job will be one which involves a considerable amount of routine work. It may seem rather dull and not very challenging. As has been pointed out by various employers, however, the real and frequently unrecognized challenge of such a job may be to prove that you can take on and handle a given task, even a routine one, in responsible fashion.

**5.** *Use tact and courtesy in all your dealings with fellow workers.* This is, of course, a good idea in all situations. It may be particularly important as a "do" during early days on a first job. Be unassuming, cheerful, willing to co-operate, and interested in others. *Do not* lose your temper, play practical jokes, be overly critical, flatter, or try too hard to be popular. Give credit where credit is due. Do not make excuses or try to cover up or shift the blame to someone else if you make a mistake.

**6.** *Accept, within reason, whatever tasks you are asked to take on and do not expect more challenging tasks and rapid advancement too soon.* The New York State Employment Service tells of Dave, a seventeen-year-old hired as an office boy, who was told to put catalogues in envelopes ready for mailing. After one month's employment the boy asked for a raise, which was refused. He wrote a letter of resignation ending with the following paragraph:

"I feel that the pay is not adequate for the amount of work expected of me. And I am inclined to think the position does not fall in the realm of an office boy's chores. It would have been entirely unnecessary for me to leave had the company adhered to my principles of an office boy's duties."

Steer clear of behavior bordering on this. It may wreck your success chances for some time.

**7.** *No matter how you really feel, try to appear interested, enthusiastic, optimistic, and energetic.* Certainly you will help to create a favorable image in the minds of those who employ you. Just one word of caution, however: don't overdo it, particularly if this is, to some extent, not entirely natural in your case.

**8.** *Look to and welcome opportunities to learn about the establishment you work for:* its history, the items it manufactures and sells, the services it offers, its various divisions, its general organization.

**9.** *Accept cheerfully orders, supervision, and criticism.* Profit from the latter, where it is justified, by trying to improve your performance.

All of the items above are important to success in any job setting. Many of them are particularly important, however, in first-job situations.

# Dolly Parton

# 9 to 5

Tumble out of bed and stumble to the
  kitchen
Pour myself a cup of ambition
Yawn and stretch and try to come to life
Jump in the shower and the blood starts
  pumping
Out on the street the traffic starts jumping
With folks like me on the job from nine to five

Working nine to five
What a way to make a living
Barely getting by
It's all taking and no giving
They just use your mind
And they never give you credit
It's enough to drive you crazy if you let it

Nine to five
For service and devotion
You would think that I
Would deserve a fair promotion
Want to move ahead
But the boss don't seem to let me
I swear sometimes that man is out to get me

They let you dream just to watch them
  shatter
You're just a step on the boss man's ladder
But you got dreams he'll never take away

In the same boat with a lot of your friends
Waiting for the day your ship will come in
Then the tide's going to turn
And it's all going to roll your way

Working nine to five
What a way to make a living
Barely getting by
It's all taking and no giving
They just use your mind
And you never get the credit
It's enough to drive you crazy if you let it

Nine to five, yeah
They got you where they want you
There's a better life
And you think about it don't you
It's a rich man's game
No matter what they call it
And you spend your life
Putting money in his wallet

Working nine to five
What a way to make a living
Barely getting by
It's all taking and no giving
They just use your mind
And they never give you credit
It's enough to drive you crazy if you let it

Hugh Garner

# The Moose and the Sparrow

"It's no longer a case
of practical jokes;
he wants to kill me!"

From the very beginning Moose Maddon picked on him. The kid was bait for all of Maddon's cruel practical jokes around the camp. He was sent back to the toolhouse for left-handed saws, and down to the office to ask the pay cheater if the day's mail was in, though the rest of us knew it was only flown out every week.

The kid's name was Cecil, and Maddon used to mouth it with a simpering mockery, as if it pointed to the kid being something less than a man. I must admit though that the name fitted him, for Cecil was the least likely lumberjack I've seen in over twenty-five years in lumber camps. Though we knew he was intelligent enough, and a man too, if smaller than most of us, we all kidded him, in the good-natured way a bunkhouse gang will. Maddon however always lisped the kid's name as if it belonged to a woman.

Moose Maddon was as different from Cecil as it is possible for two human beings to be and still stay within the species. He was a big moose of a man, even for a lumber stiff, with a round, flat, unshaven face that looked down angrily and dourly at the world. Cecil on the other hand was hardly taller than an axe-handle, and almost as thin. He was about nineteen years old, with the looks of an inquisitive sparrow behind his thick horn-rimmed glasses. He had been sent out to the camp for the summer months by a distant relative who had a connection with the head office down in Vancouver.

That summer we were cutting big stuff in an almost inaccessible stand of Douglas fir about fifty miles out of Nanaimo. The logs were catted five miles down to the river where they were bunked waiting for the drive. Cecil had signed on as a whistle punk, but after a few days of snarling the operation

with wrong signals at the wrong time and threatening to hang the rigging-slingers in their own chokers, he was transferred to Maddon's gang as a general handyman. Besides going on all the ridiculous and fruitless errands for Moose, he carried the noon grub to the gangs from the panel truck that brought it out from camp, made the tea, and took the saws and axes in to old Bobbins, the squint eye, to be sharpened.

For the first two weeks after he arrived, the jokes were the usual ones practised on a greenhorn, but when they seemed to be having little or no effect on his bumbling habits and even temper Moose devised more cruel and intricate ones. One night Moose and a cohort of his called Lefevre carried the sleeping Cecil, mattress and all, down to the river and threw him in. The kid almost drowned, but when he had crawled up on shore and regained his breath he merely smiled at his tormentors and ran back to the bunkhouse, where he sat shivering in a blanket on the springs of his bunk till the sun came up.

Another time Moose painted a wide mustache with tar on Cecil's face while he slept. It took him nearly a week to get it all off, and his upper lip was red and sore-looking for longer than that.

Nearly all of us joined in the jokes on Cecil at first, putting a young raccoon in his bunk, kicking over his tea water, hiding his clothes or tying them in knots, all the usual things. It wasn't long though until the other men noticed that Moose Maddon's jokes seemed to have a grim purpose. You could almost say he was carrying out a personal vendetta against the kid for refusing to knuckle under or cry "Uncle." From then on everybody but Moose let the kid alone.

One evening as a few of us sat outside the bunkhouse shooting the guff, Moose said, "Hey, Cecil dear, what do you do over on the mainland?"

"Go to school," Cecil answered.

Moose guffawed. "Go to school? At your age?"

Cecil just grinned.

"What school d'ya go to, Cecil? Kindergarten?" Moose asked him, guffawing some more.

"No."

"You afraid to tell us?"

"No."

"Well, what school d'ya go to?"

"U.B.C."

"What's that, a hairdressin' school?"

"No, the university."

"University! You!"

Moose, who was probably a Grade Four dropout himself, was flabbergasted. I'm sure that up until that minute he'd been living in awe of anybody with a college education.

"What you takin' up?" he asked, his face angry and serious now.

"Just an arts course," Cecil said.

"You mean paintin' pictures an' things?"

"No, not quite," the kid answered.

For once Moose had nothing further to say.

From then on things became pretty serious as far as Moose and Cecil were concerned. On at least two occasions the other men on the gang had to prevent Moose from beating the boy up, and old Bobbins even went so far as to ask Mr. Semple, the walking boss, to transfer the youngster to another gang. Since learning that Cecil was a college boy, Moose gave him no peace at all, making him do jobs that would have taxed the strength of any man in the camp, and cursing him out when he was unable to do them, or do them fast enough.

The kid may not have been an artist, as Moose had thought, but he could make beautiful things out of wire. Late in the evenings he would sit on his bunk and fashion belt-buckles, rings, and tie-clips from a spool of fine copper wire he'd found in the tool shed. He made things for several of the men, always refusing payment for them. He used to say it gave him something to do, since he couldn't afford to join in the poker games.

One evening late in the summer as I was walking along the river having an after-supper pipe, I stumbled upon Cecil curled up on a narrow sandy beach. His head was buried in his arms and his shoulders were heaving with sobs. I wanted to turn around without letting him know he'd been seen, but he looked so lonely crying there by himself that I walked over and tapped him on the shoulder.

He jumped as if I'd prodded him with a peavey, and swung around, his eyes nearly popping from his head with fright. The six weeks he'd spent working under Moose Maddon hadn't done his nerves any good.

"It's all right, kid," I said.

"Oh! Oh, it's you, Mr. Anderson!"

He was the only person in camp who ever called me anything but "Pop."

"I don't mean to butt in," I said. "I was just walking along here, and couldn't help seeing you. Are you in trouble?"

He wiped his eyes on his sleeve before answering me. Then he turned and stared out across the river.

"This is the first time I broke down," he said, wiping his glasses.

"Is it Moose?"

"Yes."

"What's he done to you now?"

"Nothing more than he's been doing to me all along. At first I took it...you know that, Mr. Anderson, don't you?"

I nodded.

"I thought that after I was out here a couple of weeks it would stop," he said. "I expected the jokes that were played on me at first. After all I was pretty green when I arrived here. When they got to know me the other men stopped, but not that...that Moose."

He seemed to have a hard time mouthing the other's name.

"When are you going back to school?" I asked him.

"In another couple of weeks."

"Do you think you can stand it until then?"

"I need all the money I can make, but it's going to be tough."

I sat down on the sand beside him and asked him to tell me about himself. For the next ten or fifteen minutes he poured out the story of his life; he was one of those kids who are kicked around from birth. His mother and father had split up while he was still a baby, and he'd been brought up in a series of foster homes. He'd been smart enough, though, to graduate from high school at seventeen. By a miracle of hard work and self-denial he'd managed to put himself through the first year of university, and his ambition was to continue on to law school. The money he earned from his summer work here at the camp was to go toward his next year's tuition.

When he finished we sat in silence for a while. Then he asked, "Tell me, Mr. Anderson, why does Maddon pick on me like he does?"

I thought about his question for a long time before answering it. Finally I said, "I guess that deep down Moose knows you are smarter than he is in a lot of ways. I guess he's – well, I guess you might say he's jealous of you."

"No matter what I do, or how hard I try to please him, it's no good."

"It never is," I said.

"How do you mean?"

I had to think even longer this time. "There are some men, like Moose Maddon, who are so twisted inside that they want to take it out on the world. They feel that most other men have had better breaks than they've had, and it rankles inside them. They try to get rid of this feeling by working it out on somebody who's even weaker than they are. Once they pick on you there's no way of stopping them short of getting out of their way or beating it out of their hide."

Cecil gave me a wry grin. "I'd never be able to beat it out of the...the Moose's hide."

"Then try to keep out of his way."

"I can't for another two weeks," he said. "I'm afraid that before then he'll have really hurt me."

I laughed to reassure him, but I was afraid of the same thing myself. I knew that Moose was capable of going to almost any lengths to prevent Cecil leaving the camp without knuckling under at least once; his urge seemed to me to be almost insane. I decided to talk to George Semple myself in the morning, and have the boy flown out on the next plane.

"I don't think Moose would go as far as to really hurt you," I told him.

"Yes he would! He would, Mr. Anderson, I know it! I've seen the way he's changed. All he thinks about any more are ways to make me crawl. It's no longer a case of practical jokes; he wants to kill me!"

My reassuring laugh stuck in my throat this time. "In another two weeks, son, you'll be back in Vancouver, and all this will seem like a bad dream."

"He'll make sure I leave here crippled," Cecil said.

We walked back to the camp together, and I managed to calm him down some.

The next day I spoke to Semple, the walking boss, and convinced him we should get the boy out of there. There was never any thought of getting rid of Moose, of course. Saw bosses were worth their weight in gold, and the top brass were calling for more and more production all the time. Whatever else Moose was, he was the best production foreman in the camp. When Semple spoke to Cecil, however, the kid refused to leave. He said he'd made up his mind to stick it out until his time was up.

Though my gang was working on a different side than Maddon's, I tried to keep my eye on the boy from then on. For a week things went on pretty much as usual, then one suppertime Cecil came into the dining hall without his glasses. Somebody asked him what had happened, and he said there'd been an accident, and that Moose had stepped on them. We all knew how much of an accident it had been: luckily the kid had an old spare pair in his kit. Few of his gang had a good word for Moose any more, which only seemed to make him more determined to take his spite out on the kid.

That evening I watched Cecil fashioning a signet ring for one of the men out of wire and a piece of quartz the man had found. The way he braided the thin wire and shaped it around a length of thin sapling was an interesting thing to see. Moose was watching him too, but pretending not to. You could see he hated the idea of Cecil getting along so well with the other men.

"I was going to ask you to make me a new watch strap before you left," I said to Cecil. "But it looks like you're running out of wire."

The kid looked up. "I still have about twenty-five feet of it left," he said. "That'll be enough for what I have in mind. Don't worry, Mr. Anderson, I'll make you the watch strap before I leave."

The next afternoon there was quite a commotion over where Maddon's gang were cutting, but I had to wait until the whistle blew to find out what had happened. Cecil sat down to supper with his right hand heavily bandaged.

"What happened?" I asked one of Maddon's men.

"Moose burned the kid's hand," he told me. "He heated the end of a saw blade in the tea fire, and then called the kid to take it to the squint eye to be sharpened. He handed the hot end to Cecil, and it burned his hand pretty bad."

"But – didn't any of you...?"

"None of us was around at the time. When we found out, big Chief went after Moose with a cant hook, but the rest of us held him back. He would have killed Moose. If Maddon doesn't leave the kid alone, one of us is going to have to cripple him for sure."

Moose had been lucky that The Chief, a giant Indian called Danny Corbett, hadn't caught him. I made up my mind to have Cecil flown out in the morning without fail, no matter how much he protested.

That evening the kid turned in early, and we made sure there was always one of us in the bunkhouse to keep him from being bothered by anybody. He refused to talk about the hand-burning incident at all, but turned his head to the wall when anybody tried to question him about it. Moose left shortly after supper to drink and play poker in Camp Three, about a mile away through the woods.

I woke up during the night to hear a man laughing near the edge of the camp, and Maddon's name being called. I figured it was Moose and Lefevre coming home drunk from Camp Three, where the bull cook bootlegged homebrew.

When I got up in the morning, Cecil was already awake and dressed, sitting on the edge of his bunk plaiting a long length of his copper wire, using his good hand and the ends of the fingers of the one that was burned.

"What are you doing up so early?" I asked him.

"I went to bed right after chow last night, so I couldn't sleep once it got light." He pointed to the plaited wire. "This is going to be your watch strap."

"But you didn't need to make it now, Cecil," I said. "Not with your hand bandaged and everything."

"It's all right, Mr. Anderson," he assured me. "I can manage it okay, and I want to get it done as soon as I can."

Just as the whistle blew after breakfast one of the jacks from Camp Three came running into the clearing shouting that Moose Maddon's body was lying at the bottom of a deep, narrow ravine outside the camp. This ravine was crossed by means of a fallen log, and Moose must have lost his footing on it coming home drunk during the night. There was a free fall of more than forty feet down to a rocky stream bed.

None of us were exactly broken-hearted about Moose kicking off that way, but the unexpectedness of it shocked us. We all ran to the spot, and the boys rigged a sling from draglines and hauled the body to the top of the ravine. I asked Lefevre if he'd been with Moose the night before, but he told me he hadn't gone over to Camp Three. Later in the day the district coroner flew out from Campbell River or somewhere, and after inspecting the log bridge made us rig a handline along it. He made out a certificate of accidental death.

When they flew the body out, Cecil stood with the rest of us on the river bank, watching the plane take off. If I'd been in his place I'd probably have been cheering, but he showed no emotion at all, not relief, happiness, or anything else.

He worked on my watch strap that evening, and finished it the next day, fastening it to my watch and attaching my old buckle to it. It looked like a real professional job, but when I tried to pay him for it he waved the money aside.

It was another week before Cecil packed his things to leave. His hand had begun to heal up nicely, and he was already beginning to lose the nervous twitches he'd had while Moose was living. When he was rowed out to the company plane, all the boys from his bunkhouse were on the river bank to see him go. The last we saw of Cecil was his little sparrow smile, and his hand waving to us from the window.

One day in the fall I went out to the ravine to see how the handline was making it. It still shocked me to think that Maddon, who had been as sure-footed as a chipmunk, and our best man in a log-rolling contest, had fallen to his death the way he had. Only then did I notice something nobody had looked for before. In the bark of the trunks of two small trees that faced each other diagonally across the fallen log were burn marks that could have been made by wire loops. A length of thin wire rigged from one to the other would have crossed the makeshift footbridge just high enough to catch a running man on the shin, and throw him into the ravine. Maddon could have been running across the log that night, if he'd been goaded by the laughter and taunts of somebody waiting at the other end. I remembered the sound of laughter and the shouting of Maddon's name.

I'm not saying that's what happened, you understand, and for all I know nobody was wandering around outside the bunkhouses on the night of Maddon's death, not Cecil or anybody else. Still, it gives me a queer feeling sometimes, even yet, to look down at my wrist. For all I know I may be the only man in the world wearing the evidence of a murder as a wristwatch strap.

# Alden Nowlan

# Warren Pryor

When every pencil meant a sacrifice
his parents boarded him at school in town,
slaving to free him from the stony fields,
the meagre acreage that bore them down.

They blushed with pride when, at his graduation,
they watched him picking up the slender scroll,
his passport from the years of brutal toil
and lonely patience in a barren hole.

When he went in the Bank their cups ran over.
They marvelled how he wore a milk-white shirt
work days and jeans on Sundays. He was saved
from their thistle-strewn farm and its red dirt.

And he said nothing. Hard and serious
like a young bear inside his teller's cage,
his axe-hewn hands upon the paper bills
aching with empty strength and throttled rage.

Reprinted by permission of the author.

# Robert Frost

# The Road
# Not
# Taken

Two roads diverged in a yellow wood,
And sorry I could not travel both
And be one traveller, long I stood
And looked down one as far as I could
To where it bent in the undergrowth;

Then took the other, as just as fair,
And having perhaps the better claim,
Because it was grassy and wanted wear;
Though as for that the passing there
Had worn them really about the same,

And both that morning equally lay
In leaves no step had trodden black.
Oh, I kept the first for another day!
Yet knowing how way leads on to way,
I doubted if I should ever come back.

I shall be telling this with a sigh
Somewhere ages and ages hence:
Two roads diverged in a wood, and I –
I took the one less travelled by,
And that has made all the difference.

# W. Somerset Maugham

# The Verger

He wore it with complacence, for it was the dignified symbol of his office, and without it . . . he had the disconcerting sensation of being somewhat insufficiently clad.

There had been a christening that afternoon at St. Peter's, Neville Square, and Albert Edward Foreman still wore his verger's gown. He kept his new one, its folds as full and stiff as though it were made not of alpaca but of perennial bronze, for funerals and weddings (St. Peter's, Neville Square, was a church much favored by the fashionable for these ceremonies), and now he wore only his second-best. He wore it with complacence, for it was the dignified symbol of his office, and without it (when he took it off to go home) he had the disconcerting sensation of being somewhat insufficiently clad. He took pains with it; he pressed it and ironed it himself. During the sixteen years he had been verger of this church he had had a succession of such gowns, but he had never been able to throw them away when they were worn out, and the complete series, neatly wrapped up in brown paper, lay in the bottom drawers of the wardrobe in his bedroom.

The verger busied himself quietly, replacing the painted wooden cover on the marble font, taking away a chair that had been brought for an infirm old lady, and waited for the vicar to have finished in the vestry so that he could tidy up in there and go home. Presently he saw him walk across the chancel, genuflect in front of the high altar, and come down the aisle; but he still wore his cassock.

"What's he 'anging about for?" the verger said to himself. "Don't 'e know I want my tea?"

The vicar had been but recently appointed, a red-faced, energetic man in the early forties, and Albert Edward still regretted his predecessor, a clergyman of the old school who preached leisurely sermons in a silvery voice and dined out a great deal

Reprinted by permission of The Estate of W. Somerset Maugham and William Heinemann Ltd.

with his more aristocratic parishioners. He liked things in church to be just so, but he never fussed; he was not like this new man who wanted to have his finger in every pie. But Albert Edward was tolerant. St. Peter's was in a very good neighborhood and the parishioners were a very nice class of people. The new vicar had come from the East End and he couldn't be expected to fall in all at once with the discreet ways of his fashionable congregation.

"All this 'ustle," said Albert Edward. "But give 'im time, he'll learn."

When the vicar had walked down the aisle so far that he could address the verger without raising his voice more than was becoming in a place of worship he stopped.

"Foreman, will you come into the vestry for a minute. I have something to say to you."

"Very good, sir."

The vicar waited for him to come up and they walked up the church together.

"A very nice christening, I thought, sir. Funny 'ow the baby stopped cryin' the moment you took him."

"I've noticed they very often do," said the vicar, with a little smile. "After all I've had a good deal of practice with them."

It was a source of subdued pride to him that he could nearly always quiet a whimpering infant by the manner in which he held it and he was not unconscious of the amused admiration with which mothers and nurses watched him settle the baby in the crook of his surpliced arm. The verger knew that it pleased him to be complimented on his talent.

The vicar preceded Albert Edward into the vestry. Albert Edward was a trifle surprised to find the two churchwardens there. He had not seen them come in. They gave him pleasant nods.

"Good afternoon, my lord. Good afternoon, sir," he said to one after the other.

They were elderly men, both of them, and they had been churchwardens almost as long as Albert Edward had been verger. They were sitting now at a handsome refectory table that the old vicar had brought many years before from Italy and the vicar sat down in the vacant chair between them. Albert Edward faced them, the table between him and them, and wondered with slight uneasiness what was the matter. He remembered still the occasion on which the organist had got into trouble and the bother they had all had to hush things up. In a church like St. Peter's, Neville Square, they couldn't afford a scandal. On the vicar's red face was a look of resolute benignity, but the others bore an expression that was slightly troubled.

"He's been naggin' them, he 'as," said the verger to himself. "He's jockeyed them into doin' something, but they don't 'alf like it. That's what it is, you mark my words."

But his thoughts did not appear on Albert Edward's clean-cut and distinguished features. He stood in a respectful but not obsequious attitude. He had been in service before he was appointed to his ecclesiastical office, but only in very good houses, and his deportment was irreproachable. Starting as a page-boy in the household of a merchant-prince, he had risen by due degrees from the position of fourth to first footman; for a year he had been single-handed butler to a widowed peeress and, till the vacancy occurred at St. Peter's, butler with two men under him in the house of a retired ambassador. He was tall, spare, grave, and dignified. He looked, if not like a duke, at least like an actor of the old school who specialized in dukes' parts. He had tact, firmness, and self-assurance. His character was unimpeachable.

The vicar began briskly.

"Foreman, we've got something rather

226

unpleasant to say to you. You've been here a great many years and I think his lordship and the general agree with me that you've fulfilled the duties of your office to the satisfaction of everybody concerned."

The two churchwardens nodded.

"But a most extraordinary circumstance came to my knowledge the other day and I felt it my duty to impart it to the churchwardens. I discovered to my astonishment that you could neither read nor write."

The verger's face betrayed no sign of embarrassment.

"The last vicar knew that, sir," he replied. "He said it didn't make no difference. He always said there was a great deal too much education in the world for 'is taste."

"It's the most amazing thing I ever heard," cried the general. "Do you mean to say that you've been verger of this church for sixteen years and never learned to read or write?"

"I went into service when I was twelve, sir. The cook in the first place tried to teach me once, but I didn't seem to 'ave the knack for it, and then what with one thing and another I never seemed to 'ave the time. I've never really found the want of it. I think a lot of these young fellows waste a rare lot of time readin' when they might be doin' something useful."

"But don't you want to know the news?" said the other churchwarden. "Don't you ever want to write a letter?"

"No, me lord, I seem to manage very well without. And of late years now they've all these pictures in the papers I get to know what's goin' on pretty well. Me wife's quite a scholar and if I want to write a letter she writes it for me. It's not as if I was a bettin' man."

The two churchwardens gave the vicar a troubled glance and then looked down at the table.

"Well, Foreman, I've talked the matter over with these gentlemen and they quite agree with me that the situation is impossible. At a church like St. Peter's, Neville Square, we cannot have a verger who can neither read nor write."

Albert Edward's thin, sallow face reddened and he moved uneasily on his feet, but he made no reply.

"Understand me, Foreman, I have no complaint to make against you. You do your work quite satisfactorily; I have the highest opinion both of your character and of your capacity; but we haven't the right to take the risk of some accident that might happen owing to your lamentable ignorance. It's a matter of prudence as well as of principle."

"But couldn't you learn, Foreman?" asked the general.

"No, sir, I'm afraid I couldn't, not now. You see, I'm not as young as I was and if I couldn't seem able to get the letters in me 'ead when I was a nipper I don't think there's much chance of it now."

"We don't want to be harsh with you, Foreman," said the vicar. "But the churchwardens and I have quite made up our minds. We'll give you three months and if at the end of that time you cannot read and write I'm afraid you'll have to go."

Albert Edward had never liked the new vicar. He'd said from the beginning that they'd made a mistake when they gave him St. Peter's. He wasn't the type of man they wanted with a classy congregation like that. And now he straightened himself a little. He knew his value and he wasn't going to allow himself to be put upon.

"I'm very sorry, sir, I'm afraid it's no good. I'm too old a dog to learn new tricks. I've lived a good many years without knowin' 'ow to read and write, and without wishin' to praise myself, self-praise is no recommendation, I don't mind sayin' I've done my duty in that state of life in which it 'as pleased a merciful providence to place me, and if I *could* learn now I don't know as I'd want to."

"In that case, Foreman, I'm afraid you must go."

"Yes, sir, I quite understand. I shall be 'appy to 'and in my resignation as soon as you've found somebody to take my place."

But when Albert Edward with his usual politeness had closed the church door behind the vicar and the two churchwardens he could not sustain the air of unruffled dignity with which he had borne the blow inflicted upon him and his lips quivered. He walked slowly back to the vestry and hung up on its proper peg his verger's gown. He sighed as he thought of all the grand funerals and smart weddings it had seen. He tidied everything up, put on his coat, and hat in hand walked down the aisle. He locked the church door behind him. He strolled across the square, but deep in his sad thoughts he did not take the street that led him home, where a nice strong cup of tea awaited him; he took the wrong turning. He walked slowly along. His heart was heavy. He did not know what he should do with himself. He did not fancy the notion of going back to domestic service; after being his own master for so many years, for the vicar and churchwardens could say what they liked, it was he that had run St. Peter's, Neville Square, he could scarcely demean himself by accepting a situation. He had saved a tidy sum, but not enough to live on without doing something, and life seemed to cost more every year. He had never thought to be troubled with such questions. The vergers of St. Peter's, like the popes of Rome, were there for life. He had often thought of the pleasant reference the vicar would make in his sermon at evensong the first Sunday after his death to the long and faithful service, and the exemplary character, of their late verger, Albert Edward

Foreman. He sighed deeply. Albert Edward was a non-smoker and a total abstainer, but with a certain latitude; that is to say he liked a glass of beer with his dinner and when he was tired he enjoyed a cigarette. It occurred to him now that one would comfort him and since he did not carry them he looked about him for a shop where he could buy a packet of Gold Flakes. He did not at once see one and walked on a little. It was a long street, with all sorts of shops in it, but there was not a single one where you could buy cigarettes.

"That's strange," said Albert Edward.

To make sure he walked right up the street again. No, there was no doubt about it. He stopped and looked reflectively up and down.

"I can't be the only man as walks along this street and wants a smoke," he said. "I shouldn't wonder but what a fellow might do very well with a little shop here. Tobacco and sweets, you know."

He gave a sudden start.

"That's an idea," he said. "Strange 'ow things come to you when you least expect it."

He turned, walked home, and had his tea.

"You're very silent this afternoon, Albert," his wife remarked.

"I'm thinkin'," he said.

He considered the matter from every point of view and next day he went along the street and by good luck found a little shop to let that looked as though it would exactly suit him. Twenty-four hours later he had taken it and when a month after that he left St. Peter's, Neville Square, forever, Albert Edward Foreman set up in business as a tobacconist and news agent. His wife said it was a dreadful comedown after being verger of St. Peter's, but he answered that you had to move with the times, the church wasn't what it was, and 'enceforward he was going to render unto Caesar what was Caesar's. Albert Edward did very well. He did so well that in a year or so it struck him that he might take a second shop and put a manager in. He looked for another long street that hadn't got a tobacconist in it and when he found it, and a shop to let, took it and stocked it. This was a success too. Then it occurred to him that if he could run two he could run half a dozen, so he began walking about London, and whenever he found a long street that had no tobacconist and a shop to let he took it. In the course of ten years he had acquired no less than ten shops and he was making money hand over fist. He went round to all of them himself every Monday, collected the week's takings, and took them to the bank.

One morning when he was there paying in a bundle of notes and a heavy bag of silver the cashier told him that the manager would like to see him. He was shown into an office and the manager shook hands with him.

"Mr. Foreman, I wanted to have a talk to you about the money you've got on deposit with us. D'you know exactly how much it is?"

"Not within a pound or two, sir; but I've got a pretty rough idea."

"Apart from what you paid in this morning it's a little over thirty thousand pounds. That's a very large sum to have on deposit and I should have thought you'd do better to invest it."

"I wouldn't want to take no risk, sir. I know it's safe in the bank."

"You needn't have the least anxiety. We'll make you out a list of absolutely gilt-edged securities. They'll bring you in a better rate of interest than we can possibly afford to give you."

A troubled look settled on Mr. Foreman's distinguished face. "I've never 'ad anything to do with stocks and shares and I'd 'ave to leave it all in your 'ands," he said.

The manager smiled. "We'll do everything. All you'll have to do next time you come in is just to sign the transfers."

"I could do that all right," said Albert uncertainly. "But 'ow should I know what I was signin'?"

"I suppose you can read," said the manager a trifle sharply.

Mr. Foreman gave him a disarming smile.

"Well, sir, that's just it. I can't. I know it sounds funny-like, but there it is, I can't read or write, only me name, an' I only learnt to do that when I went into business."

The manager was so surprised that he jumped up from his chair.

"That's the most extraordinary thing I ever heard."

"You see, it's like this, sir, I never 'ad the opportunity until it was too late and then some'ow I wouldn't. I got obstinate-like."

The manager stared at him as though he were a prehistoric monster.

"And do you mean to say that you've built up this important business and amassed a fortune of thirty thousand pounds without being able to read or write? Good God, man, what would you be now if you had been able to?"

"I can tell you that, sir," said Mr. Foreman, a little smile on his still aristocratic features. "I'd be verger of St. Peter's, Neville Square."

# Ted Engstrom

AND

# David Juroe

# Out
# of the Work
# Trap

## Learn to leave your work at work!

Myron is obsessed by his work. His family, friends, and business associates at times describe him as a robot. Everything he does seems to be mechanical, and he appears to be consumed by his work.

• Jack feels guilty much of the time. Just about everyone can see it. He walks with his shoulders slumped, his eyes never focus on yours when you talk with him – a dead giveaway. He's seldom at home. If you want to reach him, try calling him at work first.

• Phil is highly devoted to his work. He constantly puts himself down with negative remarks about his weaknesses. He gets angry if members of his family call to ask him to go to a social function in the evening. He's not much interested in having fun.

These three typical workaholic types dis-

close additional underlying factors behind the work trap. People become work addicted because they become obsessed with it, are loaded with guilt, and dislike themselves intensely. Recognizing the defences used by the ego to ward off stress is fundamental to an understanding of the problem. But the person caught in the work trap may be there because of other unconscious needs as well.

There is a humorous gibe which indicates that psychotics build castles in the sky, neurotics live in them, and psychiatrists collect rent on them.

The fact is, a person becomes psychotic when his mental functioning is sufficiently impaired to interfere with his meeting the demands of life. This impairment is due to a serious distortion of reality. Hallucinations or delusions distort reality and an individual's inability to focus may be so profound that his ability to respond appropriately to various situations is grossly impaired.

A neurosis, on the other hand, has a different psychological base. Anxiety is the main characteristic evident in the neurotic. Someone has put it this way: "A psychotic believes that two and two equals five, a neurotic believes that two and two equals four, but can't stand it!"

"What does all this have to do with the workaholic?" you may ask. Just this: One of the basic themes we are seeking to set forth is that workaholism is a neurotic way some people choose to deal with their deep inner problems.

Workaholics have an obsession – work, work, work – even if they drop dead. What is an obsession? The dictionary indicates that the term *obsession* is a state of being whereby a person is ruled by an idea, desire, or behavior pattern. It is an idea, emotion, or impulse that is repetitive. It is normal if it does not interfere with thinking or behavior – and it is often short-lived.

One tragedy of the workaholic is that, due to his isolation from the real emotional world, he is usually caught up in preparations – always working for the future and never being able to experience the present. Consequently, he doesn't live in a real world. He experiences the world as did one client who rejoiced in the walk uphill because he thought of the downhill walk coming later, but was always sad on the downhill trip because he would reflect upon a later uphill climb!

The unfortunate thing about the obsessive workaholic is that work is used to hide his feelings from either himself or others. As an avoidance technique, it becomes a self-destructive mechanism. He becomes alienated from himself.

Most authorities agree with a multicausation theory when studying addictive behavior. This includes cultural, biological, and psychosociological factors that interact in a complex pattern. Workaholism falls into the category of addictive behavior. For that reason, several factors may go into the underlying causes of why people get themselves into a work trap.

All very well, you may say – but, once caught in the work trap, how the devil does one get out?

Here, it is important for the recognized workaholic to follow a strategic plan for his life – not only for the present but for the future as well. Following are several practical and helpful steps one can follow to obtain relief from stressful situations:

• Accept ability for what it is. Stress is often created because one has a reputation to live up to or else has the need to excel at some particular thing.

As Socrates wisely stated, we should know and understand ourselves, our gifts, our abilities. "Know thyself" was the theme of ancient Greek society. We, therefore, must learn to recognize our limitations.

• Try to develop wider interests. Stress is frequently a by-product of lack of interest in the broader areas of satisfying living. We need to allow for the development of the creative drive within ourselves.

• Learn to accept the fact that our work is really never completed. This fact keeps us going and can add zest to our living.

• Learn how to drain off the built-up energy created by stress. The reduction of this tension can be handled in various ways. Instead of anger, frustration, and such nagging feelings being repressed or acted out in our work, they need to be expressed in other ways – exercise, for one.

Someone has rightly said that stress never leaves you where it consumed you. It will always render some change within you. It will either make you more frustrated, weaker, tougher, harder, colder, angrier – or it will turn you into a softer, gentler, more understanding human being. The way you deal with stress many times helps determine your future. Many workaholics are yes-men, bound by others' wishes, commands, or approval. Thus, learning to say no is a strong step in the right direction when a person already overloaded with work and responsibility sees that added responsibility is about to be thrust upon him. There are at least four basic ways to assert oneself when objecting to accepting overloads or taking on extra work: (1) say no; (2) say no with a truthful reason; (3) say no with a "maybe next time" answer; (4) say no with an excuse.

It takes a person with self-worth to be capable of treating others so as to gain and retain their respect and affection. This is the sort of person who, instead of climbing over his fellow workers whom he has pulled down, sets himself to help everyone around him in order that he may move up with them.

### Avoiding workaholism

If you think you are a workaholic or on the way to becoming one and wish to change, here are some proven guideposts:

**1.** Don't allow yourself to indulge in guilt and shame.

**2.** Look for the causes of your behavior within your current situation and not in personality defects within yourself.

**3.** Remind yourself that there are alternative views with every event. This attitude will enable you to be more tolerant in your interpretation of others' intentions and more generous in dismissing what might appear to be their rejection of you.

**4.** Don't allow others to criticize you as a person. It is your specific actions that are open for evaluation and improvement. Accept constructive feedback graciously if it will help you.

**5.** Remember that failure and disappointments are sometimes blessings in disguise which tell you that your goals were not right for you, or that your effort wasn't worth it.

**6.** Do not tolerate people, jobs, and situations which make you feel inadequate. If you can't change them or yourself enough to make you feel worthwhile, walk out on them or pass them by. Life is too short to fill with "downers."

**7.** Enjoy feeling the energy that other people transmit – the unique qualities and range of variability of your fellow human beings. Imagine what their fears and insecurities might be and how you could help them. Decide what you need from them and what you have to give. Then let them know that you are open to sharing with them.

It is important for the workaholic to develop a strong sense of his individuality. This is not to be confused with isolation or the uniqueness of standing alone, or refusing to interact with others. It is the process of interaction. This is a mark of maturity, the ability to relate or deal with others when there is anxiety or conflict.

Intimacy avoidance is a major hallmark of the workaholic. The reason he is often oblivious to needs is that he denies the presence of need in others. This makes him oblivious to opportunities to satisfy that need. It is like a person who denies the reality of pain; he is often unaware of the source of the pain.

The fear of getting close to others is behind intimacy avoidance. The workaholic needs to take a good look at this. "Am I using my work to avoid dealing with people or conflicts in my personal life?" If so, he needs to seek and to find solutions that will change his relationships.

It may be difficult at first to discover this about yourself, but healing will not take

232

place until you do something about it. Facing reality may not only be uncomfortable, but you may be confronted with the necessity of taking positive action which – you may fear – will be hazardous and disagreeable because it will force you to open up.

Avoiding change and close involvement in the personal lives of those we love comes down to one thing: a lack of concern for others' welfare. The workaholic needs to strengthen his personal relationships and seek a balance between work and friends. A person who desires to discipline his life can have the best of both worlds – satisfying personal relationships and meaningful work.

And now, a final word: One of the tragedies of life is that second chances seldom occur. Far too often, we wait too long – until sickness, accidents, or calamities happen – before we make significant decisions or provide for changes to be made. Many die without ever enjoying the fullness of life because they have lacked the courage to alter their lifestyle before some circumstance changed it for them.

When you have been able to cut loose from the tyranny of excessive work, to be free at last to enlarge your horizons and become a greater part of your family and society, bear in mind that you will not want to slip back into the old patterns. Hopefully, those modes of doing and thinking will lose their meaning in light of the new behavior. One of the wonderful freedoms is that you no longer see yourself as indispensable. And you will no longer be threatened by the thought of it.

Hard work is good; consuming work is wrong. We must constantly guard against overwork that will deprive us of health, family, and a strong, effective spiritual life.

Learn to leave your work at work!

# Raymond Souster

# Evening in the Suburbs

*after Jacques Prévert*

Around six he arrives
from a hard day at the office
His dog greets him
his children greet him
even his wife greets him
He sits down
his wife sits down
his children sit down
even his dog sits down
and they eat supper
Then he lights his cigar
reads the evening paper
the sports page
the markets
the comics
Gets up
goes into the garden
where he adjusts the sprinkler
turns the water on
sits down again
watching the drops
fall through the air
and goes to sleep
in the deck chair
When he wakes up
it's dark outside
the sprinkler's off
He lights a cigar

and goes inside
the house is empty
the lights are out
then he remembers
his wife's at the church
his children next door
watching TV
even his dog's gone
He takes a beer
from the refrigerator
but the beer doesn't taste right
he sits down again
in his easy chair
picks up the paper
but his eyes are tired
he doesn't feel like reading
Still he feels like doing something
and he takes the paper
and rips it down the middle
he goes to the kitchen
and takes the beer bottle
and throws it through the window
his dog coming from the cellar
gets booted in the rear
Then he feels better
he feels good again
sits down in his chair
falls asleep like a child.

"Evening in the Suburbs" by Raymond Souster is reprinted from *Ten Elephants on Yonge Street* by permission of Oberon Press.

# Erma Bombeck

# Put Down Your Brother

What to do
when togetherness
becomes
an obscene word.

There are all kinds of camping, of course. There are the primitives who sleep on a blanket of chipmunks under the stars and exist only on wild berries and what game they are able to trap in the zippers of their sleeping bags. There are the tent enthusiasts who use cots, ice coolers, matches, transistor radios, and eat store-bought bread, but who draw the line at electricity and indoor plumbing. Finally, there are the wheelsvilles. They run the gamut from the family that converts the old pickup truck to a home on wheels to those who rough it with color TV, guitars, outdoor lounge furniture, flaming patio torches, ice crushers, electric fire lighters, showers, make-up mirrors, hoods over the campfire, plastic logs, Hondas for short trips to the city, and yapping dogs that have had their teeth capped.

It doesn't matter how you camp. The point is that a few practical suggestions could keep you from going bananas:

*What to do when it rains.* Rearrange canned foods, plan a side trip, write letters home, remembering to lie. Read all the wonderful books you brought and promised yourself to read. (*The Red Badge of Courage* and *The American Journal on Tooth Decay*.)

*And rains.* Pick grains of sand out of the butter, sit in the car and pretend you're going home, find out who really has gym shoes that smell like wet possum.

*And rains.* Send the kids out to find traffic to play in. Call in friends and watch the clothing mildew. Pair off and find an ark.

Otherwise camping can be loads of fun. Tips from my woodland log:

*How to bed down without hurting yourself or anyone else.*

1. Don't kneel on the stove to let the cot down from the wall until all the burners are off.

2. If the table converts to a bed, make sure it has been cleared.

3. Whoever brought the guitar along sleeps with it.

4. If the wind is blowing southward, sleep northward of the person who bathed in mosquito repellent.

5. Place the kid who had three bottles of pop before bedtime nearest the door. Oil the zipper of his sleeping bag before retiring.

6. If you are sleeping on the ground, make it as comfortable as possible by using a rollaway bed.

7. Make sure all the cupboard doors are closed and traffic areas cleared before the light is extinguished. Statistics show that more campers are lost through carelessly placed ice coolers and clotheslines than through crocodile bites.

*How to live among our furry friends.*

1. Forget Disney. Remember, not all bears have their own television series. Some of them are unemployed wild animals.

2. Never argue with a bear over your picnic basket, even though deep in your heart you know the green onions will repeat on him.

3. Any woman in the laundry room who tries to assure you snakes are as afraid of you as you are of them should be watched.

*How to know when you are there.*

1. When you are reading the road map and your husband accuses you of moving Lake Michigan over two states.

2. When the kids start playing touch football in the back seat with a wet diaper and the baby is in it.

3. When not only starvation sets in, but your stomach begins to bloat and your vision becomes blurred.

4. When Daddy screams, "Stop kicking my seat!" and the kids are all asleep.

5. When you find a haven the size of a football field that you don't have to back a trailer into (even if it is a football field).

*What to do when togetherness becomes an obscene word.*

No one, not even a man and a woman, can endure two weeks of complete togetherness – especially when they are married. Thus, being confined with two or three children in an area no larger than a sandbox often has the appeal of being locked in a bus-station restroom over the weekend. Planning your activities will help avoid this.

1. Keep busy. Rotate the tires on the car. This gets you out in the fresh air and at the same time gives you a feeling of accomplishment.

2. Play games like "Look for Daddy" or "Bury the Motorcycle" (the one that runs up and down through the campgrounds all night).

3. Have a roster of chores. One child could be in charge of water for the radiator. Another could be in charge of killing that last mosquito in the tent at night.

4. Have family dialogues around the campfire. Suggested topics: Who was the idiot who had to bring the ping-pong table and "Harvey, where are you getting the drinking water and what did you hope to find when you put a slideful of it under your new microscope?"

5. Make new friends (assuming your marriage is stable).
   If it happens to be Be Kind to Campers Month (July 19-26), observe it by taking a camper to the city for a day.

Will R. Bird

# The Movies Come to Gull Point

For a heartbeat
it seemed they must capsize.

Four men were mending nets in a shack behind the fish wharf at Granny Cove. Spring had come grudgingly, but now the warm sun was melting the ice and sending steamy vapors from tarred roofs. The Cove front murmured with activity as all its men prepared for the sea.

The four worked in silence, seated on benches, half-hidden by the drab folds that hung from the crossbeams overhead, their hands flicking in and out among the meshes, tying, knotting, threading. All at once they paused and listened. There were new voices outside.

"Them's the two back from pulp-cuttin'," said Simon Holder. He was a small, lean man.

"Wonder if they got their pay," said Dick Berry, a red-faced man with big bony shoulders.

The two working in the rear were young, and brothers, Ben and Matthew Crowdy, proud of being hired with Simon. Ben was only seventeen, and slim, but he carried himself as seriously as the other three.

"Ho, Willyum," shouted Berry as a man passed the open door. "Don't rush yourself. What's the word down along?"

The man came back and peered in at them. "Not much new," he said. "They're havin' movin' pictures...."

"Movin'!" Berry's mouth fell open. "How?"

"The man's got a machine'n engine to drive her. He's over't Gull Point tonight givin' a showin'."

"Over't Gull Point!" Berry rose from his bench, his red face glowing. "Simon, let's go over?"

"What's he chargin'?" asked Simon.

"Twenty-five cents, but he's got good pictures. There's one..."

Reprinted by permission of the author.

"Don't tell us," blurted Matthew. "That would spoil it. What say we go, Simon?" He had a solemn face, like Ben, but his eyes were bright.

Simon left his bench and went outside. The others followed him and they stood, gazing at the sea.

The ice was breaking up. The warm sun had been aided by a strong wind off land and a lane of black water was steadily widening along the foot of the cliffs, while smaller leads angled in all directions, opening as the pack surged and loosened. Southward, toward Gull Point, there seemed plenty of open sea.

"Risky," pronounced Simon.

"Chancy," agreed Berry, "but not too much."

"Wind's favourin', too," added Matthew.

There was a slow, shrill screaming of the ice. Floes and pans were grinding together; the harsh noises never stilled.

Ben looked up. There were no clouds and the sky was a blue that seemed to reflect the endless ice.

"Looks fairish weather," he said, "but it's comin' tonight."

"You boys got money?" asked Simon.

They shook their heads and Berry grinned.

"That makes a dollar," Simon said gravely. "That's a lot of money."

"There ain't never been," said Ben, "movin' pictures up here. I never seen any in my life."

"Bet she's open to the Point," said Berry. "We'd do fine with a lugsail."

Simon rubbed his salt-bitten chin. They four were the best in the Cove. "Git geared," he said suddenly.

"It's six mile," Simon said an hour later. They had launched their dory and were well into the wide lead but the lugsail was proving a menace. A stiffer breeze caught them and tipped the boat. He pulled the canvas in. "Mebbe we're fools."

They had lost much time. Matthew had broken a thole pin in his eagerness and they had not turned back to repair it. They had trusted in the sail, and his oars were idle.

"The wind'll be strong outside," said Berry. He was rowing and he grunted his words.

They were true enough. Once away from the shelter of the high black cliffs, the wind caught the dory and they swung along sharply. There were many wide lanes and the sea was running higher than it had seemed, and spray flung over them.

Simon steered with a long sweep and Matthew was seated next him, squatted low but ready to lend a hand. As they swayed with the dory all four seemed a jumble of sou'westers and oilskins.

They did not attempt conversation. The shrieking, jarring crashes of the ice mingled with the whistling of the breeze and drowned all lesser sounds. The rapidly widening lane they were in became a sea of racing, tumbling water that spewed spray as it struck the dory. Simon's oilskins dripped and his cheeks were wet but his expression never changed. He was gauging every wave with the instinct of one born to the sea.

Suddenly each man braced himself for action. A loose floe hove in their path and the waves pitched it about dangerously. Simon and Berry used all their strength and skill as they managed to avoid it, but neither man spoke. Matthew was bailing instantly and they moved slowly until he had scooped from the dory the gallons of water shipped during the swinging manoeuvre. It seemed, in that short time, to become night.

The rocky point behind them had cut off the sun as it sank rapidly, and with its going the wind keened to a penetrating chill. The darkness added greatly to their risks and Matthew peered ahead.

"She's started to fog," he shouted. "She's a bank now."

The shore, hazy before, had become mist-drowned, shrouded with a thick white creeping veil. It seemed to permeate the air.

"She's come behind the same," yelled Ben.

They were half their journey and a swirling blanket of grey vapors closed about them. They would have to chance their passage ahead where the contour of the coast veered so that the slow-moving field of ice might bar their way.

It was Matthew who first saw that they had entered a wide lane and were between shifting ice. He peered again.

"Keep straight on!" he cried.

Short waves were deluging the boat with freezing spray. Berry rowed with quick strokes, and the roar of wind and grinding ice filled the night.

The water became smoother. Matthew reached and touched Berry on the back and at the signal the bigger man changed places with him. They were tense and watchful; only men of their experience could know the risk of a channel between rafted ice. Deep booming sounds seemed to pass over them as though they had sunk in a trough of the sea, and it grew darker.

"Look!" yelled Ben. "She's closin' in."

There was a muttered undertone beneath the booming and their lane of open water had narrowed to feet in width.

They slipped awkwardly in their sealskin boots as each man scrambled onto the floe, but they secured footing and with desperate hurried strength dragged the heavy dory from the water. It taxed them to their utmost and no one spoke. The ice was an uneven surging field and a blurred greyness covered everything.

"She's bad," said Berry. "We should have..."

He did not finish. There was a crash of

giant floes colliding and they were sprawled beside the dory. In an instant the night was a wilder chaos of wind and clamor.

"Watch out!" Simon's voice rose above the tumult like a cracking whip. "She's breakin'."

The floe buckled. It rose and lowered under them. There were sudden surgings that pitched them about. They seized the dory sides and pushed landward. The roaring of surf at the face of the floe came clearly.

"Watch her!" It was a scream more than a shout. The ice was parting.

The floe rocked and settled. Water sloshed over the ice, reached them. There was another settling.

"There!" yelled Ben.

The field had opened and the sea drove into the vent with foaming fury. It poured over the ice to meet them. Then, its weight, and the driving surf, heaved the floe.

They slid backward in the wash. Ben, caught by the dory, fell, and water washed over him. He rose, sobbing with his immersion, clinging to the dory, and, as if a signal were given, they rushed the boat toward the open water. The lane had widened into a broad lead.

Again the floe surged, and the dory slid into the water. Ben leaped into it, tilting it dangerously. Matthew sprang in beside him, rocking it to a safer keel. Berry had given a great thrust forward to clear them from the ice and as he sprang he lunged against Simon, knocking him backward.

For a heartbeat it seemed they must capsize. The churning water had caught them as the dory took its plunge. Berry grasped his oars and threw his weight against the surge. Behind them, in the screaming murk, Simon was lost to view.

Ben had seized Simon's sweep and they toiled to bring the dory about. The lane was a smother of surf. Danger hovered over every move and the water boiled with changing currents.

They drove back alongside, catching, with perfect co-ordination, a minute lull at the ice edge, and Simon, gauging their move, joined them. It was a risky plunge, challenging all their chances, but once more Berry's strength saved the dory and then they had swung away and Ben was bailing.

In the thick darkness the surf seemed wilder than before but the worst was soon behind them. Then, just ahead, a pinpoint of light shone steadily.

Within ten minutes they were in calmer waters, and lamp glows began to pierce the gloom. They landed and hurried Ben, shaking and almost numbed with cold, to the nearest house.

"Us is from Granny Cove," announced Simon. "Ben were wet on the ice. Could us dry him here?"

"Sure, the stove's red-hot." A woman wrapped in a thick jacket and ready to leave for the hall where the movies were to be shown, answered them. "I'll git a rig for him to put on and his'll dry while we're gone."

Ben was shaking as with ague and tiny pools formed on the floor beside him as the warmth of the stove softened his frozen clothing. He drank a scalding mixture the woman provided and his trembling ceased. He stripped his sodden clothing and Matthew ranged it on a chair back alongside the stove. Then Ben dressed in a makeshift outfit and they followed the path the woman had taken.

The building where the movies were being shown was packed with people. It was a low-roofed structure and heated by a huge box stove. There were high odors of perspiration and many faces were beaded with moisture. Children were sandwiched among their elders and every seat was taken. Simon led the way along one wall and they stood against it, tightly wedged by others who crowded after. Ben struggled from the borrowed reefer that blanketed him.

"We're lucky," he gasped. "She's jist startin'."

There were gasps and murmurings as the lamps were extinguished and the hum of a motor began. Headings appeared on the screen and a dozen voices tried to read them.

"Let teacher read 'em," bellowed a husky voice at the rear.

"'She Knew She War Wrong'," a high-pitched voice shrilled in the darkness as "teacher" assumed her task. "Pretty Virginia..."

The audience had stilled. It was seeing the incredible...mirrored eating places... ladies with bare backs and cigarettes... bewildering dances...racing cars...a bathing beach teeming with thousands. And one face dominated.

"See that one!" said Berry hoarsely. "Her's..."

"Keep shut," ordered Simon in a sibilant whisper.

They watched the heroine driving in city traffic and there were cries of admiration.

"Ho!" shouted Berry. "Look at she." He clapped his hands.

"She's won'erful sharp in steerin'," responded Simon, "but..." He couldn't express himself.

Another picture began and all voices stilled. It was a story of rival airmen, and the planes in action did marvellous stunting. A flight of machines gave a thrilling performance, all manner of stunt flying.

Berry tensed, his big hands gripping a seat back. Simon breathed with sharp little intakes. Ben and Matthew gave shrill exclamations, unable to restrain themselves.

"They're hittin'!"

"No – yes – there!"

"Lookit – lookit – *lookit*!"

A dozen voices yelled with him. The airmen were shooting earthward at dizzy speed, headed toward each other.

There was a dull grinding sound and the screen went blank.

A lamp was lighted and the operator of the movie machine worked desperately with various tools. Then he came forward.

"Sorry, folks," he said, "but the machine's broke and I've got to send the piece away. I can't show any more."

There were sighs of disappointment but no one gave criticism. They began filing from the building and the night was filled with excited voices.

Ben went to change his clothes again and the woman insisted on their stopping to drink scalding tea and to eat slices of hard bread.

"Stay the night," she urged. "I've blankets enough to fix you up on the kitchen floor."

"No," refused Simon. "The fog's cleared and she's light as day. We've got a mortal sight of work to do, gettin' ready to fish."

Berry ate and drank hugely but said nothing. The unexpected ending of the show had given him vast disappointment.

It was breaking day as the dory swung to the wharf at Granny's Cove. The sea had been much rougher than they anticipated and they had been forced to keep near the shore line all the way. For hours there had been but the creak of boat timbers and the slap of heavy water; each was silent, and dull-minded.

A slight breeze stirred the morning. It was from the west and warm. There would be a perfect day. The sunrise began in a fire of orange and crimson that merged into soft pinks and changing blues. The heavens were a mass of color.

The light spread over the hills and reached the sleeping houses. It found iced places in the hollows and they glittered like jewels.

They dragged the dory to its landing and stood away from it. Ben was bruised and stiff. Matthew had lost a mitten and each was conscious of clothing damp with spray.

"We're back," said Simon tersely, "but it were worth it."

"Sure," agreed Berry, yawning mightily. "That girl were a prime one."

"It must be great," said Matthew, "to live where you kin see won'erful sights all the time."

The light strengthened and the sea was blue as sapphire where the sun rays reached it slantingly. Still they stood, as if each were laboring with thoughts they could not put into words. Then Simon spat and faced them.

"I don't know what youse think," he said, "but takin' all them risks to make a picture don't seem right to me."

Matthew nodded gravely. "Us been thinkin' just that," he said. "It's for nothin' but pleasurin' and it's queer they ain't laws to stop it."

"Sure," added Ben, "there should be a law ag'in it. They might have been killed."

There was no further comment. Smoke began to curl from a chimney. Ben yawned again. They had expressed that which stirred them most, so they turned and filed soberly to their homes.

## Shirley Jackson

# One Ordinary Day, with Peanuts

He had given away
almost all of his candy,
and had fed all the
rest of his peanuts
to the pigeons. . . .

**M**r. John Philip Johnson shut his front door behind him and came down his front steps in the bright morning with a feeling that all was well with the world on this best of all days, and wasn't the sun warm and good, and didn't his shoes feel comfortable after the resoling, and he knew that he had undoubtedly chosen the precise very tie which belonged with the day and the sun and his comfortable feet, and, after all, wasn't the world just a wonderful place? In spite of the fact that he was a small man, and the tie was perhaps a shade vivid, Mr. Johnson irradiated this feeling of wellbeing as he came down the steps and onto the dirty sidewalk, and he smiled at people who passed him, and some of them even smiled back. He stopped at the newsstand on the corner and bought his paper, saying "Good morning" with real conviction to the man who sold him the paper and the two or three other people who were lucky enough to be buying papers when Mr. Johnson skipped up. He remembered to fill his pockets with candy and peanuts, and then he set out to get himself uptown. He stopped in a flower shop and bought a carnation for his buttonhole, and stopped almost immediately afterward to give the carnation to a small child in a carriage, who looked at him dumbly, and then smiled, and Mr. Johnson smiled, and the child's mother looked at Mr. Johnson for a minute and then smiled too.

When he had gone several blocks uptown, Mr. Johnson cut across the avenue and went along a side street, chosen at random; he did not follow the same route every morning, but preferred to pursue his eventful way in wide detours, more like a puppy than a man intent upon business. It happened this morning that halfway down the block a moving van was parked, and the furniture from an upstairs apartment stood half on the sidewalk, half on the steps, while an amused group of people loitered, examining the scratches on the tables and the worn spots on the chairs, and a harassed woman, trying to watch a young child and the movers and the furniture all at the same time, gave the clear impression of endeavoring to shelter her private life from the people staring at her belongings. Mr. Johnson stopped, and for a moment joined the crowd, and then he came forward and, touching his hat civilly, said, "Perhaps I can keep an eye on your little boy for you?"

The woman turned and glared at him distrustfully, and Mr. Johnson added hastily, "We'll sit right here on the steps." He beckoned to the little boy, who hesitated and then responded agreeably to Mr. Johnson's genial smile. Mr. Johnson brought out a handful of peanuts from his pocket and sat on the steps with the boy, who at first refused the peanuts on the grounds that his mother did not allow him to accept food from strangers; Mr. Johnson said that probably his mother had not intended peanuts to be included, since elephants at the circus ate them, and the boy considered, and then agreed solemnly. They sat on the steps cracking peanuts in a comradely fashion, and Mr. Johnson said, "So you're moving?"

"Yep," said the boy.

"Where you going?"

"Vermont."

"Nice place. Plenty of snow there. Maple sugar, too; you like maple sugar?"

"Sure."

"Plenty of maple sugar in Vermont. You going to live on a farm?"

"Going to live with Grandpa."

"Grandpa like peanuts?"

"Sure."

"Ought to take him some," said Mr. Johnson, reaching into his pocket. "Just you and Mommy going?"

"Yep."

"Tell you what," Mr. Johnson said. "You take some peanuts to eat on the train."

The boy's mother, after glancing at them frequently, had seemingly decided that Mr. Johnson was trustworthy, because she had devoted herself wholeheartedly to seeing that the movers did not—what movers rarely do, but every housewife believes they will—crack a leg from her good table, or set a kitchen chair down on a lamp. Most of the furniture was loaded by now, and she was deep in that nervous stage when she knew there was something she had forgotten to pack—hidden away in the back of a closet somewhere, or left at a neighbor's and forgotten, or on the clothesline—and was trying to remember under stress what it was.

"This all, lady?" the chief mover said, completing her dismay.

Uncertainly, she nodded.

"Want to go on the truck with the furniture, sonny?" the mover asked the boy, and laughed. The boy laughed too and said to Mr. Johnson, "I guess I'll have a good time at Vermont."

"Fine time," said Mr. Johnson, and stood up. "Have one more peanut before you go," he said to the boy.

The boy's mother said to Mr. Johnson, "Thank you so much; it was a great help to me."

"Nothing at all," said Mr. Johnson gallantly. "Where in Vermont are you going?"

The mother looked at the little boy accusingly, as though he had given away a secret of some importance, and said unwillingly, "Greenwich."

"Lovely town," said Mr. Johnson. He took out a card, and wrote a name on the back.

"Very good friend of mine lives in Greenwich," he said. "Call on him for anything you need. His wife makes the best doughnuts in town," he added soberly to the little boy.

"Swell," said the little boy.

"Goodbye," said Mr. Johnson.

He went on, stepping happily with his new-shod feet, feeling the warm sun on his back and on the top of his head. Halfway down the block he met a stray dog and fed him a peanut.

At the corner, where another wide avenue faced him, Mr. Johnson decided to go on uptown again. Moving with comparative laziness, he was passed on either side by people hurrying and frowning, and people brushed past him going the other way, clattering along to get somewhere quickly. Mr. Johnson stopped on every corner and waited patiently for the light to change, and he stepped out of the way of anyone who seemed to be in any particular hurry, but one young lady came too fast for him, and crashed wildly into him when he stooped to pat a kitten which had run out onto the sidewalk from an apartment house and was now unable to get back through the rushing feet.

"Excuse me," said the young lady, trying frantically to pick up Mr. Johnson and hurry on at the same time, "terribly sorry."

The kitten, regardless now of danger, raced back to its home. "Perfectly all right," said Mr. Johnson, adjusting himself carefully. "You seem to be in a hurry."

"Of course I'm in a hurry," said the young lady. "I'm late."

She was extremely cross and the frown between her eyes seemed well on its way to becoming permanent. She had obviously awakened late, because she had not spent any extra time in making herself look pretty, and her dress was plain and unadorned with collar or brooch, and her lipstick was noticeably crooked. She tried to brush past Mr. Johnson, but, risking her suspicious displeasure, he took her arm and said, "Please wait."

"Look," she said ominously, "I ran into you and your lawyer can see my lawyer and I will gladly pay all damages and all inconveniences suffered therefrom but please this minute let me go because *I am late.*"

"Late for what?" said Mr. Johnson; he tried his winning smile on her but it did no more than keep her, he suspected, from knocking him down again.

"Late for work," she said between her teeth. "Late for my employment. I have a job and if I am late I lose exactly so much an hour and I cannot really afford what your pleasant conversation is costing me, be it *ever* so pleasant."

"I'll pay for it," said Mr. Johnson. Now these were magic words, not necessarily because they were true, or because she seriously expected Mr. Johnson to pay for anything, but because Mr. Johnson's flat statement, obviously innocent of irony, could not be, coming from Mr. Johnson, anything but the statement of a responsible and truthful and respectable man.

"What *do* you mean?" she asked.

"I said that since I am obviously responsible for your being late I shall certainly pay for it."

"Don't be silly," she said, and for the first time the frown disappeared. "*I* wouldn't expect you to pay for anything – a few minutes ago I was offering to pay *you.* Anyway," she added, almost smiling, "it *was* my fault."

"What happens if you don't go to work?"

She stared. "I don't get paid."

"Precisely," said Mr. Johnson.

"What do you mean, precisely? If I don't show up at the office exactly twenty minutes ago I lose a dollar and twenty cents an hour, or two cents a minute, or . . ." She thought,

"…almost a dime for the time I've spent talking to you."

Mr. Johnson laughed, and finally she laughed, too. "You're late already," he pointed out. "Will you give me another four cents' worth?"

"I don't understand why."

"You'll see," Mr. Johnson promised. He led her over to the side of the walk, next to the buildings, and said, "Stand here," and went out into the rush of people going both ways. Selecting and considering, as one who must make a choice involving perhaps whole years of lives, he estimated the people going by. Once he almost moved, and then at the last minute thought better of it and drew back. Finally, from half a block away, he saw what he wanted, and moved out into the centre of the traffic to intercept a young man, who was hurrying, and dressed as though he had awakened late, and frowning.

"Oof," said the young man, because Mr. Johnson had thought of no better way to intercept anyone than the one the young woman had unwittingly used upon him. "Where do you think you're going?" the young man demanded from the sidewalk.

"I want to speak to you," said Mr. Johnson ominously.

The young man got up nervously, dusting himself and eying Mr. Johnson. "What for?" he said. "What'd *I* do?"

"That's what bothers me most about people nowadays," Mr. Johnson complained broadly to the people passing. "No matter whether they've done anything or not, they always figure someone's after them. About what you're going to do," he told the young man.

"Listen," said the young man, trying to brush past him, "I'm late, and I don't have any time to listen. Here's a dime, now get going."

"Thank you," said Mr. Johnson, pocketing the dime. "Look," he said, "what happens if you stop running?"

"I'm late," said the young man, still trying to get past Mr. Johnson, who was unexpectedly clinging.

"How much you make an hour?" Mr. Johnson demanded.

"A communist, are you?" said the young man. "Now will you please let me…"

"No," said Mr. Johnson insistently, "*how* much?"

"Dollar fifty," said the young man. "And *now* will you…"

"You like adventure?"

The young man stared, and, staring, found himself caught and held by Mr. Johnson's genial smile; he almost smiled back and then repressed it and made an effort to tear away. "I got to *hurry*," he said.

"Mystery? Like surprises? Unusual and exciting events?"

"You selling something?"

"Sure," said Mr. Johnson. "You want to take a chance?"

The young man hesitated, looked longingly up the avenue toward what might have been his destination, and then, when Mr. Johnson said "I'll pay for it" with his own peculiar convincing emphasis, turned and said, "Well, O.K. But I got to *see* it first, what I'm buying."

Mr. Johnson, breathing hard, led the young man over to the side where the girl was standing; she had been watching with interest Mr. Johnson's capture of the young man and now, smiling timidly, she looked at Mr. Johnson as though prepared to be surprised at nothing.

Mr. Johnson reached into his pocket and took out his wallet. "Here," he said, and handed a bill to the girl. "This about equals your day's pay."

"But no," she said, surprised in spite of herself. "I mean, I *couldn't*."

"Please do not interrupt," Mr. Johnson told her. "And *here*," he said to the young man, "this will take care of *you*." The young man accepted the bill dazedly, but said, "Probably counterfeit" to the young woman out of the side of his mouth. "Now," Mr. Johnson went on, disregarding the young man, "what is your name, miss?"

"Kent," she said helplessly. "Mildred Kent."

"Fine," said Mr. Johnson. "And you, sir?"

"Arthur Adams," said the young man stiffly.

"Splendid," said Mr. Johnson. "Now, Miss Kent, I would like you to meet Mr. Adams. Mr. Adams, Miss Kent."

Miss Kent stared, wet her lips nervously, made a gesture as though she might run, and said, "How do you do?"

Mr. Adams straightened his shoulders, scowled at Mr. Johnson, made a gesture as though he might run, and said, "How do you do?"

"Now *this*," said Mr. Johnson, taking several bills from his wallet, "should be enough for the day for both of you. I would suggest, perhaps, Coney Island – although I personally am not fond of the place – or perhaps a nice lunch somewhere, and dancing, or a matinee, or even a movie, although take care to choose a really *good* one; there are *so* many bad movies these days. You might," he said, struck with an inspiration, "visit the Bronx Zoo, or the Planetarium. Anywhere, as a matter of fact," he concluded, "that you would like to go. Have a nice time."

As he started to move away Arthur Adams, breaking from his dumbfounded stare, said, "But see here, mister, you *can't* do this. Why – how do you know – I mean, *we* don't even know – I mean, how do you know we won't just take the money and not do what you said?"

"You've taken the money," Mr. Johnson said. "You don't have to follow any of my suggestions. You may know something you prefer to do – perhaps a museum, or something."

"But suppose I just run away with it and leave her here?"

"I know you won't," said Mr. Johnson gently, "because you remembered to ask *me* that. Goodbye," he added, and went on.

As he stepped up the street, conscious of the sun on his head and his good shoes, he heard from somewhere behind him the young man saying, "Look, you know you don't *have* to if you don't want to," and the girl saying, "But unless *you* don't want to..." Mr. Johnson smiled to himself and then thought that he had better hurry along; when he wanted to he could move very quickly, and before the young woman had gotten around to saying, "Well, *I* will if *you* will," Mr. Johnson was several blocks away and had already stopped twice, once to help a lady lift several large packages into a taxi and once to hand a peanut to a seagull. By this time he was in an area of large stores and many more people and he was buffeted constantly from either side by people hurrying and cross and late and sullen. Once he offered a peanut to a man who asked him for a dime, and once he offered a peanut to a bus driver who had stopped his bus at an intersection and had opened the window next to his seat and put out his head as though longing for fresh air and the comparative quiet of the traffic. The man wanting a dime took the peanut because Mr. Johnson had wrapped a dollar bill around it, but the bus driver took the peanut and asked ironically, "You want a transfer, Jack?"

On a busy corner Mr. Johnson encountered two young people – for one minute he thought they might be Mildred Kent and Arthur Adams – who were eagerly scanning a newspaper, their backs pressed against a storefront to avoid the people passing, their heads bent together. Mr. Johnson, whose curiosity was insatiable, leaned onto the storefront next to them and peeked over the man's shoulder; they were scanning the "Apartments Vacant" columns.

Mr. Johnson remembered the street where the woman and her little boy were going to Vermont and he tapped the man on the shoulder and said amiably, "Try down on West Seventeen. About the middle of the block, people moved out this morning."

"Say, what do you..." said the man, and then, seeing Mr. Johnson clearly, "Well, thanks. Where did you say?"

"West Seventeen," said Mr. Johnson. "About the middle of the block." He smiled again and said, "Good luck."

"Thanks," said the man.

"Thanks," said the girl, as they moved off.

"Goodbye," said Mr. Johnson.

He lunched alone in a pleasant restaurant, where the food was rich, and only Mr. Johnson's excellent digestion could encompass two of their whipped-cream-and-chocolate-and-rum-cake pastries for dessert. He had three cups of coffee, tipped the waiter largely, and went out into the street again into the wonderful sunlight, his shoes still comfortable and fresh on his feet. Outside he found a beggar staring into the windows of the restaurant he had left and, carefully looking through the money in his pocket, Mr. Johnson approached the beggar and pressed some coins and a couple of bills into his hand. "It's the price of the veal cutlet lunch plus tip," said Mr. Johnson. "Goodbye."

After his lunch he rested; he walked into the nearest park and fed peanuts to the pigeons. It was late afternoon by the time he was ready to start back downtown, and he had refereed two checker games and watched a small boy and girl whose mother had fallen asleep and awakened with surprise and fear which turned to amusement when she saw Mr. Johnson. He had given away almost all of his candy, and had fed all the rest of his peanuts to the pigeons, and it was time to go home. Although the late afternoon sun was pleasant, and his shoes were still entirely comfortable, he decided to take a taxi downtown.

He had a difficult time catching a taxi, because he gave up the first three or four empty ones to people who seemed to need them more; finally, however, he stood alone on the corner and – almost like netting a frisky fish – he hailed desperately until he succeeded in catching a cab which had been proceeding with haste uptown and seemed to draw in toward Mr. Johnson against its own will.

"Mister," the cab driver said as Mr. Johnson climbed in, "I figured you was an omen, like. I wasn't going to pick you up at all."

"Kind of you," said Mr. Johnson ambiguously.

"If I'd of let you go it would of cost me ten bucks," said the driver.

"Really?" said Mr. Johnson.

"Yeah," said the driver. "Guy just got out of the cab, he turned around and give me ten bucks, said take this and bet it in a hurry on a horse named Vulcan, right away."

"Vulcan?" said Mr. Johnson, horrified. "A fire sign on a Wednesday?"

"What?" said the driver. "Anyway, I said to myself if I got no fare between here and there I'd bet the ten, but if anyone looked like they needed the cab I'd take it as a omen and I'd take the ten home to the wife."

"You were very right," said Mr. Johnson heartily. "This is Wednesday, you would have lost your money. Monday, yes, or even Saturday. But never never never a fire sign on a Wednesday. Sunday would have been good, now."

"Vulcan don't run on Sunday," said the driver.

"You wait till another day," said Mr. Johnson. "Down this street, please, driver. I'll get off on the next corner."

"He *told* me Vulcan, though," said the driver.

"I'll tell you," said Mr. Johnson, hesitating with the door of the cab half open. "You take that ten dollars and I'll give you another ten dollars to go with it, and you go right ahead and bet that money on any Thursday on any horse that has a name indicating...let me see, Thursday...well, grain. Or any growing food."

"Grain?" said the driver. "You mean a horse named, like, Wheat or something?"

"Certainly," said Mr. Johnson. "Or, as a matter of fact, to make it even easier, any horse whose name includes the letters C, R, L. Perfectly simple."

"Tall corn?" said the driver, a light in his eye. "You mean a horse named, like, Tall Corn?"

"Absolutely," said Mr. Johnson. "Here's your money."

"Tall Corn," said the driver. "Thank *you*, mister."

"Goodbye," said Mr. Johnson.

He was on his own corner and went straight up to his apartment. He let himself in and called "Hello?" and Mrs. Johnson answered from the kitchen, "Hello, dear, aren't you early?"

"Took a taxi home," Mr. Johnson said. "I remembered the cheesecake, too. What's for dinner?"

Mrs. Johnson came out of the kitchen and kissed him; she was a comfortable woman, and smiling as Mr. Johnson smiled. "Hard day?" she asked.

"Not very," said Mr. Johnson, hanging his coat in the closet. "How about you?"

"So-so," she said. She stood in the kitchen doorway while he settled into his easy chair and took off his good shoes and took out the paper he had bought that morning. "Here and there," she said.

"I didn't do so badly," Mr. Johnson said. "Couple young people."

"Fine," she said. "I had a little nap this afternoon, took it easy most of the day. Went into a department store this morning and accused the woman next to me of shoplifting, and had the store detective pick her up. Sent three dogs to the pound – *you* know, the usual thing. Oh, and listen," she added, remembering.

"What?" asked Mr. Johnson.

"Well," she said, "I got onto a bus and asked the driver for a transfer, and when he helped someone else first I said that he was impertinent, and quarrelled with him. And then I said why wasn't he in the army, and I said it loud enough for everyone to hear, and I took his number and I turned in a complaint. Probably got him fired."

"Fine," said Mr. Johnson. "But you do look tired. Want to change over tomorrow?"

"I *would* like to," she said. "I could do with a change."

"Right," said Mr. Johnson. "What's for dinner?"

"Veal cutlet."

"Had it for lunch," said Mr. Johnson.